**Did You Know That
51 Million Americans Take Tranquilizers
Prescribed by Their Doctors?
28 Million Take Sedatives?
17 Million Take Stimulants?**

Now the general public can easily understand
and accurately identify the medicines their
doctors prescribe. Written especially for the
consumer, *THE PILL BOOK* describes prac-
tically everything you should know about almost 1,000 prescription drugs, including the
medicine's generic and brand names, type and
general data, cautions and warnings, side effects, adverse effects, usual dosages, overdose potential, and much, much more . . .

The purpose of this book is to provide educational information to the public concerning the majority of various types of prescription drugs which are presently utilized by physicians. It is not intended to be complete or exhaustive or in any respect a substitute for personal medical care. Only a physician may prescribe these drugs as well as their dosages.

While every effort has been made to reproduce products on the cover and insert of this book in an exact fashion, certain variations of size or depiction may be expected as a result of the photographic process. In any event, the reader should not rely upon the photographic image in any manner to identify any pills depicted herein, but should rely solely upon the physician's prescription as dispensed by the pharmacist.

THE PILL BOOK

The Illustrated Guide to the Most Prescribed Drugs in the United States

by
Harold M. Silverman, Pharm.D.
and
Gilbert I. Simon, D.Sc.

**Introduction by
Dr. Frank Field**

BANTAM BOOKS
TORONTO · NEW YORK · LONDON

THE PILL BOOK
A Bantam Book / June 1979
2nd printing
3rd printing
4th printing
5th printing
6th printing
7th printing
8th printing
9th printing

ISBN 0-553-12781-0

Published simultaneously in the United States and Canada

PRINTED IN THE UNITED STATES OF AMERICA

Contents

Producer/Photography: Bert Stern

Editor-in-Chief: Lawrence D. Chilnick

Designer: Milton Glaser

ACKNOWLEDGMENTS

The editors and authors would like to acknowledge
the assistance of the following individuals, without
whom this project could not have been completed:
John DeLorenzo, R.Ph., Janet S. Chilnick, Richard
Berman, Mamie Harris, Rosemarie Vitrano, Kenneth
Gilberg, and Trista Stern.

DEDICATION

To Barbara and Mimi without whose patience,
support, understanding, insights and love;
this project could not have been completed.

—Harold M. Silverman
Gilbert I. Simon

Introduction

If you've never swallowed a pill and don't ever intend to, stop reading this book, put it down, and save yourself the purchase price. But if you're like most of us who occasionally do take pills when we're ill, then read on. Because what's in the following pages may increase your awareness about the drugs you are taking and may even be instrumental in saving your life.

How? Well, let's say you're not feeling well and you decide to visit your family doctor. Predictably, his waiting room is filled with patients, some sitting quietly, others coughing, sneezing, wheezing, and worse. To benefit from the visit, you have to stay alive. And to do that, you must breathe. But the air you're inhaling is the same air that others have exhaled in the form of those coughs, sneezes, wheezes, and worse. And the waiting time seems to crawl along.

So the scene is set. When you're finally ushered into the doctor's office, you're not only ill but tense and impatient.

Yes, the doctor tells you after his examination, there's a pill to help you. And as he hands you the prescription, he says something about meals and times-a-day. But by then you're already stuffing the prescription into your pocket and eagerly waiting to pay the fee and make your exit.

Once on your way, you breathe a sigh of relief—until those nagging doubts start to creep in: What did he say about those pills? Take them before or after meals? How many a day? Oh, I forgot to tell him I'm allergic to egg yolks. I didn't mention that my stomach gets upset easily. What shall I do?

If you've asked yourself such questions or feel that someday you might, then let me suggest that the following pages contain just the type of information to counter the embarrassment and danger of not having listened closely or asked key questions about the pills prescribed by your doctor.

This book has been designed for use by you, the consumer. Among its many features, *The Pill Book* has almost 400 pills, pictured by color, each with its name and reference to more information on other pages. This is only one of the many reasons that no home should be without this book. Think of the value of color pictures of pills if, for example, the label has fallen off your bottle. In fact, this is the only book you can buy that has this unique color index.

It lists the most commonly prescribed drugs in the United States, alphabetically, by both brand name and generic name. It tells you the reasons they're prescribed and their possible side effects. It spells out the usual dosage and what to do if you overdose. There's a summary of how various drugs work—among them, antibiotics, high blood pressure pills, and heart drugs. Questions are answered on how the food you eat affects drug therapy and how drugs you take affect diet and nutrition. The book contains a handy list of important questions and points to remember to raise with your doctor. (In fact, why not carry the list with you when you visit him?) There's a chart telling which drugs may interact with one another and what may happen as a result.

Let me emphasize that this book is not meant to substitute for the professional care of a trained physician. Nor is it designed to be the final word on whether a particular pill is dangerous or safe for your body. Only a doctor should advise conclusively on that.

But this book will provide the kind of information that either can set your mind at ease because it confirms what you thought you heard the doctor say, or can point you in the right direction if you discover or even suspect that your body may not be suited to a certain drug.

If you're faced with such a situation, you never know when, as a lawyer friend of mine would say, time is of the essence. And just then, an inexpensive ready-reference book like this, sitting within reach by the medicine chest, can suddenly be worth all the money in the world, and maybe more.

—Dr. Frank Field, Science Editor, WNBC TV, New York

How to Use This Book

The Pill Book, like pills themselves, should be used with caution. Used properly, this book can save you money and perhaps your life.

Our book's unique visual identifier contains life-sized pictures of the drugs most often prescribed in America. A few drugs that have had an important impact on medical care, such as cancer chemotherapy and heart drugs, have also been included.

The pill identification section is alphabetically organized by color so that you can match the pill you have with a picture to assure yourself that you have the correct medicine. You can then check the descriptive material in the text (page numbers are given) to find out more about these drugs. The pill section of the text provides a complete description of over 950 generic and brand-name drugs. These are the drugs prescribed to Americans 99 percent of the time. The descriptions should amplify what your doctor and pharmacist have told you about your prescription. The pills are listed under their generic classification or major brand name. Every brand and generic name is cross-referenced in the index beginning on page 407.

Each drug entry contains the following information:

Generic or **Brand Name:** The generic name, the common name of the drug approved by the Food and Drug Administration, is listed along with the current brand names for each generic name.

Most prescription drugs are sold in more than one strength. Some, such as the oral contraceptive drugs, come in packages with different numbers of pills in them. A few manufacturers reflect this fact by adding letters and/or numbers to the basic drug name; others do not. An example: Norlestrin 21 1/50, Norlestrin 21

2.5/50, Norlestrin 28 1/50, Norlestrin 28 2.5/50. (The numbers here refer to the number of tablets in each monthly supply—28 or 21—and the strength of medication found in the tablets.) Other drugs come in different strengths: this is often indicated by a notation such as "DS" (double strength) or "Forte" (stronger).

The Pill Book lists only the basic generic or brand names (e.g., Norlestrin) where there are no differences in the basic ingredients, only in amounts of ingredients.

Type of Drug: Describes the general pharmacologic use of each drug: "antidepressant," "tranquilizer," "decongestant," "expectorant," and so on. A separate index begins on page 416 and gives page references for all the pills of a particular type.

Prescribed for: The reasons for which a drug is most often prescribed. Most drugs are given for certain symptoms, but often a drug may be prescribed in combination with another for a quite different reason. Check with your doctor if you are not sure why you have been given a certain pill.

Cautions and Warnings: Any drug can be harmful if the patient is sensitive to any of its actions. The information given alerts you to possible allergic reactions and to certain personal physical conditions such as pregnancy and heart disease which should be taken into consideration if the drug is prescribed for you.

Possible Side Effects: These are the more common side effects to be expected from a drug.

Possible Adverse Drug Effects: More uncommon effects of a pill that can be cause for concern. If you are not sure whether you are experiencing an adverse reaction, ALWAYS call your doctor.

Drug Interactions: This section gives you information on what drugs should not be taken at the same time. This important information is also summarized in a general chart in the color section of the book. Drug interactions with other pills, alcohol, food, or other substances can be a cause of drug-related death. Interactions are more common than overdoses! In fact, many drug overdoses actually consist of a high but not fatal amount of a drug plus a reaction to another substance, often alcohol. Obviously, it is important to be careful when taking several medications at the same time. Be sure to inform your doctor of any medication that you have been taking. Your pharmacist should also keep a record of all your prescription and nonprescription medicines. This listing, generally called a Patient Drug Profile, is used to review your record for any potential problems.

Usual Dose: The maximum and minimum amounts of a drug usually prescribed; however, you may be given different dosage instructions by your doctor. It is important to check with your doctor if you are confused about how often to take a pill and when. Dosages differ for different age groups and this general information is also given.

Overdosage: Symptoms of an overdose of drugs and the immediate steps to take if you suspect a drug overdose. If you suspect you've taken an overdose, call your doctor immediately, or go to a hospital. Bring the medicine bottle with you!

Storage: Information on any special considerations about where or for how long you should keep the medicine in your home.

Special Information: More information, which may not directly relate to the clinical use of a drug, to amplify your general knowledge about it.

The Pill Book also describes how some of the most common drug types (MAO inhibitors, heart drugs, etc.) work. It suggests some questions you may want to ask your doctor or pharmacist about your medicine.

This book is a unique visual reference tool. It should be kept in the medicine cabinet or with your most valuable references such as the dictionary or encyclopedia. Its use, however, is only intended to amplify the information given by your doctor and pharmacist.

If you read something in *The Pill Book* which does not jibe with your instructions, call your doctor. Any drug can have serious side effects if abused or used improperly.

The Most Commonly Prescribed Drugs in the United States

Generic Name

Acetaminophen

Brand Names

A'Cenol	Panex
Aceta	Panofen
Actamin	Panpyro
Anuphen	Parten
Apamide	Phenaphen
APAP	Pirin
Capital	Proval
Dapa	Pyrogesic
Datril	Relenol
Dimindol	SK-APAP
Febrinol	Sonapane
Febrogesic	Sudoprin
G-1	Tapar
Hi-Temp	Temlo
NAPAP	Tempra
Nebs	Tylenol
Neopap Supprettes	Tylenol Extra Strength
Nilprin	Valadol
Nylorac	Valorin

Type of Drug

Antipyretic analgesic.

Prescribed for

Symptomatic relief of pain and fever for people who cannot take Aspirin.

General Information

Acetaminophen is generally used to provide symptomatic relief from pain and fever associated with the common cold, flu, viral infections, or other disorders where pain or fever may be a problem. It is also used to relieve pain in people with an Aspirin allergy or those who cannot take Aspirin because of potential interactions with other drugs such as oral anticoagulants.

Cautions and Warnings

Do not take Acetaminophen if you are allergic or sensitive to it. Do not take more than is prescribed for you or recommended on the package.

Possible Side Effects

This drug is relatively free from side effects. For this reason it has become extremely popular, especially among those who cannot take Aspirin.

Possible Adverse Drug Effects

Taking large doses of Acetaminophen for a long time may cause skin rash, itching, fever, lowered blood sugar, stimulation, and/or yellowing of the skin or whites of the eyes. Other effects of overuse may be a change in the composition of your blood.

Usual Dose

Adult: 325 to 650 milligrams 3 to 4 times per day. Do not take more than 2.6 grams (8 of the 325-milligram tablets) per day.

Child (ages 7 to 12): 162 to 325 milligrams 3 to 4 times per day. Do not take more than 1.3 grams per day.

Child (ages 3 to 6): 120 milligrams 3 to 4 times per day. Do not take more than 480 milligrams per day.

Overdosage

Symptoms are development of bluish color of the lips, fingertips, etc., rash, fever, stimulation, excitement, delirium, depression, nausea and vomiting, abdominal pain, diarrhea, yellowing of the skin and/or eyes, convulsions, and coma. The patient should be taken to a hospital emergency room immediately. ALWAYS bring the medicine bottle.

Special Information

Unless abused, Acetaminophen is a beneficial, effective, and relatively nontoxic drug.

Acetazolamide

Brand Names

Diamox

Type of Drug

Carbonic anhydrase inhibitor.

Prescribed for

General elimination of excess body water. Treatment of glaucoma where it is desirable to lower the pressure inside the eye. Acetazolamide is generally thought of as a weak diuretic and is most often used for its effects on glaucoma. It may also be used as part of the treatment of certain epileptic seizure disorders.

General Information

Acetazolamide inhibits an enzyme in the body called carbonic anhydrase. This effect allows the drug to be used as a weak diuretic, and as part of the treatment of glaucoma by helping to reduce pressure inside the eye. The same effect on carbonic anhydrase is thought to make Acetazolamide a useful drug in treating certain epileptic seizure disorders. The exact way in which the effect is produced is not understood.

Cautions and Warnings

Do not take Acetazolamide if you are pregnant. If you become pregnant and are taking Acetazolamide, discuss it with your doctor.

Possible Side Effects

Side effects of short-term Acetazolamide therapy are usually minimal. Those which have been noted include tingling feeling in the arms and legs, loss of appetite, increased frequency in urination (to be expected since this drug has a weak diuretic effect), occasional drowsiness and/or confusion. Transient myopia has been reported.

Possible Adverse Drug Effects

Infrequent: itching, rash, blood in stool or urine, increased blood sugar, convulsions, diarrhea, loss of weight, nausea, vomiting, constipation, weakness, nervousness, depression, dizziness, dry mouth, disorientation, muscle spasms, ringing in the ears.

Drug Interactions

Acetazolamide will inhibit the action of methenamine used for the treatment of urinary tract infection. Consult your doctor if you receive a prescription for a drug to treat urinary tract infection. (Most such drugs are not affected by Acetazolamide.)

Avoid over-the-counter drug products which contain stimulants or anticholinergics, which tend to aggravate glaucoma or cardiac disease. Ask your pharmacist about ingredients contained in the over-the-counter drugs.

Usual Dose

From 250 milligrams to 1 gram per day, according to disease and patient's condition.

Special Information

Acetazolamide may cause minor drowsiness and confusion, particularly during the first 2 weeks of therapy. Take care while performing tasks which require concentration, such as driving or operating appliances or machinery.

Brand Name

Actifed-C Expectorant

Ingredients

Codeine Phosphate
Guiafenesin
Pseudoephedrine
  Hydrochloride
Triprolidine
  Hydrochloride

Other Brand Names

Sherafed-C
Tri-Profed Expectorant with Codeine

Type of Drug

Decongestant; expectorant.

Prescribed for

Relief of cough, nasal congestion, runny nose, and other symptoms associated with the common cold, viruses, or other upper respiratory diseases. It may also be used as part of the treatment for allergies, asthma, ear infections, or sinus infections.

General Information

Actifed-C is one of almost 100 products marketed to relieve the symptoms of the common cold and other respiratory infections. These products contain medicine to relieve congestion, act as an antihistamine, relieve or suppress cough, and help cough up mucus. They may contain medicine for each purpose, or may contain a combination of medicines. Some combinations leave out the antihistamine, the decongestant, or the expectorant. You must realize while taking Actifed-C or similar products that these drugs are good only for the relief of symptoms and will not treat the underlying problem, such as a cold virus or other infections.

Cautions and Warnings

Can cause excessive tiredness or drowsiness.

Possible Side Effects

Dry mouth, blurred vision, difficulty passing urine, and possibly constipation, nervousness, restlessness or even inability to sleep.

Drug Interactions

Taking Actifed-C with Marplan, Parnate, or other MAO inhibitors can produce severe interaction. Consult your doctor first.

Actifed-C contains Codeine. Drinking alcoholic beverages while taking this drug may produce excessive drowsiness and/or sleepiness, or inability to concentrate.

Usual Dose

1 to 2 teaspoons 4 times per day.

Special Information

Take with a full glass of water to reduce stomach upset and help remove excessive mucus from the throat.

Brand Name

Actifed Tablets

Ingredients

Pseudoephedrine Hydrochloride
Triprolidine

Other Brand Names

Actamine Tablets   Sudahist Tablets
Edlefed Tablets   Suda-Prol Tablets
Sherafed Tablets

Type of Drug

Decongestant; antihistamine.

Prescribed for

Relief of sneezing, runny nose, and nasal congestion associated with the common cold, allergy, or other upper respiratory condition.

General Information

Actifed Tablets is one of many products marketed to relieve the symptoms of the common cold. Most of these products contain ingredients to relieve nasal congestion or to dry up runny noses or relieve a scratchy throat; and several of them may contain ingredients to suppress cough, or to help eliminate unwanted mucus. All these products are good only for the relief of symptoms and do not treat the underlying problem such as the cold virus or other infections.

Cautions and Warnings

Can cause excessive tiredness or drowsiness, restlessness, nervousness with an inability to sleep.

Possible Side Effects

Tremor, headache, palpitations, elevation of blood pressure, sweating, sleeplessness, loss of appetite, nausea, vomiting, dizziness, constipation.

Drug Interactions

Interaction with alcoholic beverages may produce excessive drowsiness and/or sleepiness, or inability to concentrate.

Do not self-medicate with additional over-the-counter drugs for the relief of cold symptoms: taking Actifed Tablets with such drugs may result in aggravation of high blood pressure, heart disease, diabetes, or thyroid disease.

Do not take Actifed Tablets if you are taking or suspect you may be taking a monoamine oxidase (MAO) inhibitor: severe elevation in blood pressure may result.

Usual Dose

Adult: 1 tablet 2 to 3 times per day. Syrup preparation, 1 or 2 teaspoons 3 times per day.

Child (age 6 and over): 1 tablet 3 times per day. Syrup preparation, 2 teaspoons 3 times per day.

Child (ages 4 months to 6 years): 1 teaspoon 3 times per day.

Child (up to age 4 months): ½ teaspoon 3 times per day.

Brand Name

Aldactazide

Ingredients

Hydrochlorothiazide
Spironolactone

Type of Drug

Diuretic.

Prescribed for

High blood pressure or any condition where it is desirable to eliminate excess fluid from the body.

General Information

Aldactazide is a combination of two diuretics which act by different mechanisms and is a convenient, effective approach for the treatment of diseases where the elimination of excess fluids is required. One of the ingredients in Aldactazide has the ability to hold potassium in the body while producing a diuretic effect. This balances off the other ingredient, Hydrochlorothiazide, which normally causes a loss of potassium. The two drugs counterbalance one another, and save the patient the trouble of taking extra potassium from outside sources.

Cautions and Warnings

Do not use Aldactazide if you have nonfunctioning kidneys, if you think you may be allergic to this drug or any sulfa drug, or if you have a history of allergy or bronchial asthma. Aldactazide may be used to treat specific conditions in pregnant women, but the decision to use this medication by pregnant women should be weighed carefully because the drug may cross the placental barrier into the blood of the unborn child. Aldactazide may appear in the breast milk of nursing mothers. Do not take any potassium supplements together with Aldactazide unless specifically directed to do so by your doctor.

Possible Side Effects

Drowsiness, lethargy, headache, gastrointestinal upset, cramping and diarrhea, rash, mental confusion, fever, feeling of ill health, enlargement of the breasts, inability to achieve or maintain erection in males, irregular menstrual cycle or deepening of the voice in females.

Possible Adverse Drug Effects

Loss of appetite, headache, tingling in the toes and fingers, restlessness, anemias or other effects on components of the blood, unusual sensitivity to sunlight, dizziness when rising quickly from a sitting or lying position. Aldactazide can also produce muscle spasms, weakness, and blurred vision.

Drug Interactions

Aldactazide will add to (potentiate) the action of other blood-pressure-lowering drugs. This is beneficial, and is frequently used to help lower blood pressure in patients with hypertension.

The possibility of developing imbalances in body fluids (electrolytes) is increased if you take medications such as Digitalis and adrenal corticosteroids while you take Aldactazide.

If you are taking an oral antidiabetic drug and begin taking Aldactazide, the antidiabetic dose may have to be altered.

Lithium Carbonate should not be taken with Aldactazide because the combination may increase the risk of lithium toxicity.

Avoid over-the-counter cough, cold, or allergy remedies containing stimulant drugs which can aggravate your condition.

Usual Dose

Two to 4 tablets per day, adjusted by your doctor until desired therapeutic effect is achieved.

Special Information

Take Aldactazide exactly as prescribed.

Brand Name

Aldoril

Ingredients

Hydrochlorothiazide
Methyldopa

Type of Drug

Antihypertensive combination.

Prescribed for

High blood pressure.

General Information

Be sure to take this medicine exactly as prescribed: if you don't, it cannot exert its maximum effect.

An ingredient in this drug can cause loss of potassium. Potassium loss leads to a condition known as hypokalemia. Warning signs of hypokalemia or other electrolyte imbalances that can be due to Aldoril are dryness of the mouth, excessive thirst, weakness, drowsiness, restlessness, muscle pains or cramps, muscular fatigue, lack of urination, abnormal heart rhythms, and upset stomach. If this happens, call your doctor. You may have to take extra potassium to supplement loss due to Aldoril. This may be taken as a potassium supplement (tablet, powder, liquid) or as a high concentration of foods in your diet which contain potassium. Some of these foods are bananas, citrus fruits, melons, and tomatoes.

Cautions and Warnings

Do not take Aldoril if you are allergic to either ingredient contained in it, if you have any liver disease such as hepatitis or active cirrhosis, or if previous therapy with Methyldopa has been associated with signs of liver reaction (jaundice or unexplained fever).

Possible Side Effects

Loss of appetite, stomach upset, nausea, vomiting, cramps, diarrhea, constipation, dizziness, headache, tingling in the extremities, restlessness, chest pains, abnormal heart rhythms, temporary drowsiness during the first few days of therapy.

Possible Adverse Drug Effects

Aldoril can cause abnormal liver function in the first 2 to 3 months of therapy. Watch for jaundice (yellowing of the skin or whites of the eyes), with or without fever. If you are taking Aldoril for the first time, be sure the doctor checks your liver function, particularly during the first 6 to 12 weeks of therapy. If fever or jaundice appears, notify your doctor immediately and discontinue therapy. Other adverse effects: stuffed nose, breast enlargement, lactation (in females), impotence or decreased sex drive, mild arthritis, skin reactions such as mild eczema.

Drug Interactions

Interaction with Digitalis or Quinidine can develop abnormal heart rhythms.

Interaction with lithium products can lead to lithium toxicity unless appropriate dose adjustments are made.

Do not self-medicate with over-the-counter cough, cold, or allergy remedies containing stimulant drugs which may raise your blood pressure. If you are not sure which over-the-counter drugs are safe for you, ask your pharmacist.

Usual Dose

Individualized to suit the patient. The usual starting dose, of 1 tablet 2 to 3 times per day for the first 2 days, is adjusted up or down as needed.

Special Information

Aldoril may cause temporary mild sedation. Contact your doctor if your normal urine output is dropping or you are less hungry or nauseated.

Be aware that Aldoril can cause orthostatic hypotension (dizziness when rising from a sitting or lying position). Alcohol will worsen this effect, so avoid alcohol at the beginning of Aldoril therapy.

Generic Name

Allopurinol

Brand Name

Zyloprim

Type of Drug

Anti-gout, anti-uric acid medication.

Prescribed for

Gout or high blood levels of uric acid.

General Information

Unlike other anti-gout drugs which affect the elimination of uric acid from the body, Allopurinol acts on the system that manufactures uric acid in your body. A high level of uric acid can mean that you have gout or that you have one of many other diseases, including various cancers and malignancies, or psoriasis. High uric acid levels can be caused by taking some drugs, including diuretic medicines. The fact that you have a high blood level of uric acid does not point to a specific disease.

Cautions and Warnings

Do not take this medication if you have ever developed a severe reaction to it in the past. If you develop a skin rash or any other adverse effects while taking Allopurinol, stop taking the medication immediately and contact your doctor. Allopurinol should be used by children only if they have high uric acid levels due to neoplastic disease. A nursing mother should not take this medication, since it will pass through the mother's milk into the child. Allopurinol can affect the development of the unborn child if taken throughout pregnancy; pregnant women should not use this medication without specifically discussing it with a doctor.

Possible Side Effects

You may develop skin rash. Such rashes have been associated with severe, allergic, or sensitivity reactions to Allopurinol. If you develop an unusual skin rash or other sign of drug toxicity, stop taking this medication and contact your doctor. Other side effects: nausea, vomiting, diarrhea, intermittent stomach pains, effects on blood components, drowsiness or lack of ability to concentrate, and, rarely, effects on the eyes.

Possible Adverse Drug Effects

Loss of hair, fever, chills, arthritislike symptoms, itching.

Drug Interactions

Avoid interaction with iron tablets or vitamins with iron: Allopurinol can cause iron to concentrate in your liver.

Interaction with drugs used to treat cancer is important and should be taken into account by your physician.

Allopurinol may interact with anticoagulant (blood-thinning) medication such as Dicoumarol. The importance of this interaction is not yet known.

Usual Dose

Adult: 200 to 600 milligrams per day depending on disease and patient's response.

Child (ages 6 to 10): 300 milligrams per day.

Child (under age 6): 150 milligrams per day.

The dose should be reviewed periodically by your doctor to be sure that it is producing the desired therapeutic effect.

Special Information

Drink large amounts of water, juices, soda, or other liquids to avoid the formation of crystals in your urine and/or kidneys.

Allopurinol can make you sleepy or make it difficult for you to concentrate: take care while driving a car or using other equipment or machinery.

Brand Name

Ambenyl Expectorant

Ingredients

Ammonium Chloride
Bromodiphenhydramine
  Hydrochloride
Codeine Sulfate
Diphenhydramine
Potassium
  Guaiacolsulfonate

Type of Drug

Cough suppressant and expectorant combination.

Prescribed for

Coughs.

General Information

Ambenyl Expectorant may make you tired or drowsy. Avoid other drugs which may have the same effect, since they will add to the drowsiness.

Cautions and Warnings

Do not take this medicine if you are allergic to any of its ingredients.

Possible Side Effects

Drowsiness, dry mouth, blurred vision, difficulty in urination, constipation.

Possible Adverse Drug Effects

Palpitations—pounding of the heart.

Drug Interactions

Avoid alcohol, sedatives, tranquilizers, antihistamines, or other medication which can cause tiredness and/or drowsiness.

Taking Ambenyl Expectorant with Isocarboxazid (Marplan), Tranylcypromine Sulfate (Parnate), Phenelzine Sulfate (Nardil), or other MAO inhibitor drugs can produce a severe interaction. Consult your doctor first.

Usual Dose

Adult: 2 teaspoons 4 times per day.

Child (over age 1): ½ to 1 teaspoon 3 or 4 times per day.

Take with a full glass of water. This will help the expectorant effect of the drug and may reduce stomach upset.

Special Information

Be aware of the potential depressive effects of Ambenyl Expectorant; be careful when driving or operating heavy or dangerous machinery.

Generic Name
Amitriptyline

Brand Names

Amitril	Endep
Elavil	Rolavil

Type of Drug

Antidepressant.

Prescribed for

Depression with or without symptoms of anxiety.

General Information

Amitriptyline and other members of this group are effective in treating symptoms of depression. They can elevate your mood, increase physical activity and mental alertness, improve appetite and sleep patterns. These drugs are mild sedatives and therefore useful in treating mild forms of depression associated with anxiety. You should not expect instant results with this medicine: results are usually seen after 1 to 4 weeks. If symptoms are not affected after 6 to 8 weeks, contact your doctor. Occasionally this drug and other members of the group of drugs have been used in treating nighttime bed-wetting in the young child, but they do not produce long-lasting relief and therapy with one of them for nighttime bed-wetting is of questionable value.

Cautions and Warnings

Do not take Amitriptyline if you are allergic or sensitive to this or other members of this class of drug: Doxepin, Nortriptyline, Imipramine, Desipramine, and Protriptyline. The drugs should not be used if you are recovering from a heart attack. Amitriptyline may be taken with caution if you have a history of epilepsy or other convulsive disorders, difficulty in urination, glaucoma, heart disease, or thyroid disease. Amitriptyline can interfere with your ability to perform tasks which require concentration, such as driving or operating machinery. Amitriptyline will pass from mother to unborn child:

17

consult your doctor before taking this medicine if you are pregnant.

Possible Side Effects

Changes in blood pressure (both high and low), abnormal heart rates, heart attack, confusion, especially in elderly patients, hallucinations, disorientation, delusions, anxiety, restlessness, excitement, numbness and tingling in the extremities, lack of coordination, muscle spasms or tremors, seizures and/or convulsions, dry mouth, blurred vision, constipation, inability to urinate, skin rash, itching, sensitivity to bright light or sunlight, retention of fluids, fever, allergy, changes in composition of blood, nausea, vomiting, loss of appetite, stomach upset, diarrhea, enlargement of the breasts in males and females, increased or decreased sex drive, increase or decrease of blood sugar.

Possible Adverse Drug Effects

Infrequent: agitation, inability to sleep, nightmares, feeling of panic, development of a peculiar taste in the mouth, stomach cramps, black coloration of the tongue, yellowing eyes and/or skin, changes in liver function, increased or decreased weight, perspiration, flushing, frequent urination, drowsiness, dizziness, weakness, headache, loss of hair, nausea, not feeling well.

Drug Interactions

Interaction with monoamine oxidase (MAO) inhibitors can cause high fevers, convulsions, and occasionally death. Don't take MAO inhibitors until at least 2 weeks after Amitriptyline has been discontinued.

Amitriptyline interacts with Guanethidine, a drug used to treat high blood pressure: if your doctor prescribes Amitriptyline and you are taking medicine for high blood pressure, be sure to discuss this with him.

Amitriptyline increases the effects of barbiturates, tranquilizers, other depressive drugs, and alcohol. Don't drink alcohol if you take this medicine.

Taking Amitriptyline and thyroid medicine will enhance the effects of the thyroid medicine. The combination can cause abnormal heart rhythms.

Large doses of Vitamin C (Ascorbic Acid) can reduce

the effect of Amitriptyline. Drugs such as Bicarbonate of Soda or Acetazolamide will increase the effect of Amitriptyline.

Usual Dose

25 milligrams 3 times per day, which may be increased to 150 milligrams per day if necessary. The medication must be tailored to the needs of the patient.

Adolescent or elderly: Lower doses are recommended: generally, 30 to 50 milligrams per day.

Overdosage

Symptoms are confusion, inability to concentrate, hallucinations, drowsiness, lowered body temperature, abnormal heart rate, heart failure, large pupils of the eyes, convulsions, severely lowered blood pressure, stupor, and coma (as well as agitation, stiffening of body muscles, vomiting, and high fever). The patient should be taken to a hospital emergency room immediately. ALWAYS bring the medicine bottle.

Generic Name

Amoxicillin

Brand Names

Amoxil	Robamox
Larotid	Sumox
Polymox	Trimox

Type of Drug

Broad-spectrum antibiotic.

Prescribed for

Gram-positive bacterial infections. Gram-positive bacteria (pneumococci, streptococci, and staphylococci) are organisms which usually cause diseases such as pneumonia, infections of the tonsils and throat, venereal disease, meningitis (infection of the spinal column), and septicemia (general infection of the bloodstream).

Infections of the urinary tract and some infections of the gastrointestinal tract can also be treated with Amoxicillin.

General Information

Amoxicillin is manufactured in the laboratory by the process known as fermentation and by general chemical reaction and, as such, is classified as a semisynthetic antibiotic. Because the effectiveness of the antibiotic is determined by the drug's ability to destroy the cell wall of the invading bacteria, it is very important that the patient completely follow the doctor's prescribing directions. These directions include spacing of doses as well as the number of days the patient should continue taking the medicine. If they are not followed, the effect of the antibiotic is severely reduced. To ensure the maximum effect of this antibiotic, you should take the medication on an empty stomach, either 1 hour before or 2 hours after meals.

Cautions and Warnings

If you have a known history of allergy to Penicillin you should avoid taking Amoxicillin, since the drugs are chemically very similar. The most common allergic reaction to Amoxicillin, as well as to the other penicillins, is a hivelike rash over the body with itching and redness. It is important to tell your doctor if you have ever taken this drug or penicillins before and if you have experienced any adverse reaction to the drug such as skin rash, itching, or difficulty in breathing.

Possible Side Effects

Common side effects: stomach upset, nausea, vomiting, diarrhea, and possible skin rash. Less common side effects: hairy tongue, itching or irritation around the anus and/or vagina. If these symptoms occur, you should contact your doctor immediately.

Drug Interactions

The effect of Amoxicillin can be significantly reduced when taken with other antibiotics. Consult your doctor if you are taking both. Otherwise, Amoxicillin is generally free of interactions with other medications.

Usual Dose

Adult: 250 milligrams every 8 hours.

Child: 9 milligrams per pound of body weight per day in 3 divided doses (every 8 hours). Amoxicillin pediatric drops (under 3 pounds), 1 milliliter every 8 hours; (3 to 4 pounds), 2 milliliters every 8 hours. Dose may be halved for less serious infections or doubled for severe infections.

Storage

Amoxicillin can be stored at room temperature.

Special Information

Do not take Amoxicillin after the expiration date on the label.

The safety of Amoxicillin in pregnancy has not been established.

Generic Name

Ampicillin

Brand Names

Alpen	Pensyn
Amcill	Polycillin
Ampi-Co	Principen
Omnipen	SK-Ampicillin
Pen A	Supen
Penbritin	Totacillin

Type of Drug

Broad-spectrum antibiotic.

Prescribed for

Gram-positive bacterial infections. Gram-positive bacteria (pneumococci, streptococci, and staphylococci) are organisms which usually cause diseases such as pneumonia, infections of the tonsils and throat, venereal disease, meningitis (infection of the spinal column), and septicemia (infection of the bloodstream).

Infections of the urinary tract and some infections of the gastrointestinal tract can also be treated with Ampicillin.

General Information

Ampicillin is manufactured in the laboratory by the process known as fermentation and by general chemical reaction, and as such, is classified as a semisynthetic antibiotic. Because the effectiveness of the antibiotic is determined by the drug's ability to affect the cell wall of the invading bacteria, it is very important that the patient completely follow the doctor's prescribing directions. These directions include spacing of doses as well as the number of days the patient should continue taking the medicine. If they are not followed, the effect of the antibiotic is severely reduced. To ensure the maximum effect of this antibiotic, you should take the medication on an empty stomach, either 1 hour before or 2 hours after meals.

Cautions and Warnings

If you have a known history of allergy to Penicillin you should avoid taking Ampicillin, since the drugs are chemically similar. The most common allergic reaction to Ampicillin, as well as to the other penicillins, is a hivelike rash over the body with itching and redness. It is important to tell your doctor if you have ever taken Ampicillin or penicillins before and if you have experienced any adverse reaction to the drug such as skin rash, itching, or difficulty in breathing.

Possible Side Effects

Common side effects: stomach upset, nausea, vomiting, diarrhea, possible skin rash. Less common: hairy tongue, itching or irritation around the anus and/or vagina. If these symptoms occur, contact your doctor immediately.

Drug Interactions

The effect of Ampicillin can be significantly reduced when taken with other antibiotics. Consult your doctor if you are taking both during the same course of therapy.

Otherwise, Ampicillin is generally free of interactions with other medications.

Usual Dose

Adult: 250 to 500 milligrams every 6 hours.

Child (44 pounds and over): 250 to 500 milligrams every 6 hours.

Child (under 44 pounds): 50 to 100 milligrams every 6 to 8 hours.

Storage

Ampicillin can be stored at room temperature.

Special Information

Do not take Ampicillin after the expiration date on the label.

The safety of Ampicillin in pregnancy has not been established.

Brand Name

Anusol-HC

Ingredients

Benzyl Benzoate
Bismuth Resorcin Compound
Bismuth Subgallate
Hydrocortisone Acetate
Zinc Oxide

Type of Drug

Hemorrhoid relief compound.

Prescribed for

The relief of rectal pain and itching due to hemorrhoids or local itching.

General Information

Although its ingredients are unique, Anusol-HC is one of many products available for the relief of rectal pain and itching. The bismuth compounds and Zinc Oxide act to help shrink hemorrhoids, and the Hydrocortisone acts to reduce inflammation throughout the general area. This and similar products provide effective relief but do not treat the underlying cause of the problem.

Cautions and Warnings

Do not use if the area is infected or if you have herpes cold sores, tuberculosis of the skin or other generalized skin infections, or glaucoma. Use with caution if you experience urinary difficulties, are elderly, or suffer from prostate disease.

Possible Side Effects

Local irritation, aggravation of glaucoma, or infection.

Possible Adverse Effects

A lot of the Hydrocortisone in this drug will be absorbed into the bloodstream and it is possible to experience the adverse effects seen when a corticosteroid drug is taken by mouth. This will not become a serious problem except in cases where the medicine is used for too long or when used by someone also taking corticosteroids by mouth.

Usual Dose

Children: Should be used with caution in children under age 6.

Cream: Apply locally, twice a day, for up to 7 days.

Suppository: One suppository, twice a day, for up to 7 days.

Storage

Keep away from excessive heat.

Special Information

Do not use for more than 7 days unless specifically directed to do so. Stop taking or call your doctor if you experience dry mouth, blurred vision, eye pain, or dizziness.

A.P.C. with Codeine

Ingredients

Aspirin
Caffeine
Codeine Sulfate
Phenacetin

Brand Names

Anexsia with Codeine
APA-Deine Tablets
A.S.A. and Codeine
Buff-A Comp Tablets
Empirin Compound with
  Codeine

Lemidyne with Codeine
Monacet with Codeine
P-A-C Compound with
  Codeine
Salatin with Codeine

Type of Drug

Narcotic analgesic combination.

Prescribed for

Relief of mild to moderate pain.

General Information

A.P.C. with Codeine is one of many combination products containing narcotics and analgesics. These products often also contain barbiturates or tranquilizers, and Acetaminophen may be substituted for Aspirin, or Phenacetin and/or Caffeine may be omitted. All these products are used for the relief of mild to moderate pain.

Cautions and Warnings

Do not take Codeine if you know you are allergic or sensitive to it. Long-term use of Codeine may cause drug dependence or addiction. Codeine is a respiratory depressant. Use this drug with extreme caution if you suffer from asthma or other breathing problems. Codeine affects the central nervous system, producing sleepiness, tiredness, and/or inability to concentrate. If you are pregnant or suspect that you are pregnant do not take this drug.

Possible Side Effects

Most frequent: light-headedness, dizziness, sleepiness, nausea, vomiting, loss of appetite, sweating. If these effects occur, consider calling your doctor and asking him about lowering the dose of Codeine you are taking. Usually the side effects disappear if you simply lie down.

More serious side effects of A.P.C. with Codeine are shallow breathing or difficulty in breathing.

Possible Adverse Drug Effects

Adverse effects of A.P.C. with Codeine include euphoria (feeling high), weakness, sleepiness, headache, agitation, uncoordinated muscle movement, minor hallucinations, disorientation and visual disturbances, dry mouth, loss of appetite, constipation, flushing of the face, rapid heartbeat, palpitations, faintness, urinary difficulties or hesitancy, reduced sex drive and/or potency, itching, skin rashes, anemia, lowered blood sugar, and a yellowing of the skin and/or whites of the eyes. Narcotic analgesics may aggravate convulsions in those who have had convulsions in the past.

Drug Interactions

Interaction with alcohol, tranquilizers, barbiturates, or sleeping pills produces tiredness, sleepiness, or inability to concentrate, and seriously increases the depressive effect of A.P.C. with Codeine.

The Aspirin component of A.P.C. with Codeine can affect anticoagulant (blood-thinning) therapy. Be sure to discuss this with your doctor so that the proper dosage adjustment can be made.

Interaction with adrenal cortical steroids, Phenylbutazone, or alcohol can cause severe stomach irritation with possible bleeding.

Usual Dose

1 to 2 tablets 3 to 4 times per day.

Overdosage

Symptoms are depression of respiration (breathing), extreme tiredness progressing to stupor and then coma, pinpointed pupils of the eyes, no response to stimulation such as a pin stick, cold and clammy skin, slowing down of the heartbeat, lowering of blood pressure, convulsions, and cardiac arrest. The patient should be taken to a hospital emergency room immediately. ALWAYS bring the medicine bottle.

Special Information

Drowsiness may occur: be careful when driving or operating hazardous machinery.

Take with food or ½ glass of water to prevent stomach upset.

The Phenacetin ingredient of A.P.C. with Codeine may be toxic to your kidneys: do not take this medication for longer than 10 days unless directed by your doctor.

Brand Name

AVC Cream

Ingredients

Allantoin
Aminacrine
Sulfanilamide

Other Brand Names

Avsul	Triconol
Benegyn	Vagidine
Deltavac	Vagimine
Femguard	Vaginal Sulfa
Nil	Vagi-Nil
Sufamal	Vagitrol

Type of Drug

Vaginal anti-infective.

Prescribed for

Relief of vaginal infection.

General Information

AVC Cream should only be used to treat vaginal irritation due to an infection. In such cases, relief may be within a few days, but the drug should be used through an entire menstrual cycle. If no relief occurs within a few days or if the symptoms return, do not continue this drug. Consult your doctor as a new medication may be required.

Cautions and Warnings

Do not use if you are allergic to sulfa drugs. If a skin rash develops, stop using the drug and consult your doctor.

Possible Side Effects

Most frequent: vaginal burning or discomfort. Less frequent: skin rash or other side effects associated with sulfa drug toxicity.

Usual Dose

One applicator full of cream inserted into the vagina, once or twice a day.

Generic Name

Azathioprine

Brand Name

Imuran

Type of Drug

Immunosuppressive.

Prescribed for

Part of the treatment of any disease where it is desirable to suppress the normal immune responses of the body.

General Information

Azathioprine is a unique medicine used to suppress the body's immune response mechanism, which normally allows us to respond to infection, outside agents that cause allergies, or other foreign objects. When it is artificially suppressed with this medication, as in the case of a transplanted kidney it permits the new kidney to continue functioning in the body of the transplant patient. Without Azathioprine the body would see a new kidney as a foreign object and soon destroy it. People taking this drug are unusually susceptible to infection and must be constantly alert to any changes. Normal responses (fever, etc.) may not be present or may be delayed by Azathioprine treatment.

Cautions and Warnings

This drug should be avoided by pregnant women if possible. Although Azathioprine has been used by some women throughout pregnancy without adverse effect, complete blood counts should be taken weekly to check for any unusual changes.

Possible Side Effects

The most often seen and most severe side effects are related to components of the blood. These may manifest themselves by unusual bleeding or be detected by a weekly blood count.

Possible Adverse Drug Effects

Sores in the mouth, drug fever, loss of hair, joint pains, nausea, vomiting, diarrhea and loss of appetite, yellowing of skin or whites of the eye.

Drug Interactions

Allopurinol markedly reduces the rate at which Azathioprine is eliminated from the body. This effect is so important that it may be necessary to reduce the Azathioprine dose to 25 to 30 percent of the original dose while taking Allopurinol.

Usual Dose

1½ to 2½ milligrams per pound of body weight per day to start. The dose may be reduced to ½ to 1 milligram per pound per day, according to patient response.

Special Information

Contact your doctor immediately if you develop sores in the mouth or unusual bleeding.

Brand Name

Azo Gantrisin

Ingredients

Phenazopyridine
Sulfisoxazole

Other Brand Names

Ameri-EZP   Azosul
Azo-Soxazole   Suldiazo

Type of Drug

Urinary anti-infective.

Prescribed for

Urinary tract infections.

General Information

Azo Gantrisin is one of many combination products used to treat urinary tract infections. The primary active ingredient is Sulfisoxazole. The other ingredient, Phenazopyridine, is added as a pain reliever.

Cautions and Warnings

Do not take Azo Gantrisin if you know you are allergic to sulfa drugs, salicylates, or similar agents. Do not take this drug if you are pregnant or nursing a young child since the drug can pass from the mother into the unborn child. Azo Gantrisin should not be considered if you have advanced kidney disease.

Possible Side Effects

Headache, itching, skin rash, sensitivity to strong sunlight, nausea, vomiting, abdominal pains, feeling of tiredness or lassitude, hallucinations, dizziness, ringing in the ears, chills, feeling of ill health.

Possible Adverse Drug Effects

Blood diseases or alterations of normal blood components, itching of the eyes, arthritis-type pain, diarrhea, loss of appetite, stomach cramps or pains, hearing loss, drowsiness, fever, chills, loss of hair, yellowing of the skin and/or eyes, reduction in sperm count.

Drug Interactions

When Azo Gantrisin is taken with an anticoagulant (blood-thinning) drug, any drug used to treat diabetes, or Methotrexate, it will cause unusually large amounts of these drugs to be released into the bloodstream, producing symptoms of overdosage. If you are going to take Azo Gantrisin for an extended period, your physician should reduce the dosage of these interactive drugs. Also, avoid large doses of Vitamin C.

Usual Dose

Adult: First dose, 4 to 6 tablets; then 2 tablets every 4 hours.

Take each dose with a full glass of water.

Overdosage

Induce vomiting and give a rectal enema; then take the patient to a hospital emergency room. ALWAYS bring the medicine bottle.

Special Information

Azo Gantrisin can cause photosensitivity—a severe reaction to strong sunlight. Avoid prolonged exposure to strong sunlight while taking it.

Sore throat, fever, unusual bleeding or bruising, rash, and feeling tired are early signs of serious blood disorders and should be reported to your doctor immediately.

The Phenazopyridine ingredient in Azo Gantrisin is an orange-red dye and will color the urine. Do not be worried, since this is a normal effect of the drug; but note that if you are diabetic, the dye may interfere with testing your urine for sugar.

Brand Name

Bendectin

Ingredients

Doxylamine Succinate
Pyridoxine Hydrochloride

Type of Drug

Antivomiting, antidizziness combination.

Prescribed for

Control of nausea, vomiting, and morning sickness.

General Information

Bendectin is often used to control the symptoms of morning sickness because of its relative safety in pregnant women. However, there is no proof that Pyridoxine Hydrochloride adds anything to the effectiveness of the combination. Doxylamine Succinate, the primary ingredient, is an antihistamine with antiemetic properties. It works by antagonizing any histamine present as a result of any sort of allergic or sensitivity reaction.

Cautions and Warnings

Bendectin should be avoided or used with extreme caution if you have glaucoma or certain types of stomach ulcer. Bendectin can reduce the body's ability to produce and excrete urine, but this is mostly seen in elderly or debilitated patients.

Possible Side Effects

Difficulty in urination, blurred vision, change in heartbeat, sensitivity to light, headache, flushing of the skin, nervousness, dizziness, weakness, drowsiness, nausea, inability to sleep, vomiting, fever, nasal stuffiness, heartburn, constipation, feeling of being bloated, and occasionally, drug allergy.

Drug Interactions

The drug should be used with caution with alcohol or alcoholic beverages, depressants such as sleeping medicines, sedatives, tranquilizers, or other drugs which may cause drowsiness or other signs of depression.

Do not take if you are taking monoamine oxidase (MAO) inhibitor drugs.

Usual Dose

2 tablets at bedtime. If nausea occurs during the day, 1 tablet may be taken in the morning and afternoon if needed.

Special Information

Bendectin may produce tiredness or inability to concentrate. Be very careful when driving an automobile or operating other machinery.

Brand Name

Bentyl with Phenobarbital

Ingredients

Dicyclomine Hydrochloride
Phenobarbital

Type of Drug

Gastrointestinal anticholinergic agent.

Prescribed for

Symptomatic relief of stomach upset and spasms. Frequently this medication is prescribed to treat morning sickness associated with the first trimester of pregnancy.

General Information

Bentyl with Phenobarbital works by reducing spasms in muscles of the stomach and other parts of the gastrointestinal tract. In doing so, it helps relieve some of the uncomfortable symptoms associated with peptic ulcer, irritable bowel and/or colon, spastic colon, and other gastrointestinal disorders. It only relieves symptoms. It does not cure the underlying disease.

Cautions and Warnings

Bentyl with Phenobarbital should not be used if you know you are sensitive or allergic to Dicyclomine Hydrochloride. Do not use this medicine if you have glaucoma, asthma, obstructive disease of the gastrointestinal tract, or other serious gastrointestinal disease. Because this drug reduces your ability to sweat, its use in hot climates may cause heat exhaustion.

Possible Side Effects

Occasional: difficulty in urination, blurred vision, rapid heartbeat, palpitations, sensitivity to light, headache, flushing, nervousness, dizziness, weakness, drowsiness, inability to sleep, nausea, vomiting, fever, nasal congestion, heartburn, constipation, feeling of being bloated. There is also occasionally drug allergy or a drug idiosyncratic reaction, which may include itching or other skin manifestations.

Possible Adverse Drug Effects

Use of this drug in elderly patients may be associated with some degree of mental confusion and/or excitement.

Drug Interactions

Interaction with antihistamines, phenothiazines, tranquilizers, antidepressants, and some narcotic painkillers may cause blurred vision, dry mouth, or drowsiness.

Do not use with Tranylcypromine Sulfate (Parnate), Isocarboxazid (Marplan), Phenelzine Sulfate (Nardil), or other MAO inhibitor drugs, which will tend to prevent excretion of Bentyl with Phenobarbital from the body and thus potentiate it (increase its effect).

Usual Dose

One capsule every 3 to 4 hours as needed for relief of symptoms. If necessary, capsules may be given up to 8 times per day, tablets up to 4 times per day.

Syrup, 1 teaspoon 3 to 4 times per day, but as many as 8 teaspoons per day may be required.

Special Information

Dry mouth produced by Bentyl with Phenobarbital can be relieved by chewing gum or sucking hard candy; constipation can be treated with a stool softener (rather than a harsh cathartic).

Benylin Cough Syrup

Ingredients

Ammonium Chloride
Diphenhydramine Hydrochloride
Sodium Citrate

Other Brand Names

Benachlor Cough Syrup
Diphenallin Cough Syrup
Diphen-Ex

Diphenhydramine
  Hydrochloride Cough
  Syrup
Noradryl Cough Syrup
Tusstat Expectorant

Type of Drug

Cough syrup expectorant.

Prescribed for

Coughs associated with the common cold and other upper respiratory infections.

General Information

Benylin Cough Syrup is one of many products marketed for the relief of coughs. Its major active ingredient is an antihistamine; therefore, the drug is most effective in relieving the symptoms of excess histamine production. Basically, Benylin Cough Syrup is only able to help you feel well. It cannot help you recover more quickly, only more comfortably.

Cautions and Warnings

Do not use Benylin Cough Syrup if you have glaucoma (increased pressure in the eye).

Possible Side Effects

Tiredness, inability to concentrate, blurred vision, dry mouth, difficulty in urination, constipation.

Drug Interactions

Benylin Cough Syrup contains an antihistamine and may produce some depression, drowsiness, or inability to concentrate. Don't drink large quantities of alcoholic beverages, which can add to this depressant effect.

Usual Dose

One or 2 teaspoons 4 times per day.

Special Information

Take with a full glass of water to reduce stomach upset and help loosen mucus that may be present in the breathing passages.

Generic Name

Benztropine Mesylate

Brand Name

Cogentin

Type of Drug

Anticholinergic.

Prescribed for

Treatment of Parkinson's disease or prevention or control of muscle spasms caused by other drugs, particularly phenothiazine drugs.

General Information

Benztropine Mesylate has an action on the body similar to that of Atropine Sulfate, but side effects are less frequent and less severe. It is an anticholinergic and has the ability to reduce muscle spasms. This property makes the drug useful in treating Parkinson's disease and other diseases associated with spasm of skeletal muscles.

Cautions and Warnings

Benztropine Mesylate should be used with caution if you have narrow angle glaucoma, stomach ulcers, obstructions in the gastrointestinal tract, prostatitis, or myasthenia gravis.

Possible Side Effects

The same as with any other anticholinergic drug: difficulty in urination, constipation, blurred vision, and increased sensitivity to strong light. The effects may increase if Benztropine Mesylate is taken with antihistamines, phenothiazines, antidepressants, or other anticholinergic drugs.

Drug Interactions

Interaction with other anticholinergic drugs, including tricyclic antidepressants, may cause severe stomach upset or unusual abdominal pain. If this happens, contact your doctor. Avoid over-the-counter remedies which contain Atropine or similar drugs. Your pharmacist can tell you the ingredients of over-the-counter drugs.

Usual Dose

0.5 to 6 milligrams per day, depending upon the disease being treated and patient response.

Special Information

Side effects of dry mouth, constipation, and increased sensitivity to strong light may be relieved by, respectively, chewing gum or sucking on hard candy, taking a stool softener, and wearing sunglasses. Such side effects are easily tolerated in the absence of undesirable drug interaction.

Generic Name

Betamethasone Topical Ointment/Cream/Lotion/Gel/ Aerosol

Brand Names

Benisone Benzoate
  Cream/Gel
Celestone Cream
Diprosone Dipropionate
  Ointment/Cream/
  Lotion/Aerosol

Flurobate Benzoate
  Cream/Lotion/Gel
Uticort Benzoate Gel
Valisone Valerate
  Ointment/Cream/
  Lotion/Aerosol

Type of Drug

Corticosteroid.

Prescribed for

Relief of inflammation, itching, or other skin problems in a localized area.

General Information

Betamethasone is used to relieve the symptom of any itching, rash, or inflammation of the skin. It does not treat the underlying cause of the skin problem, only the symptom. It exerts this effect by interfering with natural body mechanisms that produced the rash, itching, etc., in the first place. If you use this drug without finding the cause of the problem, the problem may return after you stop using the drug. Betamethasone should not be used without your doctor's consent because it could cover an important reaction, one that may be valuable to him in treating you.

Cautions and Warnings

Betamethasone should not be used if you have viral diseases of the skin (herpes), fungal infections of the skin (athlete's foot), or tuberculosis of the skin, nor should it be used in the ear if the eardrum has been perforated. Don't use this medicine if you are allergic to any of the components of the ointment, cream, lotion, gel, or aerosol (check the label).

Possible Side Effects

Burning sensations, itching, irritation, dryness of the skin, secondary infection.

Special Information

Clean the skin before applying Betamethasone in a very thin film. Effectiveness is based on contact area and not on the thickness of the layer applied.

Generic Name

Brompheniramine Maleate

Brand Names

Dimetane
Rolabromophen
Veltane

Type of Drug

Antihistamine.

Prescribed for

Seasonal allergy, stuffed and runny nose, itching of the eyes, scratching of the throat caused by allergy, and other allergic symptoms such as itching, rash, or hives.

General Information

Antihistamines generally, and Brompheniramine Maleate specifically, act by blocking the release of the chemical substance histamine from the cell. Antihistamines work by drying up the secretions of the nose, throat, and eyes.

Cautions and Warnings

Brompheniramine Maleate should not be used if you are allergic to this drug. It should be avoided or used with extreme care if you have narrow angle glaucoma (pressure in the eye), stomach ulcer or other stomach problems, enlarged prostate, or problems passing urine. It should not be used by people who have deep-breathing problems such as asthma.

Possible Side Effects

Occasional: itching, rash, sensitivity to light, perspiration, chills, dryness of the mouth, nose, and throat, lowering of blood pressure, headache, rapid heartbeat, sleeplessness, dizziness, disturbed coordination, confusion, restlessness, nervousness, irritability, euphoria (feeling high), tingling of the hands and feet, blurred vision, double vision, ringing in the ears, stomach upset, loss of appetite, nausea, vomiting, constipation, diarrhea, difficulty in urination, tightness of the chest, wheezing, nasal stuffiness.

Possible Adverse Drug Effects

Use with care if you have a history of asthma, glaucoma, thyroid disease, heart disease, high blood pressure, or diabetes.

Drug Interactions

Brompheniramine Maleate should not be taken with the MAO inhibitors.

Interaction with tranquilizers, sedatives, and sleeping medication will increase the effect of these drugs; it is extremely important that you discuss this with your doctor so that doses of these drugs can be properly adjusted.

Be extremely cautious when drinking while taking Brompheniramine Maleate, which will enhance the intoxicating effect of alcohol. Alcohol also has a sedative effect.

Usual Dose

Adult: 4 milligrams 3 to 4 times per day.

Child (ages 6 to 12): 2 to 4 milligrams 3 to 4 times per day.

Child (under age 6): ¼ milligram per pound per day in divided doses.

Time-release doses are as follows.

Adult: 8 to 12 milligrams at bedtime or every 8 to 12 hours during the day.

Child (ages 6 to 12): 8 milligrams during the day or at bedtime.

Overdosage

Symptoms are depression or stimulation (especially in children), dry mouth, fixed or dilated pupils, flushing of the skin, and stomach upset. Take the patient to a hospital emergency room immediately, if you cannot make him vomit. ALWAYS bring the medicine bottle.

Special Information

Antihistamines produce a depressing effect: be extremely cautious when driving or operating heavy equipment.

The safety of Brompheniramine Maleate in pregnancy has not been established. A breast-feeding mother should avoid taking this medication, since it is known to pass from the mother to the baby through the milk.

Generic Name

Butabarbital

Brand Names

Butal

Buticaps

Butisol Sodium

Sarisol

Type of Drug

Hypnotic; sedative; anticonvulsive.

Prescribed for

Epileptic seizures, convulsions; as an anticonvulsive or a daytime sedative; as a mild hypnotic (sleeping medication); and for eclampsia (toxemia in pregnancy).

General Information

Butabarbital, like the other barbiturates, appears to act by interfering with nerve impulses to the brain. When used as an anticonvulsive, Butabarbital is not very effective by itself, but when used in combination with anticonvulsive agents such as Phenytoin, the action of both the Butabarbital and the Phenytoin is dramatic. This combination has been used very successfully to control epileptic seizures.

Cautions and Warnings

Butabarbital may slow down your physical and mental reflexes, so you must be extremely careful when operating machinery, driving an automobile, or performing other potentially dangerous tasks. Elderly patients on Butabarbital exhibit nervousness and confusion at times. Barbiturates are neutralized in the liver and eliminated from the body through the kidneys; consequently, people who have liver or kidney disorders—namely, difficulty in forming or excreting urine—should be monitored by their doctor when taking Butabarbital. Butabarbital is classified as a barbiturate; long-term or unsupervised use may cause addiction.

If you have known sensitivities or allergies to barbiturates, or if you have previously been addicted to sedatives or hypnotics, or if you have a disease affecting the respiratory system, you should not take Butabarbital.

Possible Side Effects

Difficulty in breathing, skin rash, and general allergic reaction such as running nose, watering eyes, and scratchy throat.

Possible Adverse Drug Effects

Drowsiness, lethargy, dizziness, hangover, nausea, vomiting, diarrhea. More severe adverse reactions may include anemia and yellowing of the skin and eyes.

Drug Interactions

Interaction with alcohol, tranquilizers, or other sedatives increases the sedative effect of Butabarbital.

Interaction with anticoagulants (blood-thinning agents) can reduce their effect. This is also true of muscle relaxants and painkillers.

Usual Dose

Adult: Daytime sedative, 15 to 30 milligrams 3 to 4 times per day; hypnotic for sleep, 50 to 100 milligrams at bedtime.

Child: 7½ to 30 milligrams as determined by age, weight, and degree of sedation desired.

Overdosage

Symptoms are difficulty in breathing, decrease in size of the pupils of the eyes, lowered body temperature progressing to fever as time passes, fluid in the lungs, and eventually coma.

Anyone suspected of having taken an overdose must be taken to the hospital for immediate care. ALWAYS bring the medicine bottle to the emergency room physician so he can quickly and correctly identify the medicine and start treatment. Severe overdosage of this medication can kill; the drug has been used many times in suicide attempts.

Generic Name

Cephalexin

Brand Name

Keflex

Type of Drug

Cephalosporin antibiotic.

Prescribed for

Bacterial infections susceptible to this medication. Cephalexin is generally prescribed for respiratory tract infections, infections of the middle ear, infections of the skin and other soft tissues, bone infections, and infections of the urinary tract.

General Information

Cephalexin is manufactured in the laboratory by the process known as fermentation and by general chemical reaction, and as such, is classified as a semisynthetic antibiotic. Because the effectiveness of the antibiotic is determined by the drug's ability to destroy the cell wall of the invading bacteria, it is very important that the patient completely follow the doctor's prescribing directions. These directions include spacing of doses as well as the number of days the patient should continue taking the medicine. If they are not followed, the effect of the antibiotic is severely reduced.

Cautions and Warnings

If you know that you are allergic or feel that you might be allergic to Penicillin, you should avoid taking Cephalexin since if you are allergic to one, there is a chance that you will be allergic to the other. The most common allergic effect experienced with any of the antibiotics similar to Penicillin is a hivelike rash over large areas of the body with itching and redness. It is extremely important that you tell your doctor if you have ever taken this drug or any of the penicillins before, and if you have experienced any adverse effects to the drug such as skin rash, itching, or difficulty in breathing. The safe use of Cephalexin in pregnant females has not been definitely established and it should be used only if there is a specific need for it, since it is possible that this drug may cross the blood barrier into the unborn child. These drugs will also pass into the milk of a nursing mother.

Possible Side Effects

If you are taking Cephalexin you may experience one or more of the following allergic reactions ranging from mild to life-threatening. Most commonly, however, re-actions are quite mild: itching, rashes, occasional fever, chills, and reactions of one or more of the components of the blood. Serious reactions are called anaphylactic reactions; although they are quite rare, some deaths have been reported from anaphylactic reactions to this or another member of the cephalosporin class.

Possible Adverse Drug Effects

Cephalexin and other cephalosporin antibiotics have been known to induce adverse effects on the blood system; it is the others that have been more definitely associated with decrease in kidney function. Taking Cephalexin induces nausea, vomiting, or diarrhea in about one-third of patients. Less frequent adverse effects: cramps in the abdomen, upset stomach, diar-rhea, as well as headache, not feeling well, dizziness, difficulty in breathing, tingling in the extremities, and (occasional) enlargement of the liver.

Drug Interactions

Cephalexin, which works by killing microorganisms which cause infections, may be inhibited by antibiotics, such as Erythromycin and Tetracycline, which do not kill, but simply stop the growth of microorganisms. The two types should not be taken together.

Usual Dose

Adult: 1 to 4 grams per day in divided doses.
Child: 12½ to 25 milligrams per pound of body weight per day in 4 divided doses.
For severe infections the doses may be doubled.

Special Information

Cephalexin, to be effective, must be taken continuously for 7 to 10 days; so take it exactly as prescribed.

The drug has maximum effect if taken 1 hour before or 2 hours after meals, but if upset stomach occurs, the drug can be taken with meals.

Generic Name

Chloral Hydrate

Brand Names

Aquachloral Supprettes (suppositories)	Noctec
	Oradrate
Cohidrate	SK-Chloral Hydrate
Felsules	Somnos

Type of Drug

Sedative-hypnotic.

Prescribed for

Insomnia or as a daytime sedative.

General Information

Chloral Hydrate is very effective in producing sleep. Most people will fall asleep within an hour after taking this medicine. This drug usually does not cause the morning "hangover" seen with other sleeping pills.

Cautions and Warnings

Do not take Chloral Hydrate if you have liver or kidney disease, severe heart disease, or stomach problems, or if you are sensitive or allergic to this or similar drugs.

The drug passes through the bloodstream of pregnant women into the unborn child and into breast milk of nursing mothers and should not be taken by women who are pregnant or nursing. Chloral Hydrate may be habit-forming or addictive. It should only be taken when absolutely necessary and only in the amounts prescribed.

Possible Side Effects

Most common: reduction in alertness. If you plan to drive a car or operate other machinery, do so with extreme caution.

Possible Adverse Drug Effects

Headache, hangover, hallucinations, drowsiness, stomach upset, nausea, vomiting, difficulty in walking, bad taste in the mouth, feeling of excitement, itching, light-headedness, dizziness, nightmares, feeling unwell, changes in the composition of the blood.

Drug Interactions

Taking Chloral Hydrate with blood-thinning drugs may require a change of dosage of the latter: consult your doctor. Chloral Hydrate is a potent depressant, so avoid drinking alcohol or taking other drugs with depressant properties such as tranquilizers, barbiturates, or sleeping pills.

Usual Dose

Adult: Sleeping medicine, 500 milligrams to 1 gram 1/2 hour before sleep. Daytime sedative, 250 milligrams 3 times per day after meals. Daily dose should not exceed 2 grams.

Child: Sleeping medicine, 20 milligrams per pound of body weight (maximum of 1 gram). Daytime sedative, half the dose for sleeping, divided into 3 equal doses.

Overdosage

Symptoms are listed in "Possible Adverse Drug Effects" above. The patient should be taken to a hospital emergency room immediately. ALWAYS bring the medicine bottle.

Storage

Store at room temperature in a night table drawer, not in an area that is hot and/or humid, such as a bathroom.

Special Information

The combination of Chloral Hydrate and alcohol is notorious as the Mickey Finn. Avoid it.

Stomach upset can be minimized if you take Chloral Hydrate with a full glass of water, juice, or other liquid.

Generic Name

Chlordiazepoxide

Brand Names

Chlordiazachel	Sereen
J-Liberty	SK-Lygen
Libritabs	Tenax
Librium	

Type of Drug

Tranquilizer.

Prescribed for

Relief of symptoms of anxiety, tension, fatigue, or agitation.

General Information

Chlordiazepoxide is a member of the chemical group of drugs known as benzodiazepines. These drugs are used as either antianxiety agents, anticonvulsants, or sedatives (sleeping pills). They exert their effects by relaxing the large skeletal muscles and by a direct effect on the brain. In doing so, they can relax you and make you either more tranquil or sleepier, depending on the drug and how much you use. Many doctors prefer Chlordiazepoxide and the other members of this class to other drugs that can be used for the same effect. Their reason is that the benzodiazepines tend to be safer, have fewer side effects, and are usually as, if not more, effective.

These drugs are generally used in any situation where they can be a useful adjunct.

Benzodiazepine tranquilizing drugs can be abused if taken for long periods of time and it is possible to develop withdrawal symptoms if you discontinue the therapy abruptly. Withdrawal symptoms include convulsions, tremor, muscle cramps, stomach cramps, vomiting, and sweating.

Cautions and Warnings

Do not take Chlordiazepoxide if you know you are sensitive or allergic to this drug or other benzodiazepines such as Diazepam, Oxazepam, Clorazepate, Lorazepam, Prazepam, Flurazepam, and Clonazepam.

Chlordiazepoxide and other members of this drug group may aggravate narrow angle glaucoma, but if you have open angle glaucoma you may take the drugs. In any case, check this information with your doctor. Chlordiazepoxide can cause tiredness, drowsiness, inability to concentrate, or similar symptoms. Be careful if you are driving, operating machinery, or performing other activities which require concentration. Avoid taking this drug during the first 3 months of pregnancy except under strict supervision of your doctor.

Possible Side Effects

Most common: mild drowsiness during the first few days of therapy, especially in the elderly or debilitated. If drowsiness persists, contact your doctor.

Possible Adverse Drug Effects

Major adverse reactions: confusion, depression, lethargy, disorientation, headache, inactivity, slurred speech, stupor, dizziness, tremor, constipation, dry mouth, nausea, inability to control urination, changes in sex drive, irregular menstrual cycle, changes in heart rhythm, lowered blood pressure, retention of fluids, blurred or double vision, itching, rash, hiccups, nervousness, inability to fall asleep, and (occasional) liver dysfunction. If you experience any of these reactions stop taking the medicine and contact your doctor immediately.

Drug Interactions

Chlordiazepoxide is a central nervous system depressant. Avoid alcohol, tranquilizers, narcotics, barbiturates, MAO inhibitors, antihistamines, and other medicine used to relieve depression.

Usual Dose

Adult: 5 to 100 milligrams per day. This tremendous variance in dosage exists because of varying response of individuals, related to age, weight, severity of disease, and other characteristics.

Child (over age 6): May be given this drug if it is deemed appropriate by the physician. Initial dose, lowest available (5 milligrams 2 to 4 times per day). Later, may increase in some children to 30 to 40 milligrams per day. The dose must be individualized to obtain maximum benefit.

Overdosage

Symptoms are confusion, sleep or sleepiness, lack of response to pain such as a pin stick, shallow breathing, lowered blood pressure, and coma. The patient should be taken to a hospital emergency room immediately. ALWAYS bring the medicine bottle.

Generic Name

Chlorothiazide

Brand Names

Diuril
Ro-Chlorozide

Type of Drug

Diuretic.

Prescribed for

Congestive heart failure, cirrhosis of the liver, kidney malfunction, high blood pressure, and other conditions where it is necessary to rid the body of excess fluid.

General Information

This drug is a member of the class known as thiazide diuretics. Thiazides act on the kidney to stimulate the production of large amounts of urine. They also cause you to lose bicarbonate, chloride, and potassium ions from the body. They are used as part of the treatment of any disease where it is desirable to eliminate large quantities of body water. These diseases include heart failure, some kidney diseases, and liver disease.

Cautions and Warnings

Do not take Chlorothiazide if you are allergic or sensitive to this drug, similar drugs of this group, or sulfa drugs. If you have a history of allergy or bronchial asthma, you may also have a sensitivity or allergy to Chlorothiazide. Although the drug has been used to treat specific conditions in pregnancy, unsupervised use by pregnant women should be avoided. Chlorothiazide will cross the placenta and pass into the unborn child, possibly causing problems. The drug will also pass into the breast milk of nursing mothers.

Possible Side Effects

Chlorothiazide will cause a lowering of potassium in the body. Signs of low potassium levels are dryness of the mouth, thirst, weakness, lethargy, drowsiness, restlessness, muscle pains or cramps, muscular tiredness, low blood pressure, decreased frequency of urination and decreased amount of urine produced, abnormal heart rate, stomach upset including nausea and vomiting.

To treat this, potassium supplements are given in the form of tablets, liquids, or powders, or by increased consumption of foods such as bananas, citrus fruits, melons, and tomatoes.

Possible Adverse Drug Effects

Loss of appetite, stomach upset, nausea, vomiting, cramping, diarrhea, constipation, dizziness, headache, tingling of the toes and fingers, restlessness, changes in blood composition, sensitivity to sunlight, rash, itching, fever, difficulty in breathing, allergic reactions, dizziness when rising quickly from a sitting or lying position, muscle spasms, weakness, blurred vision.

Drug Interactions

Chlorothiazide will add to (potentiate) the action of other blood-pressure-lowering drugs. This is beneficial, and is frequently used to help lower blood pressure in patients with hypertension.

The possibility of developing imbalances in body fluids (electrolytes) is increased if you take medications such as Digitalis and adrenal corticosteroids while you take Chlorothiazide.

If you are taking an oral antidiabetic drug and begin taking Chlorothiazide, the antidiabetic dose may have to be altered.

Lithium Carbonate should not be taken with Chlorothiazide because the combination may increase the risk of lithium toxicity.

If you are taking Chlorothiazide for the treatment of high blood pressure or congestive heart failure, avoid over-the-counter medicine for the treatment of coughs, colds, and allergies which may contain stimulants. If you are unsure about them, ask your pharmacist.

Usual Dose

Adult: ½ to 1 gram 1 to 2 times per day. Often people respond to intermittent therapy; that is, getting the drug on alternate days or 3 to 5 days per week. This reduces side effects.

Child: 10 milligrams per pound of body weight each day, in 2 equal doses.

Infant (under age 6 months): up to 15 milligrams per pound per day, in 2 equal doses.

Overdosage

Symptoms are large amount of urination, fatigue, and coma. The patient should be taken to a hospital emergency room immediately. ALWAYS bring the medicine bottle.

Generic Name
Chlorpheniramine Maleate

Brand Names

Allerbid Tymcaps	Ciramine
Allerid-O.D.	Cosea-12
Allermine	Histaspan
Al-R Capsules	Histex
Antagonate	Histrey
Chloramate Unicelles	Pyranistan
Chlormene	Ru-Hist
Chlorspan-12	Teldrin Spansules
Chlortab	Trymegen
Chlor-Trimeton	

Type of Drug

Antihistamine.

Prescribed for

Seasonal allergy, stuffed and runny nose, itching of the eyes, scratching of the throat caused by allergy, and other allergic symptoms such as itching, rash, or hives.

General Information

Antihistamines generally, and Chlorpheniramine Maleate specifically, act by blocking the release of the chemical substance histamine from the cell. Antihistamines work by drying up the secretions of the nose, throat, and eyes.

Cautions and Warnings

Chlorpheniramine Maleate should not be used if you are allergic to this drug. It should be avoided or used with extreme care if you have narrow angle glaucoma (pressure in the eye), stomach ulcer or other stomach problems, enlarged prostate, or problems passing urine. It should not be used by people who have deep-breathing problems such as asthma.

Chlorpheniramine Maleate can cause dizziness, drowsiness, and lowering of blood pressure particularly in the elderly patient. Young children can show signs of nervousness, increased tension, and anxiety.

Possible Side Effects

Occasionally seen: itching, rash, sensitivity to light, perspiration, chills, dryness of the mouth, nose, and throat, lowering of blood pressure, headache, rapid heartbeat, sleeplessness, dizziness, disturbed coordination, confusion, restlessness, nervousness, irritability, euphoria (feeling high), tingling of the hands and feet, blurred vision, double vision, ringing in the ears, stomach upset, loss of appetite, nausea, vomiting, constipation, diarrhea, difficulty in urination, tightness of the chest, wheezing, nasal stuffiness.

Possible Adverse Drug Effects

Use with care if you have a history of asthma, glaucoma, thyroid disease, heart disease, high blood pressure, or diabetes.

Drug Interactions

Chlorpheniramine Maleate should not be taken with the MAO inhibitors.

Interaction with tranquilizers, sedatives, and sleeping medication will increase the effect of these drugs; it is extremely important that you discuss this with your doctor so that doses of these drugs can be properly adjusted.

Be extremely cautious when drinking alcohol while taking Chlorpheniramine Maleate, which will enhance the intoxicating effect of alcohol. Alcohol also has a sedative effect.

Usual Dose

Adult: A 4-milligram tablet 3 to 4 times per day.

Child (ages 6 to 12): 2-milligram tablet 3 to 4 times per day.

Time-release capsules or tablets:

Adult: 8 to 12 milligrams at bedtime or every 8 to 10 hours during the day.

Child (ages 6 to 12): 8 milligrams during the day or at bedtime.

Overdosage

Symptoms are depression or stimulation (especially in children), dry mouth, fixed or dilated pupils, flushing of the skin, and stomach upset. Take the patient to a hospital emergency room immediately, if you cannot make him vomit. ALWAYS bring the medicine bottle.

Special Information

Antihistamines produce a depressing effect: be extremely cautious when driving or operating heavy equipment.
The safety of Chlorpheniramine Maleate in pregnancy has not been established. A breast-feeding mother should avoid taking this medication, since it is known to pass from the mother to the baby through the milk.

Generic Name

Chlorpromazine

Brand Names

Chlor-PZ
Promapar
Thorazine

Type of Drug

Phenothiazine antipsychotic.

Prescribed for

Psychotic disorders, moderate to severe depression with anxiety, control of agitation or aggressiveness of disturbed children, alcohol withdrawal symptoms, intractable pain, and senility. Chlorpromazine may also be used to relieve nausea, vomiting, hiccups, and restlessness, and/or apprehension before surgery or other special therapy.

General Information

Chlorpromazine and other members of the phenothiazine group act on a portion of the brain called the hypothalamus. They affect parts of the hypothalamus that control metabolism, body temperature, alertness, muscle tone, hormone balance, and vomiting, and may be used to treat problems related to any of these functions.

Cautions and Warnings

Chlorpromazine should not be taken if you are allergic to one of the drugs in the broad classification known as phenothiazine drugs. Do not take Chlorpromazine if you have any blood, liver, kidney, or heart disease, very low blood pressure, or Parkinson's disease. This medication is a tranquilizer and can have a depressive effect, especially during the first few days of therapy. Care should be taken when performing activities requiring a high degree of concentration, such as driving. If you are taking this medication and become pregnant contact your doctor immediately.

Possible Side Effects

Most common: drowsiness, especially during the first or second week of therapy. If the drowsiness becomes troublesome, contact your doctor.

Possible Adverse Drug Effects

Chlorpromazine can cause jaundice (yellowing of the whites of the eyes or skin), usually in 2 to 4 weeks. The jaundice usually goes away when the drug is discontinued, but there have been cases when it did not. If you notice this effect or if you develop symptoms such as fever and generally not feeling well, contact your doctor immediately. Less frequent: changes in components of the blood including anemias, raised or lowered blood pressure, abnormal heart rates, heart attack, feeling faint or dizzy.

Phenothiazines can produce "extrapyramidal effects," such as spasm of the neck muscles, severe stiffness of the back muscles, rolling back of the eyes, convulsions, difficulty in swallowing, and symptoms associated with Parkinson's disease. These effects look very serious but go away after the drug has been withdrawn; however, symptoms of the face, tongue, and jaw may persist for as long as several years, especially in the elderly with a history of brain damage. If you experience extrapyramidal effects contact your doctor immediately.

Chlorpromazine may cause an unusual increase in psychotic symptoms or may cause paranoid reactions, tiredness, lethargy, restlessness, hyperactivity, confusion at night, bizarre dreams, inability to sleep, depression, and euphoria. Other reactions are itching, swelling, unusual sensitivity to bright lights, red skin, and rash. There have been cases of breast enlargement, false positive pregnancy tests, changes in menstrual flow in females, and impotence and changes in sex drive in males. Chlorpromazine may also cause dry mouth, stuffy nose, headache, nausea, vomiting, loss of appetite, change in body temperature, loss of facial color, salivation, perspiration, constipation, diarrhea, changes in urine and stool habits, worsening of glaucoma, blurred vision, weakening of eyelid muscles, and spasms in bronchial and other muscles, as well as increased appetite, fatigue, excessive thirst, and changes in the coloration of skin, particularly in exposed areas.

Drug Interactions

Chlorpromazine should be taken with caution in combination with barbiturates, sleeping pills, narcotics, or any other medication which may produce a depressive effect. Avoid alcohol.

Usual Dose

Adult: 30 to 1000 milligrams or more per day, individualized according to disease and patient's response.

Child: 0.25 milligram per pound of body weight every 4 to 6 hours up to 200 milligrams or more per day (by various routes including rectal suppositories), depending on disease, age, and response to therapy.

Overdosage

Symptoms are depression, extreme weakness, tiredness, desire to go to sleep, coma, lowered blood pressure, uncontrolled muscle spasms, agitation, restlessness, convulsions, fever, dry mouth, and abnormal heart rhythms. The patient should be taken to a hospital emergency room immediately. ALWAYS bring the medicine bottle.

Chlorpropamide

Brand Name

Diabinese

Type of Drug

Oral antidiabetic.

Prescribed for

Diabetes mellitus (sugar in the urine).

General Information

Chlorpropamide is one of several oral antidiabetic drugs that work by stimulating the production and release of insulin from the pancreas. The primary difference between these drugs lies in their duration of action. Because they do not lower blood sugar directly, they require some function of pancreas cells.

Cautions and Warnings

Mild stress such as infection, minor surgery, or emotional upset reduces the effectiveness of Chlorpropamide. Remember that while you are taking this drug you should be under your doctor's continuous care.

Chlorpropamide is an aid to, not a substitute for, a diet. Diet remains of primary importance in the treatment of your diabetes. Follow the diet plan your doctor has prescribed for you.

Chlorpropamide and similar drugs are not oral Insulin, nor are they a substitute for Insulin. They do not lower blood sugar by themselves.

The treatment of diabetes is your responsibility. You should follow all instructions about diet, body weight, exercise, personal hygiene, and all measures to avoid infection. If you are not feeling well, or if you have symptoms such as itching, rash, yellowing of the skin or eyes, abnormally light-colored stools, a low-grade fever, sore throat, or diarrhea—contact your doctor immediately.

Possible Side Effects

Common: loss of appetite, nausea, vomiting, stomach upset. At times, you may experience weakness or tingling in the hands and feet. These effects can be eliminated by reducing the daily dose of Chlorpropamide or, if necessary, by switching to a different oral anti-diabetic drug. This decision must be made by your doctor.

Possible Adverse Drug Effects

Chlorpropamide may produce abnormally low levels of blood sugar when too much is taken for your immediate requirements. (Other factors which may cause lowering of blood sugar are liver or kidney disease, malnutrition, age, drinking alcohol, and diseases of the glands.)

Chlorpropamide may cause a yellowing of the whites of the eyes or skin, itching, rash, or changes in the results of laboratory tests made by your doctor. Usually these reactions will disappear in time. If they persist you should contact your doctor.

Drug Interactions

Thiazide diuretics may lessen the effect of Chlorpropamide, while Insulin, sulfa drugs, Oxyphenbutazone, Phenylbutazone, Aspirin and other salicylates, Probenecid, Dicoumarol, Bishydroxycoumarin, Warfarin, Phenyramidol, and MAO inhibitor drugs prolong and enhance the action of Chlorpropamide.

Interaction with alcoholic beverages will cause flushing of the face and body, throbbing pain in the head and neck, difficult breathing, nausea, vomiting, sweating, thirst, chest pains, palpitations, lowered blood pressure, weakness, dizziness, blurred vision, and confusion. If you experience these reactions contact your doctor immediately.

Because of the stimulant ingredients in many over-the-counter drug products for the relief of coughs, colds, and allergies, avoid them unless your doctor advises otherwise.

Usual Dose

Adult: 250 milligrams daily.
Elderly: 100 to 250 milligrams daily.
For severe cases, 500 milligrams daily.

Overdosage

A mild overdose of Chlorpropamide lowers the blood sugar, which can be treated by eating sugar in such forms as candy and orange juice. A patient with a more serious overdose should be taken to a hospital emergency room immediately. ALWAYS bring the medicine bottle.

Generic Name

Chlorthalidone

Brand Name

Hygroton

Type of Drug

Diuretic.

Prescribed for

Congestive heart failure, cirrhosis of the liver, kidney malfunction, high blood pressure, and other conditions where it is necessary to rid the body of excess fluid.

General Information

This drug is a member of the class known as thiazide diuretics. Thiazides act on the kidney to stimulate the production of large amounts of urine. They also cause you to lose bicarbonate, chloride, and potassium ions from the body. They are used as a part of the treatment of any disease where it is desirable to eliminate large quantities of body water. These diseases include heart failure, some kidney diseases, and liver diseases.

Cautions and Warnings

Do not take Chlorthalidone if you are allergic or sensitive to this drug, similar drugs of this group, or sulfa drugs. If you have a history of allergy or bronchial asthma, you may also have a sensitivity or allergy to Chlorthalidone. Although this drug has been used to treat specific conditions in pregnancy, unsupervised use by pregnant patients should be avoided. Chlorthalidone will cross the placenta and pass into the unborn child, possibly causing problems. The drug will pass into the breast milk of nursing mothers.

Possible Side Effects

Chlorthalidone will cause a lowering of potassium in the body. Signs of low potassium are dryness of the mouth, thirst, weakness, lethargy, drowsiness, restlessness, muscle pains or cramps, muscular tiredness, low blood pressure, decreased frequency of urination and decreased amount of urine produced, abnormal heart rate, stomach upset indicating nausea and vomiting.

To treat this, potassium supplements are given in the form of tablets, liquids, or powders, or by increased consumption of foods such as bananas, citrus fruits, melons, and tomatoes.

Possible Adverse Drug Effects

Loss of appetite, stomach upset, nausea, vomiting, cramping, diarrhea, constipation, dizziness, headache, tingling of the toes and fingers, restlessness, changes in blood composition, sensitivity to sunlight, rash, itching, fever, difficulty in breathing, allergic reactions, dizziness when rising quickly from a sitting or lying position, muscle spasms, weakness, blurred vision.

Drug Interactions

Chlorthalidone will add to (potentiate) the action of other blood-pressure-lowering drugs. This is beneficial, and is frequently used to help lower blood pressure in patients with hypertension.

The possibility of developing imbalances in body fluids (electrolytes) is increased if you take medications such as Digitalis and adrenal corticosteroids while you take Chlorthalidone.

If you are taking an oral antidiabetic drug and begin taking Chlorthalidone, the antidiabetic dose may have to be altered.

Lithium Carbonate should not be taken with Chlorthalidone because the combination may increase the risk of lithium toxicity.

If you are taking this drug for the treatment of high

blood pressure or congestive heart failure, avoid over-the-counter medicine for the treatment of coughs, colds, and allergies which may contain stimulants. If you are unsure about them, ask your pharmacist.

Usual Dose

50 to 100 milligrams per day; or 100 milligrams on alternate days or 3 days per week.

Some patients may require 150 or 200 milligrams per day; doses of more than 200 milligrams per day generally do not produce greater response. A single dose is taken with food in the morning. Dose often declines from the initial dose, according to individual patient's need.

Overdosage

Symptoms are large amount of urination, fatigue, and coma. The patient should be taken to a hospital emergency room immediately. ALWAYS bring the medicine bottle.

Generic Name

Cimetidine

Brand Name

Tagamet

Type of Drug

First member of a new class of drugs available in the U.S. known as histamine H_2 antagonists.

Prescribed for

Part of the treatment of stomach ulcer. Also used in the treatment of other conditions characterized by secretions of large amounts of gastrointestinal fluids.

Cautions and Warnings

Cimetidine is a relatively new drug and it is unlikely that you will be allergic to it, although allergy is a possibility. This drug should be used with extreme caution if you are pregnant or if you might become pregnant while taking Cimetidine.

Possible Side Effects

Most frequent: mild diarrhea, muscle pains, dizziness, rash.

Possible Adverse Drug Effects

A few patients have reported breast enlargement. There have been several reports, not yet verified, of adverse effects on components of the blood system.

Usual Dose

Three hundred milligrams 4 times per day, usually with meals and at bedtime.

Overdosage

The patient should be taken to a hospital emergency room immediately. ALWAYS bring the medicine bottle.

Because this is a new drug, there have been few Cimetidine overdoses. Doses of as much as 10 grams (approximately 33 tablets) have been taken, though, without any unusual effects.

Special Information

Many doctors believe that Cimetidine, properly used, will decrease the amount of ulcer surgery because the drug reduces the amount of irritating secretions produced by stomach glands. Report any unusual side effects of this drug to your doctor immediately: he will want to know about anything related to Cimetidine because of its newness in the U.S.

Generic Name

Clindamycin

Brand Name

Cleocin Hydrochloride

Type of Drug

Antibiotic.

Prescribed for

Serious infections caused by bacteria which are generally found to be susceptible to this drug.

General Information

This is one of the few drugs, given by mouth, which is effective against anaerobic organisms: (bacteria which grow only in the absence of oxygen) and are frequently found in infected wounds, lung abscesses, abdominal infections, and infections of the female genital tract. It is also effective against the organisms usually treated by Penicillin or Erythromycin.

Cautions and Warnings

Do not take Clindamycin if you are allergic to it or to Lincomycin, another antibiotic drug. It may cause a severe intestinal irritation called colitis, which may be fatal. Because of this, Clindamycin should be reserved for serious infections due to organisms known to be affected by it. It should not be taken for the casual treatment of colds or other moderate infections, or for infections which can be successfully treated with other drugs. If you develop severe diarrhea or stomach pains, call your doctor at once.

Possible Side Effects

Stomach pain, nausea, vomiting, diarrhea, pain when swallowing.

Possible Adverse Drug Effects

Itching and rash or more serious signs of drug sensitivity, such as difficulty in breathing; also yellowing of the skin or whites of the eyes and occasional effects on components of the blood.

Drug Interactions

Clindamycin may antagonize Erythromycin; these drugs should not be taken together.

Usual Dose

Adult: 150 to 450 milligrams every 6 hours.

Child: 2 to 11 milligrams per pound of body weight per day in divided doses. No child should be given less than 37½ milligrams 3 times per day, regardless of weight.

Special Information

Safety in pregnant women has not been established. Since this drug is transferred to the breast milk of nursing mothers, its use by them should be carefully considered.

Generic Name

Clofibrate

Brand Name

Atromid-S

Type of Drug

Antihyperlipidemic.

Prescribed for

Reduction of high blood levels of cholesterol and/or triglycerides.

General Information

Although we don't know exactly how Clofibrate works, we know that it works on blood cholesterol and possibly triglycerides. The lowering of blood levels of these fatty materials may be beneficial, and may have an effect on the development of heart disease. No one knows for sure. However, it is generally considered better to have low levels of both cholesterol and triglycerides in the blood. Clofibrate is only part of the therapy for high blood levels of cholesterol and/or triglycerides. Diet and weight control are also very important. You must remember that taking this medicine is not a substitute for other activities or dietary restrictions which have been prescribed for you by your doctor.

Cautions and Warnings

Clofibrate should not be used if you have severe liver or kidney disease, are pregnant, or are a nursing mother. There is the possibility that this medication may pass from you into your baby and cause an adverse effect.

Possible Side Effects

The most frequent side effect of Clofibrate is nausea. Other gastrointestinal reactions may be experienced: loose stools, stomach upset, stomach gas, abdominal pain. Less frequent: headache, dizziness, tiredness, cramped muscles, aching and weakness, skin rash, itching, brittle hair and loss of hair.

Possible Adverse Drug Effects

Abnormal heart rhythms, blood clots in the lungs or veins, enlargement of the liver, gallstones (especially in patients who have taken Clofibrate for a long time), decreased sex drive, sexual impotence. If you suffer from angina pectoris, a specific type of chest pain, Clofibrate may either increase or decrease this pain. It may cause you to produce smaller amounts of urine than usual, and has been associated with blood in the urine, tiredness, weakness, drowsiness, dizziness, headache, and increased appetite. Clofibrate has been accused of causing stomach ulcers, stomach bleeding, arthritislike symptoms, uncontrollable muscle spasms, increased perspiration, blurred vision, breast enlargement, and some effects on the blood.

Drug Interactions

If you are taking an anticoagulant and get a new prescription for Clofibrate, your anticoagulant dose will have to be reduced by as much as a third to a half. It is absolutely essential that your doctor knows you are taking these drugs in combination so that the proper dose adjustments can be made.

Usual Dose

4 capsules per day in divided doses.

Storage

Clofibrate capsules are covered with soft gelatin that must be protected from heat and moisture. They should not be stored in the refrigerator, or in a bathroom medicine chest where there may be a lot of heat or moisture in the air, but in a dresser or night table where room temperature is normal.

Generic Name

Clonidine

Brand Name

Catapres

Type of Drug

Antihypertensive.

Prescribed for

High blood pressure.

General Information

Clonidine acts in the brain by causing the dilation of certain blood vessels, thereby decreasing blood pressure. The drug produces its effect very quickly, causing a decline in blood pressure within 1 hour. If you abruptly stop taking Clonidine you may experience an unusual increase in blood pressure with symptoms of agitation, headache, and nervousness. These effects can be reversed by simply resuming therapy or by taking another drug to lower the blood pressure. Under no circumstances should you stop taking Clonidine without your doctor's knowledge. People who abruptly stop taking this medication may suffer severe reactions and even die. Be sure you always have an adequate supply on hand.

Cautions and Warnings

Some people develop a tolerance to usual doses of Clonidine. If this happens to you your blood pressure may increase and you will require a change in the Clonidine dose. Clonidine is not recommended for use by women who are pregnant or who feel they may become pregnant.

Possible Side Effects

Most common: dry mouth, drowsiness, sedation, constipation, dizziness, headache, fatigue. These effects tend to diminish as you continue taking the drug.

Possible Adverse Drug Effects

Infrequent: loss of appetite, not feeling well, nausea, vomiting, weight gain, breast enlargement, various effects on the heart, changes in dream patterns, nightmares, difficulty sleeping, nervousness, restlessness, anxiety, mental depression, rash, hives, itching, thinning or loss of scalp hair, difficulty urinating, impotence and dryness, burning of the eyes.

Drug Interactions

Clonidine has a depressive effect and will increase the depressive effects of alcohol, barbiturates, sedatives, and tranquilizers. Avoid them.

Usual Dose

Starting dose of 0.1 milligram twice per day may be raised by 0.1 to 0.2 milligram per day until maximum control is achieved. The dose must be tailored to your individual needs. It is recommended that no one should take more than 2.4 milligrams per day.

Overdosage

Symptoms are severe lowering of blood pressure, weakness, and vomiting. The patient should be taken to a hospital emergency room immediately. ALWAYS bring the medicine bottle.

Special Information

Clonidine causes drowsiness in about 35 percent of those who take it: be extremely careful while driving or operating any sort of appliance or machinery. The effect is prominent during the first few weeks of therapy, then tends to decrease.

Generic Name

Clorazepate

Brand Names

Azene
Tranxene
Tranxene-SD

Type of Drug

Tranquilizer.

Prescribed for

Relief of symptoms of anxiety, tension, fatigue, or agitation.

General Information

Clorazepate is a member of the chemical group of drugs known as benzodiazepines. These drugs are used as either antianxiety agents, anticonvulsants, or sedatives (sleeping pills). They exert their effects by relaxing the large skeletal muscles and by a direct effect on the brain. In doing so, they can relax you and make you either more tranquil or sleepier, depending on the drug and how much you use. Many doctors prefer Clorazepate and the other members of this class to other drugs that can be used for the same effect. Their reason is that the benzodiazepines tend to be safer, have fewer side effects, and are usually as, if not more, effective.

These drugs are generally used in any situation where they can be a useful adjunct.

Benzodiazepine tranquilizing drugs can be abused if taken for long periods of time and it is possible to develop withdrawal symptoms if you discontinue the therapy abruptly. Withdrawal symptoms include convulsions, tremor, muscle cramps, stomach cramps, vomiting, and sweating.

Cautions and Warnings

Do not take Clorazepate if you know you are sensitive or allergic to this drug or other benzodiazepines such as Diazepam, Chlordiazepoxide, Oxazepam, Lorazepam, Prazepam, Flurazepam, and Clonazepam.

Clorazepate and other members of this drug group may aggravate narrow angle glaucoma, but if you have open angle glaucoma you may take the drugs. In any case, check this information with your doctor. Clorazepate can cause tiredness, drowsiness, inability to concentrate, or similar symptoms. Be careful if you are driving, operating machinery, or performing other activities which require concentration. Avoid taking this drug during the first 3 months of pregnancy except under strict supervision of your doctor.

Possible Side Effects

Most common: mild drowsiness during the first few days of therapy, especially in the elderly or debilitated. If drowsiness persists, contact your doctor.

Possible Adverse Drug Effects

Major adverse reactions: confusion, depression, lethargy, disorientation, headache, inactivity, slurred speech, stupor, dizziness, tremor, constipation, dry mouth, nausea, inability to control urination, changes in sex drive, irregular menstrual cycle, changes in heart rhythm, lowered blood pressure, retention of fluids, blurred or double vision, itching, rash, hiccups, nervousness, inability to fall asleep, and (occasional) liver dysfunction. If you experience any of these reactions, stop taking the medicine and contact your doctor immediately.

Drug Interactions

Clorazepate is a central nervous system depressant. Avoid alcohol, tranquilizers, narcotics, sleeping pills, barbiturates, MAO inhibitors, antihistamines, and other medicine used to relieve depression.

Usual Dose

15 to 60 milligrams daily; average dose 30 milligrams in divided quantities. Must be adjusted to individual response for patient to receive maximum effect.

Tranxene-SD, a long-acting form of Clorazepate, may be given as a single dose, either 11.25 or 22.5 milligrams once every 24 hours. The daily dose of Azene, another brand name, is slightly different, from 12 to 52 milligrams per day according to patient response. The drug may be given as a single daily dose at bedtime; usual starting dose for helping patients go to sleep is 13 milligrams.

Overdosage

Symptoms are confusion, sleep or sleepiness, lack of response to pain such as a pin stick, shallow breathing, lowered blood pressure, and coma. The patient should be taken to a hospital emergency room immediately. ALWAYS bring the medicine bottle.

Generic Name

Clotrimazole

Brand Name

Lotrimin

Type of Drug

Antifungal.

Prescribed for

Fungus infections of the skin and vaginal tract.

General Information

Clotrimazole is one of the newer antifungal drugs in the U.S., although it has been available in other parts of the world for some time. This drug is especially useful against a wide variety of fungus organisms which other drugs do not effect.

Cautions and Warnings

If Clotrimazole causes local itching and/or irritation, stop using it. Do not use in the eyes. Women who are in the first three months of pregnancy should only use this drug after specific direction from their doctor.

Possible Side Effects

Side effects do not occur too often and are usually mild.

Cream or solution: redness, stinging, blistering, peeling, itching and swelling of local areas. Vaginal tablets: mild burning, skin rash, mild cramps, frequent urination, and burning or itching in a sexual partner.

Usual Dose

Cream or solution: apply to affected areas, morning and night. If there is no improvement within 4 weeks, contact your doctor. Vaginal tablets: 1 tablet, inserted into the vagina at bedtime for 7 days.

Generic Name

Codeine Sulfate

Type of Drug

Narcotic analgesic and cough suppressant.

Prescribed for

Relief of moderate to moderately severe pain, and as a cough suppressant.

General Information

Codeine Sulfate is a narcotic drug with some pain-relieving and cough-suppressing activity. As an analgesic, it is useful for mild to moderate pain. 30 to 60 milligrams of Codeine Sulfate is approximately equal in pain-relieving effect to 2 Aspirin tablets (650 milligrams). Codeine Sulfate may be less active than Aspirin for types of pain associated with inflammation, since Aspirin reduces inflammation but Codeine Sulfate does not. Codeine Sulfate suppresses the cough reflex but does not cure the underlying cause of the cough. In fact, sometimes it may not be desirable to overly suppress cough because cough suppression reduces your ability to naturally eliminate excess mucus produced during a cold or allergy attack. Other narcotic cough suppressants are stronger than Codeine Sulfate, but Codeine Sulfate remains the best cough medicine available today.

Cautions and Warnings

Do not take Codeine Sulfate if you know you are allergic or sensitive to it. Long-term use of this drug may cause drug dependence or addiction. Codeine Sulfate is a respiratory depressant. Use this drug with extreme caution if you suffer from asthma or other breathing problems. Codeine Sulfate affects the central nervous system, producing sleepiness, tiredness, and/or inability to concentrate. Be careful if you are driving, operating machinery, or performing other functions requiring concentration. If you are pregnant or suspect that you are pregnant do not take this drug.

Possible Side Effects

Most frequent: light-headedness, dizziness, sleepiness, nausea, vomiting, loss of appetite, sweating. If these occur, consider calling your doctor and asking him about lowering the dose of Codeine Sulfate you are taking. Usually the side effects disappear if you simply lie down.

More serious side effects of Codeine Sulfate are shallow breathing or difficulty in breathing.

Possible Adverse Drug Effects

Euphoria (feeling high), weakness, sleepiness, headache, agitation, uncoordinated muscle movement, minor hallucinations, disorientation and visual disturbances, dry mouth, loss of appetite, constipation, flushing of the face, rapid heartbeat, palpitations, faintness, urinary difficulties or hesitancy, reduced sex drive and/or potency, itching, skin rashes, anemia, lowered blood sugar, and a yellowing of the skin and/or whites of the eyes. Narcotic analgesics may aggravate convulsions in those who have had convulsions in the past.

Drug Interactions

Because of its depressant effect and potential effect on breathing, Codeine Sulfate should be taken with extreme care in combination with alcohol, sleeping medicine, tranquilizers, or other depressant drugs.

Usual Dose

Adult: 15 to 60 milligrams 4 times per day for relief

of pain; 10 to 20 milligrams every few hours as needed
to suppress cough.

Child: 1 to 2 milligrams per pound of body weight
In divided doses for relief of pain; ½ to ¾ milligram
per pound of body weight in divided doses to suppress
cough.

Overdosage

Symptoms are depression of respiration (breathing),
extreme tiredness progressing to stupor and then coma,
pinpointed pupils of the eyes, no response to stimulation such as a pin stick, cold and clammy skin, slowing
down of the heartbeat, lowering of blood pressure, convulsions, and cardiac arrest. The patient should be taken
to a hospital emergency room immediately. ALWAYS
bring the medicine bottle.

Brand Name

Combid

Ingredients

Isopropamide
Prochlorperazine

Type of Drug

Gastrointestinal anticholinergic combination.

Prescribed for

Excess acid in the stomach, spasms of the stomach and
small intestine, and relief of anxiety and tension or
nausea and vomiting associated with gastrointestinal
disease.

General Information

The antinauseant in Combid works to relieve and prevent nausea and vomiting and the anticholinergic works
to prevent and treat stomach and intestinal spasms. By
relieving these spasms, Combid can prevent or treat
stomach or intestinal pains. Combid spansules release

their ingredients over an 8 to 12 hour period; only 2 capsules per day are usually required.

Cautions and Warnings

Do not take Combid if you have glaucoma. Other disorders where an anticholinergic drug such as Combid may be damaging are prostatic hypertrophy, pyloric obstruction, bladder-neck obstruction, and obstructive lesions of the intestine. Nausea and vomiting may be a drug side effect or a sign of disease: if you have this medication at home, do not self-medicate for nausea and vomiting until you have checked with your doctor.

Possible Side Effects

Primary: sleepiness or drowsiness, dry mouth, blurred vision, increased sensitivity to strong light, difficulty in urination.

Possible Adverse Drug Effects

Rare: sore throat, fever, unusual bleeding or bruising, rash, yellowing of the skin or whites of the eyes. If you experience any of these, contact your doctor immediately.

Drug Interactions

Combid can cause sleepiness, tiredness, or difficulty in concentration. Do not worsen the problem by adding alcoholic beverages, tranquilizers, sedatives, and other drugs that cause tiredness.

Usual Dose

1 capsule every 12 to 24 hours.

Overdosage

Symptoms (from either ingredient in Combid) are central nervous system depression possibly to the point of coma, lowered blood pressure, agitation, restlessness, convulsions, fever, dry mouth, severe stomach cramps, abnormal heart rhythms, difficulty in swallowing, extreme thirst, blurred vision, sensitivity to bright light, flushed, hot dry skin, rash, high blood pressure, confusion, and delirium. The patient should be taken to a hospital emergency room immediately. ALWAYS bring the medicine bottle.

Generic Name

Conjugated Estrogens

Brand Names

Co-Estro	Genisis
Conest	Kestrin
Conjugated Estrogenic	Menogen
Substances	Menotab
Estroate	Ovest
Estrocon	Palopause
Estropan	Premarin
Femest	Sodestrin-H
Fem-H	

Type of Drug

Estrogen.

Prescribed for

Moderate to severe symptoms associated with menopause. There is no evidence that this drug is effective for nervous symptoms or depression occurring during menopause; it should not be used to treat this condition. Conjugated Estrogens may also be used to treat various types of cancer in selected patients; and other conditions where supplementation of normal estrogenic substances is required.

General Information

Because of the potential development of secondary disease after a long period of taking Conjugated Estrogens, the decision to take this medication chronically should be made cautiously by you and your doctor.

Cautions and Warnings

Estrogens have been reported to increase the risk of certain types of cancer in postmenopausal women taking this type of drug for prolonged periods of time:

this risk tends to depend upon the duration of treatment and on the dose of the estrogen being taken. When long-term estrogen therapy is indicated for the treatment of menopausal symptoms, the lowest effective dose should be used. If you have to take Conjugated Estrogens for extended periods of time, you should see your doctor at least twice a year so that he can assess your current condition and your need to continue the drug therapy. If you are taking an estrogenic product and experience vaginal bleeding of a recurrent, abnormal, or persistent nature, contact your doctor immediately. If you are pregnant you should not use this or any other estrogenic substance since these drugs, if used during the earlier stages of pregnancy, may seriously damage the offspring. If you have active thrombophlebitis or any other disorder associated with the formation of blood clots, you probably should not take this drug. If you feel that you have a disorder associated with blood clots and you have been taking Conjugated Estrogens or a similar product, you should contact your doctor immediately so that he can evaluate your situation and decide about stopping the drug therapy.

Prolonged continuous administration of estrogenic substances to certain animal species has increased the frequency of cancer in these animals and there is evidence that these drugs may increase the risk of various cancers in humans. This drug should be taken with caution by women with a strong family history of breast cancer or those who have breast nodules, fibrocystic disease of the breast, or abnormal mammogram. Furthermore, long-term taking of Conjugated Estrogens may expose a woman to a two- to threefold increase in chance of developing gallbladder disease. It is possible that women taking Conjugated Estrogens for extended periods of time may experience some of the same development of long-term adverse effects as women who have taken oral contraceptives for extended periods of time. These long-term problems may include thromboembolic disease or the development of various disorders associated with the development of blood clots, liver cancer or other liver tumors, high blood pressure, glucose intolerance or a development of a symptom similar to diabetes or the aggravation of diabetes in patients who had this disease before they started the estrogen, and high blood levels of calcium in certain classes of patients.

Possible Side Effects

Breakthrough bleeding, spotting, changes in menstrual flow, dysmenorrhea, premenstruallike syndrome, menorrhea, vaginal infection with candida, cystitislike syndrome, enlargement or tenderness of the breasts, nausea, vomiting, abdominal cramps, feeling of bloatedness, jaundice or yellowing of the skin or whites of the eyes, skin rash, loss of scalp hair, development of new hairy areas. Lesions of the eye have been associated with estrogen therapy, and blindness has occurred in long-term estrogen therapy. If you wear contact lenses and are taking estrogens, it is possible that you will become intolerant to the lenses. You may also experience headache—possibly of a migraine variety—dizziness, depression, weight changes, retention of water, and changes in sex drive.

Usual Dose

From 0.3 to 3.75 milligrams per day, depending on the disease and patient's response.

Overdosage

Overdosage may cause nausea and withdrawal bleeding in adult females. Accidental overdosage in children has not resulted in serious adverse effects.

Brand Name

Cortisporin Otic

Ingredients

Hydrocortisone
Neomycin Sulfate
Polymyxin-B

Type of Drug

Steroid antibiotic combination product.

Prescribed for

Superficial infections, inflammation, itching, and other problems involving the outer ear.

General Information

Cortisporin Otic contains a steroid drug to reduce inflammation and two antibiotics to treat local infections. This combination can be quite useful for local infections and inflammations of the ear because of its dual method of action and its relatively broad, nonspecific applicability.

Possible Side Effects

Local irritation such as itching or burning can occur if you are sensitive or allergic to one of the ingredients in this drug.

Usual Dose

From 2 to 4 drops in the affected ear 3 to 4 times per day.

Special Information

Use only when specifically prescribed by a physician. Overuse of this or similar products can result in the growth of other organisms such as fungus. If new infections or new problems appear during the time you are using this medication, stop using the drug and contact your doctor.

Generic Name

Cyclandelate

Brand Names

Cyclanfor
Cyclospasmol
Cydel

Type of Drug

Vasodilator.

Prescribed for

Nighttime leg cramps. Also prescribed to dilate large blood vessels in the brain so that more blood can be delivered to it.

General Information

Cyclandelate relaxes various smooth muscles: it slows their normal degree of responsiveness but does not paralyze muscle cells. Cyclandelate may directly widen blood vessels in the brain and other areas, increasing the flow of blood and oxygen to these areas.

Cautions and Warnings

Do not take Cyclandelate if you are allergic or sensitive to it. Do not take Cyclandelate if you have a history of glaucoma, or of heart or other disease in which major blood vessels have been partly or completely blocked. Safe use of this drug by pregnant women has not been established.

Possible Side Effects

The most common side effect of Cyclandelate is mild stomach upset, but this can be avoided by taking the medicine with food or antacid. Cyclandelate can produce mild flushing, particularly in the face and extremities. It can also cause headache, feeling of weakness, and rapid heartbeat, especially during the first few weeks of therapy.

Possible Adverse Drug Effects

Cyclandelate can make you feel weak, dizzy, or faint when you rise quickly from a lying or sitting position: this is called orthostatic hypotension and is caused by a sudden drop in the amount of blood being supplied to your brain. You can usually avoid orthostatic hypotension by getting up slowly. If the symptom becomes a problem, contact your doctor so that he can adjust your dose or prescribe a different medicine for you.

Drug Interactions

Avoid taking over-the-counter drugs for cough, cold, or allergy as some of these can aggravate heart disease or other diseases related to blocked blood vessels. Contact your doctor or pharmacist for more specific information about over-the-counter products which could be a problem.

Usual Dose

Starting dose, 1200 to 1600 milligrams per day in divided doses before meals and at bedtime. As you begin to respond to the medication, the dose may be reduced to a lowest effective level of, usually, 400 to 800 milligrams per day given in 2 to 4 divided doses. Improvement takes several weeks to appear; do not look for immediate benefits. Use of this medication for less than several weeks is usually of little or no value and certainly of no permanent value.

Generic Name

Cyproheptadine Hydrochloride

Brand Name

Periactin

Type of Drug

Phenothiazine-type antihistamine.

Prescribed for

Relief of symptoms associated with allergies, drug allergies, colds or upper respiratory infections, infection or itching of the extremities, insect bites, and general itching.

General Information

Cyproheptadine Hydrochloride is an antihistamine. Any effect it exerts is due to its ability to counteract the effects of histamine, a chemical released by the body as part of allergic or sensitivity reactions. Histamine is also released as a part of the body's reaction to the common cold or similar respiratory infections. Cyproheptadine Hydrochloride is especially useful in treating symptoms of allergy itching, and the common cold. It has been reported to cause weight gain and has even been tried as an appetite stimulant.

Cautions and Warnings

Do not take Cyproheptadine Hydrochloride if you are allergic to it or to other phenothiazine-type drugs such as Chlorpromazine and Prochlorperazine. Signs of allergies to phenothiazines include sore throat, fever, unusual bleeding or bruising, rash, blurred vision, and yellowing of skin.

Possible Side Effects

Most frequent: sedation, sleeplessness, dizziness, disturbed coordination. Less common: itching, drug rash, drug allergy, sensitivity to sunlight, excessive perspiration, chills, dryness of the mouth, nose, and throat. Other possible side effects: lowered blood pressure, headache, palpitations, rapid heartbeat.

Possible Adverse Drug Effects

Effects on the blood system, confusion, restlessness, excitation, nervousness, irritability, sleeplessness, euphoria, tingling in the hands and feet, blurred vision, double vision, ringing in the ears, convulsions, stomach upset, loss of appetite, vomiting, nausea, diarrhea, constipation, thickening of mucus and other bronchial secretions resulting in tightness in the chest, wheezing, stuffed nose. Cyproheptadine Hydrochloride may also produce adverse effects common to the phenothiazine class of drugs, such as tremors, a spastic, uncontrollable motion, and (rarely) a form of jaundice (yellowing of the skin and eyes).

Drug Interactions

Alcohol will increase the drowsiness or sleepiness that can be produced by Cyproheptadine Hydrochloride, so avoid drinking excessive quantities of alcoholic beverages. Taking Cyproheptadine Hydrochloride with another sedative, tranquilizer, barbiturate, or hypnotic drug can increase drowsiness and other symptoms of depression.

Cyproheptadine Hydrochloride can influence the effectiveness of any high blood pressure medicine you are taking.

If you have Parkinson's disease, you probably should not be taking this type of antihistamine; it is known to produce specific adverse drug effects in people with Parkinson's disease. An MAO inhibitor may interact with Cyproheptadine Hydrochloride to prolong the drying effect of the antihistamine, causing dry mouth and blurred vision.

Usual Dose

Adult: 4 to 20 milligrams daily.

Child (ages 7 to 14): 4 milligrams 2 to 3 times per day.

Child (ages 2 to 6): 2 milligrams 2 to 3 times per day.

The maximum daily dose for adults is 32 milligrams; for children ages 7 to 14, 16 milligrams; for children ages 2 to 6, 12 milligrams.

The liquid form of this medicine is very bitter. To improve the taste you can mix it with fruit juice, milk, or any carbonated beverage.

Overdosage

Symptoms are depression or stimulation (especially in children), dry mouth, fixed or dilated pupils, flushing of the skin, and stomach upset. Take the patient to a hospital emergency room immediately. ALWAYS bring the medicine container to the hospital. Do *not* induce vomiting. After having taken this drug the patient might breathe in the vomit, causing serious lung damage.

Storage

The liquid form of Cyproheptadine Hydrochloride is sensitive to light. Keep in an amber-colored bottle and store in a dark place.

Special Information

Cyproheptadine Hydrochloride can produce sleepiness. Be careful if you are driving or operating hazardous machinery.

Generic Name:

D-Amphetamine

Brand Names

Daro	Ferndex
Dexampex	Obotan
Dexedrine	

Type of Drug

Central nervous system stimulant.

Prescribed for

Short-term (a couple of weeks) aid to diet control, minimal brain dysfunction in children, narcolepsy (uncontrollable and unpredictable desire to sleep).

General Information

When taking this medicine as part of a weight control program it is usual to experience a lessening of effect on the appetite. This represents the fact that your body is breaking down the drug faster. Do not increase the amount of drug you are taking: simply stop taking the medicine.

The use of D-Amphetamine (as well as other drugs) in the treatment of minimal brain dysfunction in children is extremely controversial and must be judged by a physician qualified to treat the disorder. Children whose problems are judged to have been produced by their surroundings or by primary psychiatric disorders may not be helped by D-Amphetamine.

Cautions and Warnings

D-Amphetamine is highly abusable and addictive. It must be used with extreme caution. People with hardening of the arteries (arteriosclerosis), heart disease, high blood pressure, thyroid disease, or glaucoma, or who are sensitive or allergic to any Amphetamine, should not take this medication. Any person with a history of abusing drugs should avoid any Amphetamine medication. D-Amphetamine should not be used by pregnant women (it may cause birth defects).

Possible Side Effects

Palpitations, restlessness, overstimulation, dizziness, sleeplessness, increased blood pressure, rapid heartbeat.

Possible Adverse Drug Effects

Euphoria, hallucinations, muscle spasms and tremors, headache, dryness of the mouth, unpleasant taste, diarrhea, constipation, stomach upset, itching, loss of sex drive, and (rarely) psychotic drug reactions.

Usual Dose

Narcolepsy, 5 to 60 milligrams per day, depending on individual need.

Minimal brain dysfunction, 2.5 to 40 milligrams per day, depending on child's age and response to the drug.

Weight control, 5 to 30 milligrams per day in divided doses ½ to 1 hour before meals; or as a long-acting dose once in the morning.

Overdosage

Symptoms are tremors, muscle spasms, restlessness, exaggerated reflexes, rapid breathing, hallucinations, confusion, panic, and overaggressive behavior, followed by depression and exhaustion after the central nervous system stimulation wears off, as well as abnormal heart rhythms, changes in blood pressure, nausea, vomiting, diarrhea, convulsions, and coma. The patient should be taken to a hospital emergency room immediately. ALWAYS bring the medicine container.

Special Information

Do not take this medicine after 6 to 8 hours before you plan to go to sleep, or it will interfere with a sound and restful night's sleep.

Brand Name

Darvocet-N

Ingredients

Acetaminophen
Propoxyphene Napsylate

Type of Drug

Analgesic.

Prescribed for

Relief of mild to moderate pain.

General Information

Propoxyphene Napsylate, the major ingredient in this product, is a chemical derivative of Methadone, a narcotic used for pain relief. It is estimated that Propoxyphene Napsylate is about half to two-thirds as strong a pain reliever as Codeine and about as effective as Aspirin.

Do not drink excessive amounts of alcohol when taking this medicine. Be extra careful when driving or operating machinery. Do not take this medicine if you are pregnant or think you may be pregnant.

Cautions and Warnings

Do not take this drug if you are allergic to either ingredient. It may produce physical or psychological drug dependence (addiction) after long periods of time. The major sign of dependence is anxiety when the drug is suddenly stopped. Darvocet-N abuse can lead to toxic effects on the kidneys from the Acetaminophen ingredient of this drug. (See "Possible Adverse Drug Effects" below.)

Possible Side Effects

Dizziness, sedation, nausea, vomiting. These effects usually go away if you lie down and relax for a few moments.

Possible Adverse Drug Effects

Darvocet-N can produce constipation, abdominal pain, skin rash, light-headedness, weakness, headache, euphoria, and minor visual disturbances. Long-term use may lead to adverse effects caused by the Acetaminophen portion of Darvocet-N: anemias and changes in the composition of blood. Allergic reactions are skin rash, itching, and fever.

Drug Interactions

Interaction with alchohol, tranquilizers, sedatives, hypnotics, or antihistamines may produce tiredness, dizziness, light-headedness, and other signs of depression.

Usual Dose

1 or 2 tablets every 4 hours to relieve pain.
Take with a full glass of water or with food to reduce the possibility of stomach upset.

Overdosage

Symptoms are difficulty in breathing, restlessness leading to stupor or coma, blue color of the skin, anemia, yellowing of the skin and/or whites of the eyes, skin rash, fever, stimulation, excitement and delirium followed by depresssion, coma, and convulsions. The patient should be taken to a hospital emergency room immediately. ALWAYS bring the medicine bottle.

Brand Name

Darvon Compound-65

Ingredients

Aspirin
Caffeine
Phenacetin
Propoxyphene Hydrochloride

Other Brand Names

Note: The following products have the same combination of ingredients in the same or different concentrations.

Bexophene Capsules
Darvon Compound
  Capsules
Dolene Compound 65
Elder Compound 65
ICN 65 Compound
  Capsules
Migesic 65
Pargesic Compound 65
  Capsules

Poxy Compound-65
Progesic Compound-65
  Capsules
Proproxychel Compound
Propoxyphene Hydrochloride Compound Capsules
Proxagesic Compound-65
Repro Compound-65
SK-65 Compound Capsules

Type of Drug

Analgesic combination.

Prescribed for

Relief of mild to moderate pain.

General Information

Propoxyphene Hydrochloride, the major ingredient in this product, is a chemical derivative of Methadone, a narcotic used for pain relief. It is estimated that Propoxyphene Hydrochloride is about half to two-thirds as strong a pain reliever as Codeine and about as effective as Aspirin.

Do not drink excessive amounts of alcohol when taking this medicine. Be extra careful when driving or operating machinery. Do not take this medicine if you are pregnant or think you may be pregnant.

Cautions and Warnings

Do not take Darvon Compound-65 if you know you are allergic or sensitive to it. Long-term use of this medicine may cause drug dependence or addiction. Use this drug with extreme caution if you suffer from asthma or other breathing problems. Darvon Compound-65 affects the central nervous system, producing sleepiness, tiredness, and/or inability to concentrate. If you are pregnant or suspect that you are pregnant do not take this drug.

Possible Side Effects

Most frequent: light-headedness, dizziness, sleepiness, nausea, vomiting, loss of appetite, sweating. If these effects occur, consider calling your doctor and asking him about lowering the dose you are taking. Usually the side effects disappear if you simply lie down.

More serious side effects of Darvon Compound-65 are shallow breathing or difficulty in breathing.

Possible Adverse Drug Effects

Adverse effects of Darvon Compound-65 include euphoria (feeling high), weakness, sleepiness, headache, agitation, uncoordinated muscle movement, minor hallucinations, disorientation and visual disturbances, dry mouth, loss of appetite, constipation, flushing of the face, rapid heartbeat, palpitations, faintness, urinary difficulties or hesitancy, reduced sex drive and/or potency, itching, skin rashes.

Drug Interactions

Interaction with alcohol, tranquilizers, barbiturates, or sleeping pills produces tiredness, sleepiness, or inability to concentrate, and seriously increases the depressive effect of Darvon Compound-65.

The Aspirin component of Darvon Compound-65 can affect anticoagulant (blood-thinning) therapy. Be sure to discuss this with your doctor so that the proper dosage adjustment can be made.

Interaction with adrenal cortical steroids, Phenylbutazone, or alcohol can cause severe stomach irritation with possible bleeding.

Usual Dose

One capsule every 4 hours as needed for pain.

Overdosage

Symptoms are depression of respiration (breathing), extreme tiredness progressing to stupor and then coma, cold and clammy skin, slowing down of the heartbeat, convulsions, and cardiac arrest. The patient should be taken to a hospital emergency room immediately. ALWAYS bring the medicine bottle.

Special Information

Drowsiness may occur: be careful when driving or operating hazardous machinery.

Take with food or ½ glass of water to prevent stomach upset.

The Phenacetin ingredient of Darvon Compound-65 may be toxic to your kidneys; do not take this medication for longer than 10 days unless directed by your doctor.

Generic Name

Dexchlorpheniramine Maleate

Brand Name

Polaramine

Type of Drug

Antihistamine.

Prescribed for

Seasonal allergy, stuffed and runny nose, itching of the eyes, scratching of the throat caused by allergy, and other allergic symptoms such as itching, rash, or hives.

General Information

Antihistamines generally, and Dexchlorpheniramine Maleate specifically, act by blocking the release of the chemical substance histamine from the cell. Antihistamines work by drying up the secretions of the nose, throat, and eyes.

Cautions and Warnings

Dexchlorpheniramine Maleate should not be used if you are allergic to this drug. It should be avoided or used with extreme care if you have narrow angle glaucoma (pressure in the eye), stomach ulcer or other stomach problems, enlarged prostate, or problems passing urine. It should not be used by people who have deep-breathing problems such as asthma.

Dexchlorpheniramine Maleate can cause dizziness, drowsiness, and lowering of blood pressure particularly in the elderly patient. Young children can show signs of nervousness, increased tension, and anxiety.

Possible Side Effects

Occasionally seen: itching, rash, sensitivity to light, perspiration, chills, dryness of mouth, nose, and throat, lowering of blood pressure, headache, rapid heartbeat, sleeplessness, dizziness, disturbed coordination, confusion, restlessness, nervousness, irritability, euphoria (feeling high), tingling of the hands and feet, blurred vision, double vision, ringing in the ears, stomach upset, loss of appetite, nausea, vomiting, constipation, diarrhea, difficulty in urination, tightness of the chest, wheezing, nasal stuffiness.

Possible Adverse Drug Effects

Use with care if you have a history of asthma, glaucoma, thyroid disease, heart disease, high blood pressure, or diabetes.

Drug Interactions

Dexchlorpheniramine Maleate should not be taken with the MAO inhibitors.

Interaction with tranquilizers, sedatives, and sleeping medication will increase the effects of these drugs; it is extremely important that you discuss this with your doctor so that doses of these drugs can be properly adjusted.

Be extremely cautious when drinking while taking Dexchlorpheniramine Maleate, which will enhance the intoxicating effect of alcohol. Alcohol also has a sedative effect.

Usual Dose

Adult: 2 milligrams 3 to 4 times per day.
Child (under age 12): 1 milligram 3 to 4 times per day.
Infant: 0.5 milligram 3 to 4 times per day.

Overdosage

Symptoms are depression or stimulation (especially in children), dry mouth, fixed or dilated pupils, flushing of the skin, and stomach upset. Take the patient to a hospital emergency room immediately, if you cannot make him vomit. ALWAYS bring the medicine bottle.

Special Information

Antihistamines produce a depressing effect; be extremely cautious when driving or operating heavy equipment.

The safety of Dexchlorpheniramine Maleate in pregnancy has not been established. A breast-feeding mother should avoid taking this medicine, since it is known to pass from the mother to the baby through the milk.

Generic Name

Diazepam

Brand Name

Valium

Type of Drug

Tranquilizer.

Prescribed for

Relief of symptoms of anxiety, tension, fatigue, or agitation.

General Information

Diazepam is a member of the chemical group of drugs known as benzodiazepines. These drugs are used as either antianxiety agents, anticonvulsants, or sedatives (sleeping pills). They exert their effects by relaxing the large skeletal muscles and by a direct effect on the brain. In doing so, they can relax you and make you either more tranquil or sleepier, depending on the drug and how much you use. Many doctors prefer Diazepam and the other members of this class to other drugs that can be used for the same effect. Their reason is that the benzodiazepines tend to be safer, have fewer side effects, and are usually as, if not more, effective.

These drugs are generally used in any situation where they can be a useful adjunct.

Benzodiazepine tranquilizing drugs can be abused if taken for long periods of time and it is possible to develop withdrawal symptoms if you discontinue the therapy abruptly. Withdrawal symptoms include convulsions, tremor, muscle cramps, stomach cramps, vomiting, and sweating.

Cautions and Warnings

Do not take Diazepam if you know you are sensitive or allergic to this drug or other benzodiazepines such as Chlordiazepozide, Oxazepam, Chlorazepate, Lorazepam, Prazepam, Flurazepam, and Clonazepam.

Diazepam and other members of this drug group may

aggravate narrow angle glaucoma, but if you have open angle glaucoma you may take the drugs. In any case, check this information with your doctor. Diazepam can cause tiredness, drowsiness, inability to concentrate, or similar symptoms. Be careful if you are driving, operating machinery, or performing other activities which require concentration. Avoid taking this drug during the first 3 months of pregnancy except under strict supervision of your doctor.

Possible Side Effects

Most common: mild drowsiness during the first few days of therapy, especially in the elderly or debilitated. If drowsiness persists, contact your doctor.

Possible Adverse Drug Effects

Major adverse reactions: confusion, depression, lethargy, disorientation, headache, lack of activity, slurred speech, stupor, dizziness, tremor, constipation, dry mouth, nausea, inability to control urination, changes in sex drive, irregular menstrual cycle, changes in heart rhythm, lowered blood pressure, retention of fluids, blurred or double vision, itching, rash, hiccups, nervousness, inability to fall asleep, and (occasional) liver dysfunction. If you experience any of these reactions stop taking the medicine and contact your doctor immediately.

Drug Interactions

Diazepam is a central nervous system depressant. Avoid alcohol, tranquilizers, narcotics, sleeping pills, barbiturates, MAO inhibitors, antihistamines, and other medicine used to relieve depression.

Usual Dose

Adult: 2 to 40 milligrams per day as individualized for maximum benefit, depending on symptoms and response to treatment, which may call for a dose outside the range given.

Elderly: If debilitated, will usually require less of the drug to control tension and anxiety.

Child: 1 to 2½ milligrams 3 to 4 times per day. Possibly more if needed to control anxiety and tension. Diazepam should not be given to children under age 6 months.

Overdosage

Symptoms are confusion, sleep or sleepiness, lack of response to pain such as a pin stick, shallow breathing, lowered blood pressure, and coma. The patient should be taken to a hospital emergency room immediately. ALWAYS bring the medicine bottle.

Special Information

Do not drink alcohol or take other depressive drugs, such as tranquilizers, sleeping pills, narcotics, or barbiturates, when taking Diazepam.

Generic Name

Dicloxacillin Sodium

Brand Names

Dycill	Pathocil
Dynapen	Veracillin

Type of Drug

Broad-spectrum antibiotic.

Prescribed for

Gram-positive bacterial infections. Gram-positive bacteria (pneumococci, streptococci, and staphylococci) are organisms which usually cause diseases such as pneumonia, infections of the tonsils and throat, venereal disease, meningitis (infection of the spinal column), and septicemia (infection of the bloodstream). This drug is best used to treat infections resistant to Penicillin, although it may be used as initial treatment for some patients.

General Information

Dicloxacillin Sodium is manufactured in the laboratory by fermentation and by general chemical reaction, and is classified as a semisynthetic antibiotic. Because the effectiveness of the antibiotic is determined by the drug's ability to affect the cell wall of the invading bacteria, it is very important that the patient completely follow the doctor's prescribing directions. These directions include spacing of doses as well as the number of days the patient should continue taking the medicine. If they are not followed, the effect of the antibiotic is severely reduced. To ensure the maximum effect, you should take the medication on an empty stomach, either 1 hour before or 2 hours after meals.

Cautions and Warnings

If you have a known history of allergy to Penicillin you should avoid taking Dicloxacillin Sodium, since the drugs are chemically similar. The most common allergic reaction to Dicloxacillin Sodium, as well as to the other penicillins, is a hivelike rash over the body with itching and redness. It is important to tell your doctor if you have ever taken Dicloxacillin Sodium or penicillins before and if you have experienced any adverse reaction to the drug such as skin rash, itching, or difficulty in breathing.

Possible Side Effects

Common: stomach upset, nausea, vomiting, diarrhea, possible skin rash. Less common: hairy tongue, itching or irritation around the anus and/or vagina. If these symptoms occur, contact your doctor immediately.

Drug Interactions

The effect of Dicloxacillin Sodium can be significantly reduced when taken with other antibiotics. Consult your doctor if you are taking both during the same course of therapy. Otherwise, Dicloxacillin Sodium is generally free of interactions with other medications.

Usual Dose

Adult (and child weighing 88 pounds or more): 125 to 250 milligrams every 6 hours. In severe infections, 500 milligrams may be needed.

Child (less than 88 pounds): 5½ to 11 milligrams per pound of body weight per day, in divided doses.

Storage

Dicloxacillin Sodium can be stored at room temperature.

Special Information

Do not take Dicloxacillin Sodium after the expiration date on the label. Its safety in pregnancy has not been established.

Generic Name

Dicyclomine Hydrochloride

Brand Names

Antispas	Dyspas
Bentyl	Or-Tyl
Dibent	Rocyclo

Type of Drug

Gastrointestinal anticholinergic agent.

Prescribed for

Relief of stomach upset and spasms. This medication is sometimes prescribed to treat morning sickness during the early months of pregnancy.

General Information

Dicyclomine Hydrochloride works by reducing spasms in muscles of the stomach and other parts of the gastrointestinal tract. In doing so, it helps relieve some of the uncomfortable symptoms associated with peptic ulcer, irritable bowel and/or colon, spastic colon, and other gastrointestinal disorders. It only relieves symptoms. It does not cure the underlying disease.

Cautions and Warnings

Dicyclomine Hydrochloride should not be used if you know you are sensitive or allergic to it. Do not use this medicine if you have glaucoma, asthma, obstructive disease of the gastrointestinal tract, or other serious gastrointestinal disease. Because this drug reduces your ability to sweat, its use in hot climates may cause heat exhaustion.

Possible Side Effects

Difficulty in urination, blurred vision, rapid heartbeat, skin rash, sensitivity to light, headache, flushing of the skin, nervousness, dizziness, weakness, drowsiness, nausea, vomiting, fever, nasal congestion, heartburn, constipation.

Possible Adverse Drug Effects

Elderly patients taking this drug may develop mental confusion or excitement.

Drug Interactions

Interaction with antihistamines, phenothiazines, tranquilizers, antidepressants, and some narcotic painkillers may cause blurred vision, dry mouth, or drowsiness.

Do not use with MAO inhibitor drugs, which will tend to prevent excretion of Dicyclomine Hydrochloride from the body and thus potentiate it (increase its effect).

Usual Dose

10 to 30 milligrams 3 to 4 times per day.

Special Information

Dry mouth from Dicyclomine Hydrochloride can be relieved by chewing gum or sucking hard candy; constipation can be treated by using a stool softening laxative.

Generic Name

Diethylpropion Hydrochloride

Brand Names

o.b.c.t.	Tepanil
Ro-Diet	Tepanil Ten-Tab
Tenuate	Weh-Less Timecelles
Tenuate Dospan	

Type of Drug

Nonamphetamine appetite suppressant.

Prescribed for

Suppression of appetite and treatment of obesity.

General Information

Although Diethylpropion Hydrochloride is not an amphetamine, it can produce the same adverse effects as the amphetamine appetite suppressants.

Cautions and Warnings

Do not use Diethylpropion Hydrochloride if you have heart disease, high blood pressure, thyroid disease, or glaucoma, or if you are sensitive or allergic to this or similar drugs. Furthermore, do not use this medication if you are emotionally agitated or have a history of drug abuse.

Possible Side Effects

Palpitations, high blood pressure, overstimulation, nervousness, restlessness, drowsiness, sedation, weakness, dizziness, inability to sleep, tremor, headache, dry mouth, nausea, vomiting, diarrhea and other intestinal disturbances, rash, itching, changes in sex drive, hair loss, muscle pain, difficulty in passing urine, sweating, chills, blurred vision, fever.

Usual Dose

Twenty-five milligrams 3 times per day 1 hour before meals; an additional tablet may be given in midevening if needed to suppress the desire for midnight snacks. Sustained-release tablets or capsules of 75 milligrams (Tenuate Dospan, Tepanil Ten-Tab, Weh-Less Timecelles), 1 per day usually in midmorning.

Overdosage

Symptoms are restlessness, tremor, shallow breathing, confusion, hallucinations, and fever, followed by fatigue and depression, with additional symptoms such as high or possibly low blood pressure, cold and clammy skin, nausea, vomiting, diarrhea, and stomach cramps. The patient should be taken to a hospital emergency room immediately. ALWAYS bring the medicine bottle.

Special Information

Use only for a few weeks as an adjunct to diet, under strict supervision of your doctor.

Medicine alone will not take off weight. You must limit and modify your food intake, preferably under medical supervision.

Generic Name

Diethylstilbestrol

Brand Name

DES

Type of Drug

Estrogen.

Prescribed for

Hormone replacement; diseases which require increases in estrogen levels in the blood for effective treatment; treatment of symptoms associated with menopause.

General Information

Because of the potential development of secondary disease after a long period of taking Diethylstilbestrol, the decision to take this medication chronically should be made cautiously by you and your doctor.

Cautions and Warnings

Estrogens have been reported to increase the risk of certain types of cancer in postmenopausal women taking this type of drug for prolonged periods of time: this risk tends to depend on the duration of treatment and on the dose of the estrogen being taken. When long-term estrogen therapy is indicated for the treatment of menopausal symptoms, the lowest effective dose should be used. If you have to take Diethylstilbestrol for extended periods of time, you should see your doctor at least twice a year so that he can assess your current condition and your need to continue the drug therapy. If you are taking an estrogenic product and experience vaginal bleeding of a recurrent, abnormal, or persistent nature, contact your doctor immediately. If you are pregnant you should not use this or any other estrogenic substance, since these drugs, if used during the earlier stages of pregnancy, may seriously damage the offspring. Damage to the offspring can also occur in women who took Diethylstilbestrol before they became pregnant. If you have active thrombophlcbitis, or any other disorder associated with the formation of blood clots, you probably should not take this drug. If you feel that you have a disorder associated with blood clots and you have been taking Diethylstilbestrol or a similar product, you should contact your doctor immediately so that he can evaluate your situation and decide about stopping the drug therapy.

Prolonged continuous administration of estrogenic substances to certain animal species has increased the frequency of cancer in these animals and there is evidence that these drugs may increase the risk of various cancers in humans. This drug should be taken with caution by women with a strong family history of breast cancer or those who have breast nodules, fibrocystic disease of the breast, or abnormal mammogram. Furthermore, long-term taking of Diethylstilbestrol may expose a woman to a two- to threefold increase in chance of developing gallbladder disease. It is possible that women taking Diethylstilbestrol for extended periods of time may experience some of the same development of long-term adverse effects as women who have taken oral contraceptives for extended periods of time. These long-term problems may include thromboembolic disease or the development of various disorders associated with the development of blood clots, liver tumors, high blood pressure, glucose intolerance or a development of a symptom similar to diabetes or the aggravation of diabetes in patients who had this disease before they started the estrogen, and high blood levels of calcium in certain classes of patients.

Possible Side Effects

Breakthrough bleeding, spotting, changes in menstrual flow, dysmenorrhea, premenstrual-type syndrome, menorrhea, vaginal infection with candida, cystitislike syndrome, enlargement or tenderness of the breasts, nausea, vomiting, abdominal cramps, feeling of bloatedness, jaundice or yellowing of the skin or whites of the eyes, skin rash, loss of scalp hair, development of new hairy areas. Lesions of the eye have been associated with estrogen therapy, and blindness has occurred in long-term estrogen therapy. If you wear contact lenses and are taking estrogens, you may become intolerant to the lenses. You may also experience headache—possibly of a migraine variety—dizziness, depression, weight changes, retention of water, and changes in sex drive.

Usual Dose

0.2 to 3 milligrams per day, depending upon the disease being treated and patient response. However, some diseases or patients may require up to 15 milligrams per day.

Overdosage

Overdosage may cause nausea and withdrawal bleeding in adult females. Serious adverse effects have not been reported after accidental overdosage in children.

Generic Name

Digoxin

Brand Names

Lanoxin
SK-Digoxin

Type of Drug

Cardiac glycoside.

Prescribed for

Congestive heart failure, and other heart disease.

General Information

This medication is generally used for long periods of

time to treat congestive heart failure and other heart abnormalities.

Cautions and Warnings

Do not use this drug if you know you are allergic or sensitive to Digitalis. Long-term use of Digoxin can cause the body to lose potassium, especially since Digoxin is generally used in combination with a diuretic drug. For this reason, be sure to eat a well-balanced diet and emphasize foods which are high in potassium such as bananas, citrus fruits, melons, and tomatoes.

Possible Side Effects

Most common side effects: loss of appetite, nausea, vomiting, diarrhea, blurred or disturbed vision. If you experience any of these problems, discuss them with your doctor immediately.

Possible Adverse Drug Effects

Enlargement of the breasts has been reported after long-term use of Digoxin, but this is uncommon. Allergy or sensitivity to Digoxin is also uncommon.

Drug Interactions

Diuretics (drugs which increase the production of urine), including Furosemide, Chlorothiazide, and Hydrochlorothiazide, can reduce the potassium in your blood and interact with Digoxin.

If you are a long-term Digoxin user avoid over-the-counter drugs used to relieve cough, cold, or allergies if they contain stimulants which may aggravate your heart condition. If you feel you must have medication to relieve the symptoms of colds, contact your doctor or pharmacist for information about medicine which does not contain stimulating ingredients.

Usual Dose

Adult: The first dose—known as the digitalizing dose—is 1 to 1.5 milligrams. Maintenance dose ranges from 0.125 to 0.5 milligram.

Elderly: Lower doses, as the elderly are more sensitive to adverse effects.

Infant or child: Substantially lower dose.

Overdosage

If symptoms of loss of appetite, nausea, vomiting, diarrhea, headache, weakness, feeling of not caring, blurred vision, yellow or green spots before the eyes, yellowing of the skin and eyes, or changes in heartbeat appear, contact your doctor immediately. Early signs of overdose in children are changes in heart rhythm; vomiting, diarrhea, and eye trouble are frequently seen in older people.

Brand Name

Dimetane Expectorant-DC

Ingredients

Brompheniramine Maleate
Codeine Phosphate
Guaifenesin
Phenylephrine
    Hydrochloride
Phenylpropanolamine
    Hydrochloride

Type of Drug

Decongestant; expectorant.

Prescribed for

Relief of cough, nasal congestion, runny nose, and other symptoms associated with the common cold, viruses, or other upper respiratory diseases. It may also be used to treat allergies, asthma, ear infections, or sinus infections.

General Information

Dimetane Expectorant-DC is one of almost 100 products marketed to relieve the symptoms of the common cold and other upper respiratory infections. These products contain medicine to relieve congestion, act as an antihistamine, relieve or suppress cough, and help you to cough up mucus. They may contain medicine for each purpose, or may contain a combination of medicines. Some combinations leave out the antihistamine, the decongestant, or the expectorant. You must realize while taking Dimetane Expectorant-DC or similar products that these drugs are good only for the relief of symptoms and will not treat the underlying problem, such as cold, virus, or other infections.

Cautions and Warnings

Can cause excessive tiredness or drowsiness.

Possible Side Effects

Dry mouth, blurred vision, difficulty passing urine, (possibly) constipation, nervousness, restlessness, or even inability to sleep.

Drug Interactions

Taking Dimetane Expectorant-DC with MAO inhibitors can produce severe interaction. Consult your doctor first.

Dimetane Expectorant-DC contains Codeine. Drinking alcoholic beverages while taking this drug may produce excessive drowsiness and/or sleepiness, or inability to concentrate.

Usual Dose

1 or 2 teaspoons 4 times per day.

Special Information

Take with a full glass of water to reduce stomach upset and help remove excessive mucus from the throat.

Brand Name

Dimetapp Extentabs

Ingredients

Brompheniramine
Phenylephrine
Phenylpropanolamine

Other Brand Names

Bromepath Tablets	Histatapp Tablets
Eldatapp Tablets	Taltapp Duradisk Tablets

Type of Drug

Long-acting combination antihistamine-decongestant.

Prescribed for

Relief of sneezing, runny nose, and other symptoms of nasal congestion associated with the common cold, allergy, or other upper respiratory condition.

General Information

Dimetapp is one of many products marketed to relieve the symptoms of the common cold. Most of these products contain ingredients to relieve nasal congestion or to dry up runny noses or relieve a scratchy throat; and several of them may contain ingredients to suppress cough, or to help eliminate unwanted mucus. All these products are good only for the relief of symptoms and do not treat the underlying problem such as the cold virus or other infections.

Cautions and Warnings

Do not take Dimetapp if you are pregnant.

Possible Side Effects

Mild drowsiness has been seen in patients taking Dimetapp.

Possible Adverse Drug Effects

Infrequent: restlessness, tension, nervousness, tremor, weakness, inability to sleep, headache, palpitations, elevation of blood pressure, sweating, sleeplessness, loss of appetite, nausea, vomiting, dizziness, constipation.

Drug Interactions

Interaction with alcoholic beverages may produce excessive drowsiness and/or sleepiness, or inability to concentrate. Also avoid sedatives, tranquilizers, antihistamines, and sleeping pills.

Do not self-medicate with additional over-the-counter

drugs for the relief of cold symptoms; taking Dimetapp with such drugs may result in aggravation of high blood pressure, heart disease, diabetes, or thyroid disease.

Do not take Dimetapp if you are taking or suspect you may be taking a monoamine oxidase (MAO) inhibitor: severe elevation in blood pressure may result.

Usual Dose

1 tablet morning and night.

Special Information

Since drowsiness may occur during use of Dimetapp, be cautious while performing mechanical tasks requiring alertness.

Generic Name

Diphenhydramine Hydrochloride

Brand Names

Benadryl   Rohydra
Bendylate   SK-Diphenhydramine
Fenylhist   Valdrene

Type of Drug

Antihistamine.

Prescribed for

Seasonal allergy, stuffed and runny nose, itching of the eyes, scratching of the throat caused by allergy, and other allergic symptoms such as itching, rash, or hives. In addition, Diphenhydramine Hydrochloride has been used for motion sickness and, with other drugs, for Parkinson's disease.

General Information

Antihistamines generally, and Diphenhydramine Hydrochloride specifically, act by blocking the release of the chemical substance histamine from the cell. Antihistamines work by drying up the secretions of the nose, throat, and eyes.

Cautions and Warnings

Diphenhydramine Hydrochloride should not be used if you are allergic to this drug. It should be avoided or used with extreme care if you have glaucoma (pressure in the eye), stomach ulcer or other stomach problems, enlarged prostate, or problems passing urine. It should not be used by people who have deep-breathing problems such as asthma.

Diphenhydramine Hydrochloride can cause dizziness, drowsiness, and lowering of blood pressure, particularly in the elderly patient. Young children can show signs of nervousness, increased tension, and anxiety.

Possible Side Effects

Occasionally seen: itching, rash, sensitivity to light, perspiration, chills, dryness of the mouth, nose, and throat, lowering of blood pressure, headache, rapid heartbeat, sleeplessness, dizziness, disturbed coordination, confusion, restlessness, nervousness, irritability, euphoria (feeling high), tingling of the hands and feet, blurred vision, double vision, ringing in the ears, stomach upset, loss of appetite, nausea, vomiting, constipation, diarrhea, difficulty in urination, tightness of the chest, wheezing, nasal stuffiness.

Possible Adverse Drug Effects

Use with care if you have a history of asthma, glaucoma, thyroid disease, heart disease, high blood pressure, or diabetes.

Drug Interactions

Diphenhydramine Hydrochloride should not be taken with MAO inhibitors.

Interaction with tranquilizers, sedatives, and sleeping medication will increase the effects of these drugs; it is extremely important that you discuss this with your doctor so that doses of these drugs can be properly adjusted.

Be extremely cautious when drinking while taking

Diphenhydramine Hydrochloride, which will enhance the intoxicating effect of the alcohol. Alcohol also has a sedative effect.

Usual Dose

Adult: 25 to 50 milligrams 3 to 4 times per day.
Child (over 20 pounds): 12½ to 25 milligrams 3 to 4 times per day.

Overdosage

Symptoms are depression or stimulation (especially in children), dry mouth, fixed or dilated pupils, flushing of the skin, and stomach upset. Take the patient to a hospital emergency room immediately, if you cannot make him vomit. ALWAYS bring the medicine bottle.

Special Information

Antihistamines produce a depressing effect: be extremely cautious when driving or operating heavy equipment.

The safety of Diphenhydramine Hydrochloride in pregnancy has not been established. A breast-feeding mother should avoid taking this medication, since it is known to pass from the mother to the baby through the milk.

Generic Name

Dipyridamole

Brand Name

Persantine

Type of Drug

Antianginal agent.

Prescribed for

Prevention of attacks of angina pectoris; generally used for chronic treatment of angina, not for the immediate pain of an attack.

General Information

Dipyridamole is one of many drugs used in the treatment of angina and is also being studied as a possible addition to the treatment of stroke. In such studies, the drug is examined for its possible ability to affect platelets, a component of blood involved in clotting. When used for angina, Dipyridamole increases the flow of blood to the heart muscle in order to provide the heart with sufficient oxygen.

Possible Side Effects

Headache, dizziness, nausea, flushing, weakness, mild stomach upset, and possible skin rash.

Possible Adverse Drug Effects

Dipyridamole has, on rare occasions, been reported to aggravate angina pectoris.

Drug Interactions

May interact with anticoagulant (blood-thinning) drugs; patients taking anticoagulants and Dipyridamole should be checked periodically by their physician. Aspirin has an effect similar to Dipyridamole on the platelets and may increase the chances of bleeding due to loss of platelet effectiveness when taken with Dipyridamole.

Usual Dose

50 milligrams three times per day.

Special Information

Dipyridamole may take 2 or 3 months to exert a therapeutic effect.

Brand Name

Diupres

Ingredients

Chlorothiazide
Reserpine

Type of Drug

Antihypertensive.

Prescribed for

High blood pressure.

General Information

Diupres is a good example of a drug taking advantage of a drug interaction. Each of the drug ingredients works by different mechanisms to lower your blood pressure. The Chlorothiazide relaxes the muscles in your veins and arteries and also helps reduce the volume of blood flowing through those blood vessels. Reserpine works on the nervous system to decrease the quality of nerve transmissions which are contributing to the increased pressure. These drugs complement each other so that their combined effect is better than the effect of the two individually.

It is essential that you take your medicine exactly as prescribed for maximum benefit.

An ingredient in this drug may cause excessive loss of potassium, which may lead to a condition called hypokalemia. Warning signs are dryness of mouth, excessive thirst, weakness, drowsiness, restlessness, muscle pains or cramps, muscular fatigue, lack of urination, abnormal heart rhythms, and upset stomach. If this happens, call your doctor. You may need potassium from some outside source. This may be done by either taking a potassium supplement or by eating foods such as bananas, citrus fruits, melons, and tomatoes, which have high concentrations of potassium.

This drug should be stopped at the first sign of despondency, early morning insomnia, loss of appetite, or sexual impotence. Drug-induced depression may persist for several months after the drug has been discontinued; it has been known to be severe enough to result in suicide attempts. This drug should be used with care by women of childbearing age.

Cautions and Warnings

Do not take this drug if you are sensitive or allergic to either of its ingredients or if you have a history of mental depression, active peptic ulcer, or ulcerative colitis.

Possible Side Effects

People taking Diupres may experience the following: loss of appetite, stomach irritation, nausea, vomiting, cramps, diarrhea, constipation, dizziness, headache, tingling in the arms and legs, restlessness, chest pains, abnormal heart rhythms, drowsiness, depression, nervousness, anxiety, nightmares, glaucoma, blood disorders, rash, itching, fever, difficulty in breathing, muscle spasms, weakness, high blood sugar, sugar in the urine, blurred vision, stuffed nose, dryness of the mouth, or rash. Occasionally, impotence or decreased sex drive occurs.

Drug Interactions

Interaction with Digitalis or Quinidine may cause abnormal heart rhythms.

Interaction with drugs containing lithium may lead to toxic effects of lithium.

Avoid over-the-counter cough, cold, or allergy remedies containing stimulant drugs which may raise your blood pressure.

Usual Dose

Must be individualized to patient's response.

Brand Name

Donnagel-PG

Ingredients

Atropine Sulfate
Hyoscine Hydrobromide
Hyoscyamine Sulfate
Kaolin
Pectin
Powdered Opium

Type of Drug

Antidiarrheal.

Prescribed for

Relief of diarrhea.

General Information

Donnagel-PG works by reducing the mobility of the intestine, reducing secretions from the stomach and other parts of the gastrointestinal tract, and by absorbing excessive fluids and other unusual materials which may be present in the stomach. This is one of many products available for the symptomatic treatment of diarrhea. Although it is effective in reducing diarrhea, it does not treat the underlying causes of the problem.

Cautions and Warnings

Do not take Donnagel-PG if you are allergic to any of its ingredients or if you have glaucoma or serious kidney or liver disease.

Possible Side Effects

Blurring of vision, dry mouth, and difficulty in urination will occur only in a small number of people, usually only when the recommended dosage is exceeded.

Drug Interactions

Donnagel-PG should not be taken at the same time as any other drug. The Kaolin and Pectin in this product will prevent other medications from being absorbed into the bloodstream. This is especially true of antibiotics.

Donnagel-PG occasionally interacts with large quantities of alcoholic beverages to cause excessive sleepiness, drowsiness, and inability to concentrate.

The Atropine Sulfate and Hyoscyamine Sulfate in Donnagel-PG can interact with antihistamines and drugs with side effects similar to those of antihistamines, exaggerating such effects as dry mouth, difficulty urinating, constipation, and blurred vision. If this becomes a problem consult your doctor.

Usual Dose

Adult: 2 tablespoons taken immediately after each episode of diarrhea; then 2 tablespoons every 3 hours as needed.

Child (30 pounds and over): 1 to 2 teaspoons every 3 hours as needed.

Child (10 to 30 pounds): 1 teaspoon every 3 hours as needed.

Child (up to 10 pounds): ½ teaspoon every 3 hours as needed.

Special Information

The Food and Drug Administration has proposed the removal of Atropine Sulfate and Hyoscyamine Sulfate from Donnagel-PG. If by the time you read this the ingredients named have been removed, reference to "Possible Side Effects" and the last paragraph of "Drug Interactions" above no longer apply. Check with your pharmacist.

Brand Name

Donnatal

Ingredients

Atropine Sulfate
Hyoscine Hydrobromide
Hyoscyamine
Phenobarbital

Other Brand Names

Paratal Tablets   Spalix Tablets
Sedralex Tablets   Spaz Tablets
Setamine

Products with slightly different concentrations of the same ingredients are:

Barbidonna Tablets   Hasp Ovalets
Belbarb Tablets   Hybephen Tablets
Donphen Tablets   Kinesed Tablets

Type of Drug

Anticholinergic combination.

Prescribed for

Symptomatic relief of stomach spasm and other forms of cramps. Donnatal may also be prescribed for the treatment of motion sickness.

General Information

Donnatal is a mild antispasmodic sedative drug. It is only used to relieve symptoms, not to treat the cause of the symptoms. In addition to the brand names listed above, there are 40 to 50 other drug products which are anticholinergic combinations with the same properties. All are used to relieve cramps and all are about equally effective. Some have additional ingredients to reduce or absorb excess gas in the stomach, to coat the stomach, or to control diarrhea.

Cautions and Warnings

Donnatal should not be used by people with glaucoma, serious kidney or liver disease, or a history of allergy to any of the ingredients of this drug.

Possible Side Effects

Most common: blurred vision, dry mouth, difficulty in urination, flushing, dryness of the skin.

Possible Adverse Drug Effects

Infrequent: rapid or unusual heartbeat, increased sensitivity to strong light, loss of taste sensation, headache, nervousness, tiredness, weakness, dizziness, inability to sleep, nausea, vomiting, fever, stuffy nose, heartburn, loss of sex drive, constipation, bloated feeling, allergic reactions such as fever and rash.

Drug Interactions

Although Donnatal contains only a small amount of Phenobarbital, it is wise to avoid excessive amounts of alcohol or other drugs which are sedative in action. Be careful when driving or operating equipment. Other Phenobarbital interactions are probably not significant, but are possible with anticoagulants, adrenal corticosteroids, tranquilizers, narcotics, sleeping pills, and antihistamines.

Some phenothiazine drugs, tranquilizers, antidepressants, and narcotics may increase the side effects of the Atropine Sulfate contained in Donnatal, causing dry mouth, difficulty in urination, and constipation.

Usual Dose

Adult: 1 or 2 tablets, capsules, or teaspoons 3 to 4 times per day.

Child: Half the adult dose If necessary.

Overdosage

Symptoms are dry mouth, difficulty in swallowing, thirst, blurred vision, sensitivity to strong light, flushed, hot dry skin, rash, fever, abnormal heart rate, high blood pressure, difficulty in urination, restlessness, confusion, delirium, and difficulty in breathing. The patient should be taken to a hospital emergency room immediately. ALWAYS bring the medicine bottle.

Special Information

Dry mouth from Donnatal can be relieved by chewing gum or sucking hard candy; constipation can be treated with a stool softening laxative.

Generic Name

Doxepin Hydrochloride

Brand Names

Adapin
Sinequan

Type of Drug

Antidepressant.

Prescribed for

Primary depression or depression secondary to disorders such as alcoholism, other major organic diseases such as cancer, or other illnesses which may have great psychological effect on a patient.

General Information

Doxepin Hydrochloride and other members of this group are effective in treating symptoms of depression. They can elevate your mood, increase physical activity and mental alertness, and improve appetite and sleep patterns. The drugs are mild sedatives and therefore useful in treating mild forms of depression associated with anxiety. You should not expect instant results with this medicine: results are usually seen after 1 to 4 weeks of therapy. If symptoms are not changed after 6 to 8 weeks, contact your doctor.

Cautions and Warnings

Unlike other tricyclic antidepressants, Doxepin Hydrochloride should not be given to children under age 12 and cannot be used to treat nighttime bed-wetting.

Possible Side Effects

Changes in blood pressure (both high and low), abnormal heart rate, heart attack, confusion, especially in elderly patients, hallucinations, disorientation, delusions, anxiety, restlessness, excitement, numbness and tingling in the extremities, lack of coordination, muscle spasm or tremors, seizures and/or convulsions, dry mouth, blurred vision, constipation, inability to urinate, skin rash, itching, sensitivity to bright light or sunlight, retention of fluids, particularly of the face, fever, allergy, changes in composition of blood, nausea, vomiting, loss of appetite, stomach upset, diarrhea, enlargement of the breasts in males and females, increased or decreased sex drive, and increased or decreased blood sugar.

Possible Adverse Drug Effects

Infrequent: agitation, inability to sleep, nightmares, feeling of panic, development of a peculiar taste in the mouth, stomach cramps, black coloration of the tongue, yellowing eyes and/or skin, changes in liver function, increased or decreased weight, perspiration, flushing, frequent urination, drowsiness, dizziness, weakness, headache, loss of hair, nausea, not feeling well.

Drug Interactions

Interaction with MAO inhibitors can cause high fevers, convulsions, and (occasionally) death. Don't take MAO inhibitors until at least 2 weeks after Doxepin Hydrochloride has been discontinued.

Doxepin Hydrochloride interacts with Guanethidine, a

drug used to treat high blood pressure: if your doctor prescribes Doxepin Hydrochloride and you are taking medicine for high blood pressure, be sure to discuss this with him.

Doxepin Hydrochloride increases the effects of barbiturates, tranquilizers, other depressive drugs, and alcohol. Don't drink alcoholic beverages if you take Doxepin Hydrochloride.

Taking Doxepin Hydrochloride and thyroid medicine will enhance the effects of the thyroid medicine. The combination can cause abnormal heart rhythms.

Large doses of Vitamin C (Ascorbic Acid) can reduce the effect of Doxepin Hydrochloride. Drugs such as Bicarbonate of Soda or Acetazolamide will increase the effect of Doxepin Hydrochloride.

Usual Dose

Initial dose is a moderate 10 to 25 milligrams 3 times per day; the low dose reduces drowsiness during the first few days. The doctor may then increase or decrease the dose according to individual response, giving 50 to 300 milligrams per day. This drug should not be given to children under age 12.

Overdosage

Symptoms are confusion, inability to concentrate, hallucinations, drowsiness, lowered body temperature, abnormal heart rate, heart failure, large pupils of the eyes, convulsions, severely lowered blood pressure, stupor, and coma (as well as agitation, stiffening of body muscles, vomiting, and high fever). The patient should be taken to a hospital emergency room immediately. ALWAYS bring the medicine bottle.

Storage

Liquid Doxepin Hydrochloride should not be diluted until just before use. Dilute in about 4 ounces of water or juice just before you take it.

Generic Name

Doxycycline

Brand Names

Doxychel
Doxy II
Vibramycin

Type of Drug

Broad-spectrum antibiotic effective against gram-positive and gram-negative organisms.

Prescribed for

Bacterial infections such as gonorrhea, infections of the mouth, gums, and teeth, Rocky Mountain spotted fever and other fevers caused by ticks and lice from a variety of carriers, urinary tract infections, and respiratory system infections such as pneumonia and bronchitis.

These diseases may be produced by gram-positive or gram-negative organisms such as diplococci, staphylococci, streptococci, gonococci, *E. coli*, and *Shigella*.

Doxycycline has also been successfully used to treat some skin infections, but is not considered the first-choice antibiotic for the treatment of general skin infections or wounds. It may be used to prevent "traveler diarrhea."

General Information

Doxycycline works by interfering with the normal growth cycle of the invading bacteria, preventing them from reproducing and thus allowing the body's normal defenses to fight off the infection. This process is referred to as bacteriostatic action. Doxycycline has also been used along with other medicines to treat amoebic infections of the intestinal tract, known as amoebic dysentery. It is also prescribed for diseases caused by ticks, fleas, and lice.

Doxycycline has been successfully used in the treatment of adolescent acne, using small doses over a long period of time. Adverse effects or toxicity in this type of therapy are almost unheard of.

117

Since the action of this antibiotic depends on its concentration within the invading bacteria, it is imperative that you, the patient, completely follow the doctor's directions.

Cautions and Warnings

You should not use Doxycycline if you are pregnant. In general, children up to age 8 should also avoid Doxycycline as it has been shown to produce serious discoloration of the permanent teeth. Doxycycline when used in children has been shown to interfere with the development of the long bones and may retard growth.

Exceptions would be when Doxycycline is the only effective antibiotic available and all risk factors have been made known to the patient.

Doxycycline should not be given to people with known liver disease. You should avoid taking high doses of Doxycycline or undergoing extended Doxycycline therapy if you will be exposed to sunlight for a long period because this antibiotic can interfere with your body's normal sun-screening mechanism, possibly causing a severe sunburn. If you have a known history of allergy to Doxycycline you should avoid taking this drug or other drugs within this category such as Aureomycin, Terramycin, Rondomycin, Declomycin, and Minocin.

Possible Side Effects

As with other antibiotics, the common side effects of Doxycycline are stomach upset, nausea, vomiting, diarrhea, and skin rash. Less common side effects include hairy tongue, itching and irritation of the anal and/or vaginal region. If these symptoms appear, consult your physician immediately. Periodic physical examinations and laboratory tests should be given to patients who are on long-term Doxycycline.

Possible Adverse Drug Effects

Doxycycline may produce loss of appetite, peeling of the skin, sensitivity to the sun, fever, chills, anemia, possible brown spotting of the skin, decrease in kidney function, and damage to the liver.

Drug Interactions

Doxycycline (a bacteriostatic drug) may interfere with

the action of bactericidal agents such as Penicillin. It is not advisable to take both.

Don't take multivitamin products containing minerals at the same time as Doxycycline, or you will reduce the antibiotic's effectiveness. Space the taking of these two medicines at least 2 hours apart.

People receiving anticoagulation therapy (blood-thinning agents) should consult their doctor, since Doxycycline will interfere with this form of therapy. An adjustment in the anticoagulation dosage may be required.

Usual Dose

Adult: First day, 200 milligrams given as 100 milligrams every 12 hours. Maintenance, 100 milligrams per day in 1 or 2 doses. The maintenance dose may be doubled in severe infections.

Child (101 pounds and over): The usual adult dose may be given.

Child (under 101 pounds): First day, 2 milligrams per pound of body weight divided in 2 doses. Maintenance, 1 milligram per pound as a single daily dose. (Double the maintenance dose for severe infections.)

An increased incidence of side effects is observed if the dose is over 200 milligrams per day.

Storage

Doxycycline can be stored at room temperature.

Special Information

Do *not* take after the expiration date on the label. The decomposition of Doxycycline produces a highly toxic substance which can cause serious kidney damage. You may take Doxycycline with food or milk to reduce stomach upset.

Brand Name

Drixoral

Ingredients

Dexbrompheniramine Maleate
Pseudoephedrine Sulfate

Type of Drug

Long-acting combination antihistamine-decongestant.

Prescribed for

Relief of sneezing, runny nose, and nasal congestion associated with the common cold, allergy, or other upper respiratory condition.

General Information

Drixoral is one of many products marketed to relieve the symptoms of the common cold. Most of these products contain ingredients to relieve nasal congestion or to dry up runny noses or relieve a scratchy throat; and several of them may contain ingredients to suppress cough, or to help eliminate unwanted mucus. All these products are good only for the relief of symptoms and do not treat the underlying problem such as the cold virus or other infections.

Cautions and Warnings

If you are pregnant you should not take this drug.

Possible Side Effects

Mild drowsiness has been seen in patients taking Drixoral.

Possible Adverse Drug Effects

Infrequent: restlessness, tension, nervousness, tremor, weakness, inability to sleep, headache, palpitations, elevation of blood pressure, sweating, sleeplessness, loss of appetite, nausea, vomiting, dizziness, constipation.

Drug Interactions

Interaction with alcoholic beverages may cause excessive drowsiness and/or sleepiness, or inability to concentrate. Do not take this drug with alcohol, sedatives, tranquilizers, antihistamines, and sleeping pills.

Do not self-medicate with over-the-counter drugs for the relief of cold symptoms: taking Drixoral with such drugs may aggravate high blood pressure, heart disease, diabetes, or thyroid disease.

Do not take Drixoral if you are taking or suspect you may be taking a monoamine oxidase (MAO) inhibitor: severe elevation in blood pressure may result.

Usual Dose

Adult and child (age 12 and over): 1 tablet morning and night.
Child (under age 12): Not recommended.

Special Information

Since drowsiness may occur during use of Drixoral, be cautious while performing mechanical tasks requiring altertness.

Brand Name

Dyazide

Ingredients

Hydrochlorothiazide
Triamterene

Type of Drug

Diuretic.

Prescribed for

High blood pressure or any condition where it is desirable to eliminate excess fluid from the body.

General Information

Dyazide is a combination of two diuretics which act by different mechanisms and is a convenient, effective approach for the treatment of diseases where the elimination of excess fluids is required. One of the ingredients in Dyazide has the ability to hold potassium in the body while producing a diuretic effect. This balances off the other ingredient, Hydrochlorothiazide, which normally causes a loss of potassium. The two drugs counterbalance one another, and save the patient the trouble of taking extra potassium from outside sources.

Cautions and Warnings

Do not use Dyazide if you have nonfunctioning kidneys, if you think you may be allergic to this drug or any sulfa drug, or if you have a history of allergy or bronchial asthma. Dyazide may be used to treat specific conditions in pregnant women, but the decision to use this medication by pregnant women should be weighed carefully because the drug may cross the placental barrier into the blood of the unborn child. Dyazide may appear in the breast milk of nursing mothers. Do not take any potassium supplements together with Dyazide unless specifically directed to do so by your doctor.

Possible Side Effects

Drowsiness, lethargy, headache, gastrointestinal upset, cramping and diarrhea, rash, mental confusion, fever, feeling of ill health, enlargement of the breasts, inability to achieve or maintain erection in males, irregular menstrual cycles or deepening of the voice in females.

Possible Adverse Drug Effects

Loss of appetite, headache, tingling in the toes and fingers, restlessness, anemias or other effects on components of the blood, unusual sensitivity to sunlight, dizziness when rising quickly from a sitting or lying position. Dyazide can also produce muscle spasms, weakness, and blurred vision.

Drug Interactions

Dyazide will add to (potentiate) the action of other blood-pressure-lowering drugs. This is beneficial, and is frequently used to help lower blood pressure in patients with hypertension.

The possibility of developing imbalances in body fluids (electrolytes) is increased if you take other medications such as Digitalis and adrenal corticosteroids while you are taking Dyazide.

If you are taking an oral antidiabetic drug and begin taking Dyazide, the antidiabetic dose may have to be altered.

Lithium Carbonate should not be taken with Dyazide because the combination may increase the risk of lithium toxicity.

Avoid over-the-counter cough, cold, or allergy remedies containing stimulant drugs which can aggravate your condition.

Usual Dose

One capsule twice per day.

Special Information

Take Dyazide exactly as prescribed.

Equagesic

Ingredients

Aspirin
Ethoheptazine
Meprobamate

Type of Drug

Analgesic combination.

Prescribed for

Pain relief in patients who have suffered muscle spasms, sprains, strains, or bad backs.

General Information

Equagesic is a combination product containing a tranquilizer, a muscle relaxant, and Aspirin: it is used for the relief of pain associated with muscle spasms. The tranquilizer (Meprobamate) in this combination opens it to many drug interactions, especially other tranquilizers or depressant drugs. Equagesic has proven itself to be effective in providing temporary relief from pain and muscle spasm. If you are taking Equagesic, you must follow any other instructions your doctor gives you to help treat the basic problem.

Cautions and Warnings

Do not take Equagesic if you are allergic to any of the ingredients contained in it. If you are pregnant, talk to your physician before you take Equagesic, because this combination may cause adverse effects in the unborn child.

Possible Side Effects

Most frequent: nausea, vomiting, stomach upset, dizziness, drowsiness. Less frequent: allergy, itching, skin rash, fever, fluid in the arms and/or legs, occasional fainting spells, spasms of bronchial muscles leading to difficulty in breathing.

Possible Adverse Drug Effects

People taking Equagesic have occasionally experienced effects on components of the blood system. Equagesic has also caused blurred vision.

Drug Interactions

Two of the ingredients in Equagesic may cause sleepiness, drowsiness, or, in high doses, difficulty in breathing. Avoid interaction with other drugs that produce the same effect, for example, barbiturates, narcotics, tranquilizers, sleeping pills, and some antihistamines. Do not drink alcoholic beverages with Equagesic, because the depressive effect of the alcohol will be exaggerated.

If you are taking an anticoagulant (blood-thinning medication) and have been given a new prescription for Equagesic, be sure that your doctor is aware that there is Aspirin in Equagesic. Aspirin affects the ability of your blood to clot and can necessitate a change in the dose of your anticoagulant.

Usual Dose

One or 2 tablets 3 to 4 times per day as needed for the relief of pain associated with skeletal muscle spasms.

Overdosage

Equagesic overdoses are serious. Symptoms are drowsiness, feeling of light-headedness, desire to go to sleep, nausea, and vomiting. The patient should be taken to a hospital emergency room immediately. ALWAYS bring the medicine bottle.

Special Information

If you experience stomach upset with Equagesic, take with food or water.

Generic Name

Ergot Alkaloids Dihydrogenated

Brand Name

Hydergine Sublingual

Type of Drug

Psychotherapeutic.

Prescribed for

Depression, confusion, antisocial behavior, and dizziness in the elderly.

General Information

Ergot Alkaloids Dihydrogenated has improved the supply of blood to the brain in test animals and reduces heart rate and muscle tone in blood vessels. Some studies have shown the drug to be very effective in relieving mild symptoms of mental impairment, while others have found it to be only moderately effective. It has been most effective in patients whose symptoms are due to high blood pressure in the brain.

Cautions and Warnings

Do not use this drug if you are allergic or sensitive to Ergot or any of its derivatives.

Possible Side Effects

Ergot Alkaloids Dihydrogenated does not produce serious side effects. Since the tablet is taken under the tongue, you may experience some irritation, nausea, or stomach upset.

Usual Dose

1 tablet under the tongue 3 times per day.

The results of this drug are gradual. Frequently they are not seen for 3 to 4 weeks.

Dissolve the tablets under the tongue: they are not effective if swallowed.

Generic Name

Erythromycin

Brand Names

Bristamycin	Ilotycin
E.E.S.	Pediamycin
E-Mycin	Pfizer-E
Erypar	Robimycin
Erythrocin	RP-Mycin
Ethril	SK-Erythromycin
Ilosone	Wyamycin

Type of Drug

Bacteriostatic antibiotic, effective against gram-positive organisms such as streptococcus, staphylococcus, and gonococcus.

Prescribed for

Infections of the upper and lower respiratory tract; infections of the mouth, gums, and teeth; infections of the nose, ears, and sinuses. May be used for mild to moderate skin infections, but is not considered the antibiotic of choice. Can also be effective against amoebas of the intestinal tract, which cause amoebic dysentery.

Erythromycin is a relatively safe antibiotic. It is used instead of Penicillin for mild to moderate infections in people who are allergic to the penicillin class of antibiotics.

Note: Erythromycin is not the antibiotic of choice for severe infections.

General Information

Erythromycin works by interfering with the normal growth cycle of the invading bacteria, preventing them from reproducing and thus allowing the body's normal defenses to fight off the infection. This process is referred to as bacteriostatic action.

Erythromycin is absorbed from the gastrointestinal tract, but it is deactivated by the acid content of the stomach. Because of this the tablet form of this drug is formulated in such a way as to bypass the stomach and dissolve in the intestine.

Erythromycin is used primarily for infections of the mouth, nose, ears, sinuses, throat, and lungs.

It can also be used to treat venereal disease and pelvic inflammatory disease in people who have allergies and/or sensitivity to the penicillin class of antibiotics.

Because the action of this antibiotic depends on its concentration within the invading bacteria, it is imperative that you follow the doctor's directions regarding the spacing of the doses as well as the number of days you should continue taking the medication. The effect of the antibiotic is severely reduced if these instructions are not followed.

Cautions and Warnings

Erythromycin is excreted primarily through the liver. People with liver disease or damage should exercise caution. Those on long-term therapy with Erythromycin are advised to have periodic blood tests.

Erythromycin is available in a variety of formulations. One formula, Erythromycin Estolate, has occasionally produced fatigue, nausea, vomiting, abdominal cramps, and fever. If you are susceptible to stomach problems, Erythromycin may cause mild to moderate stomach upset. Discontinuing the drug will reverse this condition.

Possible Side Effects

Most common: nausea, vomiting, stomach cramps, diarrhea. Less common: hairy tongue, itching, irritation of the anal and/or vaginal region. If these symptoms appear, consult your physician immediately.

Possible Adverse Drug Effects

Erythromycin should not be given to people with known sensitivity to this antibiotic. It may cause a yellowing of the skin and eyes. If this occurs, discontinue the drug and notify your doctor immediately.

Drug Interactions

Erythromycin is relatively free of interactions with other medications.

Usual Dose

Adult: 250 to 500 milligrams every 6 hours.

Children: 50 to 200 milligrams per pound of body weight per day in divided doses depending upon age, weight, and severity of infection.

Take 1 hour before or 2 hours after meals.

Doses of E.E.S., Pediamycin, and Wyamycin are 60 percent higher due to different chemical composition of the Erythromycin.

Special Information

The safety of Erythromycin in pregnancy has not been established.

Generic Name

Ethchlorvynol

Brand Name

Placidyl

Type of Drug

Sedative-hypnotic.

Prescribed for

Inability to sleep.

General Information

Sleep is produced within 30 minutes and lasts 4 to 8 hours.

Cautions and Warnings

Patients with porphyria should not take Ethchlorvynol.

Possible Side Effects

Skin rash.

Possible Adverse Drug Effects

There have been reports of nausea, morning hangover, excitation, and blurring of the vision.

Drug Interactions

The combination of Ethchlorvynol and Amitriptyline can make you become delirious. Avoid combining them.

Usual Dose

Adult: 500 milligrams by mouth at bedtime; for severe insomnia, 750 or even 1000 milligrams. Patients may be instructed, if they awaken during the night, to take an additional 100 to 200 milligrams to help them get back to sleep. Only the smallest effective dose of Ethchlorvynol should be used, since the drug can be abused and can be addictive.

Overdosage

Large amounts of Ethchlorvynol can be fatal, and the drug is frequently used in suicide attempts. Symptoms are coma, lowered body temperature followed by fever, absence of normal reflexes and pain responses after pinches and needle or pin sticks, and shallow breathing. The patient should be taken to a hospital emergency room immediately. ALWAYS bring the medicine bottle.

People who have taken Ethchlorvynol for a long time may show signs of chronic overdosage: loss of memory, inability to concentrate, shakes, tremors, loss of reflexes, slurring of speech, and general sense of depression. Abrupt discontinuation of Ethchlorvynol often causes withdrawal reactions of nervousness, anxiety, seizures, cramping, chills, numbness of the extremities, and general behavior changes. Chronic overdosage is best treated by withdrawing of the drug over a period of days or weeks.

Storage

Ethchlorvynol capsules must be protected from heat and moisture. They should not be refrigerated. The best place to keep them is at room temperature; for example, in a night or bed table.

Generic Name

Fenoprofen Calcium

Brand Name

Nalfon

Type of Drug

Nonsteroid anti-inflammatory.

Prescribed for

Relief of pain and inflammation of joints and muscles; arthritis.

General Information

Fenoprofen Calcium is one of several new drugs used to treat various types of arthritis. These drugs reduce inflammation and share side effects, the most common of which is possible formation of ulcers and upset stomach. The drugs are roughly comparable to Aspirin in controlling the symptoms of arthritis, and are used by some people who cannot tolerate Aspirin.

Cautions and Warnings

Do not take Fenoprofen Calcium if you are allergic or sensitive to this drug, Aspirin, or other nonsteroid anti-inflammatory drugs. Fenoprofen Calcium may cause stomach ulcers.

Possible Side Effects

Stomach upset, blurred vision, darkening of stool, changes in color vision, skin rash, weight gain, retention of fluids.

Possible Adverse Drug Effects

Most frequent: stomach upset, dizziness, headache, drowsiness, ringing in the ears. Other: heartburn, nausea, vomiting, bloating, gas in the stomach, stomach pain, diarrhea, constipation, dark stool, nervousness, insomnia, depression, confusion, tremor, loss of appetite, fatigue, itching, rash, double vision, abnormal heart rhythm, anemia or other changes in the composition of the blood, changes in liver function, loss of hair, tingling in the hands and feet, fever, breast enlargement, lowered blood sugar, occasional effects on the kidneys. If symptoms appear, stop taking the medicine and see your doctor immediately.

Drug Interactions

Fenoprofen Calcium increases the action of Phenytoin, sulfa drugs, drugs used to control diabetes, and drugs used to thin the blood. If you are taking any of these medicines, be sure you discuss it with your doctor, who will probably change the dose of the other drug.

Usual Dose

Adult: 300 to 600 milligrams 4 times per day, to start. Doses may be increased if needed, up to 3200 milligrams per day. If upset stomach occurs, take each dose with food, milk, or antacid.

Child: Not recommended.

Generic Name

Ferrous Sulfate

Brand Names

Arne Modified	Fero-Gradumet
Feosol	Mol-Iron
Feosol Spansules	Mol-Iron Chronosules
Fer-In-Sol	

Type of Drug

Iron-containing product.

Prescribed for

Iron deficiency of the blood.

General Information

Ferrous Sulfate is used to treat anemias due to iron deficiency. Other anemias will not be affected by this drug. Ferrous Sulfate works by being incorporated into red blood cells where it can help carry oxygen throughout the body. Iron is absorbed only in a small section of the gastrointestinal tract called the duodenum. Sustained-release preparations of iron should only be used to help minimize the stomach discomfort that Ferrous Sulfate can cause, since any drug which passes the duodenum (in the upper part of the small intestine) cannot be absorbed.

Cautions and Warnings

Do not take Ferrous Sulfate if you have a history of stomach upset, peptic ulcer, or ulcerative colitis.

Possible Side Effects

Stomach upset and irritation, nausea, diarrhea, constipation.

Drug Interactions

Ferrous Sulfate will interfere with absorption of oral Tetracycline. Separate the doses by at least 2 hours.

Antacids will interfere with the absorption of iron; again, separate doses by 2 hours.

In either case, avoid taking iron supplements (unless absolutely necessary) until your other medical condition clears up.

Usual Dose

1 to 3 tablets per day.

Overdosage

Symptoms appear after 30 minutes to several hours: lethargy (tiredness), vomiting, diarrhea, stomach upset, change in pulse to weak and rapid, and lowered blood pressure—or, after massive doses, shock, black and tarry stools due to massive bleeding in the stomach or intestine, and pneumonia. Quickly induce vomiting and feed the patient eggs and milk until he can be taken to a hospital for stomach pumping. Be sure to call a doctor right away. The patient must be taken to the hospital as soon as possible, since stomach pumping should not be performed after the first hour of iron ingestion because there is a danger of perforation of the stomach wall. In the hospital emergency room measures to treat shock, loss of water, loss of blood, and respiratory failure may be necessary. ALWAYS bring the medicine bottle.

Special Information

Iron salts impart a black color to the stools and are slightly constipating. If stools become black and tarry in consistency, however, there may be some bleeding in the stomach or intestine. Discuss it with your doctor.

Iron salts and iron-containing products are best absorbed on an empty stomach; but if they upset your stomach, take with meals or immediately after meals.

Brand Name

Fiorinal

Ingredients

Aspirin
Butalbital
Caffeine
Phenacetin

Other Brand Name

Lanorinal

Type of Drug

Nonnarcotic analgesic combination.

Prescribed for

Relief of headache pain or other types of pain.

General Information

Fiorinal is one of many combination products containing barbiturates and analgesics. These products often also contain tranquilizers or narcotics, and Acetaminophen may be substituted for Aspirin.

Cautions and Warnings

Fiorinal can cause drug dependence or addiction. Use this drug with caution if you have asthma or problems in breathing. Fiorinal can affect your ability to drive a car or operate machinery. Do not drink alcoholic beverages while taking Fiorinal. The Aspirin component in this drug can interfere with the normal coagulation of blood. This is especially important if you are taking blood-thinning medication.

Possible Side Effects

Major side effects: light-headedness, dizziness, sedation, nausea, vomiting, sweating, stomach upset, loss of appetite, or possibly mild stimulation.

Possible Adverse Drug Effects

Weakness, headache, sleeplessness, agitation, tremor, uncoordinated muscle movements, mild hallucinations, disorientation, visual disturbances, feeling "high," dry mouth, loss of appetite, constipation, flushing of the face, changes in heart rate, palpitations, faintness, difficulty in urination, skin rashes, itching, confusion, rapid breathing, diarrhea.

Drug Interactions

Interaction with alcohol, tranquilizers, barbiturates, sleeping pills, or other drugs that produce depression can cause tiredness, drowsiness, and inability to concentrate.

Interaction with Prednisone, steroids, Phenylbutazone, or alcohol can irritate your stomach.

The dose of anticoagulant (blood-thinning) drugs will have to be changed by your physician if you begin taking Fiorinal, which contains Aspirin.

Usual Dose

1 to 2 tablets or capsules every 4 hours or as needed. Maximum of 6 doses per day.

Take with a full glass of water or with food to reduce the possibility of stomach upset.

Overdosage

Symptoms are difficulty in breathing, nervousness progressing to stupor or coma, pinpointed pupils of the eyes, cold, clammy skin and lowered heart rate and/or blood pressure, nausea, vomiting, dizziness, ringing in the ears, flushing, sweating, and thirst. The patient should be taken to a hospital emergency room immediately. ALWAYS bring the medicine bottle.

Special Information

Drowsiness may occur. The Phenacetin ingredient of Fiorinal may be dangerous to your kidneys, so do not take for an extended period unless directed by your doctor.

Brand Name

Fiorinal with Codeine

Ingredients

Aspirin
Butalbital
Caffeine
Codeine Phosphate
Phenacetin

Type of Drug

Nonnarcotic analgesic combination.

Prescribed for

Relief of headache pain or other types of pain.

General Information

Fiorinal with Codeine is one of many combination products containing barbiturates and analgesics. These products often also contain tranquilizers or narcotics, and Acetaminophen may be substituted for Aspirin.

Cautions and Warnings

Fiorinal with Codeine can cause drug dependence or addiction. Use this drug with caution if you have asthma or problems in breathing. It can affect your ability to drive a car or operate machinery.

Possible Side Effects

Major side effects: light-headedness, dizziness, sedation, nausea, vomiting, sweating, stomach upset, loss of appetite, (possible) mild stimulation.

Possible Adverse Drug Effects

Weakness, headache, sleeplessness, agitation, tremor, uncoordinated muscle movements, mild hallucinations, disorientation, visual disturbances, feeling "high," dry mouth, loss of appetite, constipation, flushing of the face, changes in heart rate, palpitations, faintness, difficulty in urination, skin rashes, itching, confusion, rapid breathing, diarrhea.

Drug Interactions

Interaction with alcohol, tranquilizers, barbiturates, sleeping pills, or other drugs that produce depression can cause tiredness, drowsiness, and inability to concentrate.

Interaction with Prednisone, steroids, Phenylbutazone, or alcohol can irritate your stomach.

The dose of anticoagulant (blood-thinning) drugs will have to be changed by your physician if you begin taking Fiorinal with Codeine, which contains Aspirin.

Usual Dose

1 to 2 tablets or capsules every 4 hours or as needed. Maximum of 6 doses per day.

Take with a full glass of water or with food to reduce the possibility of stomach upset.

Overdosage

Symptoms are difficulty in breathing, nervousness progressing to stupor or coma, pinpointed pupils of the eyes, cold, clammy skin and lowered heart rate and/or blood pressure, nausea, vomiting, dizziness, ringing in the ears, flushing, sweating, and thirst. The patient should be taken to a hospital emergency room immediately. ALWAYS bring the medicine bottle.

Special Information

Drowsiness may occur. The Phenacetin ingredient of Fiorinal with Codeine may be dangerous to your kidneys, so do not take for an extended period unless directed by your doctor.

Generic Name

Fluocinolone Acetonide

Brand Names

Fluonid
Synalar

Synalar-HP
Synemol

Type of Drug

Topical corticosteroid.

Prescribed for

Relief of skin inflammation of local skin area, itching, or other skin problems.

General Information

Fluocinolone Acetonide is one of many adrenal cortical steroids used in medical practice today. The major differences between Fluocinolone Acetonide and other adrenal cortical steroids are potency of medication and variation in some secondary effects. In most cases the choice of adrenal cortical steroids to be used in a specific disease is a matter of doctor preference and past experience. Other adrenal cortical steroids are Cortisone, Hydrocortisone, Prednisone, Prednisolone, Triamcinolone, Methylprednisolone, Meprednisone, Paramethasone, Fluprednisolone, Dexamethasone, Betamethasone, and Fludrocortisone.

Cautions and Warnings

Fluocinolone Acetonide should not be used if you have viral diseases of the skin (herpes), fungal infections of the skin (athlete's foot), or tuberculosis of the skin, nor should it be used in the ear if the eardrum is perforated.

People with a history of allergies to any of the components of the ointment, cream, or gel should not use this drug.

Possible Side Effects

Itching, irritation, dryness, and redness of the skin.

Special Information

Clean the skin before applying Fluocinolone Acetonide to prevent secondary infection. Apply in a very thin film (effectiveness is based on contact area and not on the thickness of the layer applied).

Generic Name

Fluocinonide Ointment/ Cream/Gel

Brand Names

Lidex
Topsyn

Type of Drug

Topical corticosteroid.

Prescribed for

Relief of skin inflammation of local skin area, itching, or other skin problems.

General Information

Fluocinonide is used to relieve the symptom of any itching, rash, or inflammation of the skin. It does not treat the underlying cause of the skin problem, only the symptom. It exerts this effect by interfering with natural body mechanisms that produced the rash, itching, etc., in the first place. If you use this drug without finding the cause of the problem, the problem may return after you stop using the drug. Fluocinonide should not be used without your doctor's consent because it could cover an important reaction, one that may be valuable to him in treating you.

Cautions and Warnings

Fluocinonide should not be used if you have viral diseases of the skin (herpes), fungal infections of the skin (athlete's foot), or tuberculosis of the skin, nor should it be used in the ear if the eardrum is perforated. People with a history of allergies to any of the components of the ointment, cream, or gel should not use this drug.

Possible Side Effects

Itching, irritation, dryness, and redness of the skin.

Special Information

Clean the skin before applying Fluocinonide to prevent secondary infection. Apply in a very thin film (effectiveness is based on contact area and not on the thickness of the layer applied).

Generic Name

Fluoxymesterone

Brand Names

Halotestin
Ora-Testryl

Type of Drug

Androgenic (male) hormone.

Prescribed for

Diseases in which male hormone replacement or augmentation is needed; male menopause.

General Information

This is a member of the androgenic, or male hormone group, which includes Testosterone, Methyl Testosterone, Calusterone, and Dromostanolone Propionate. (The last two are used primarily to treat breast cancer in women.) Females taking any androgenic drug should be careful to watch for deepening of the voice, oily skin, acne, hairiness, increased libido, and menstrual irregularities, effects related to the so-called virilizing effects of these hormones. Virilization is a sign that the drug is starting to produce changes in secondary sex characteristics. The drugs should be avoided if possible by young boys who have not gone through puberty.

Cautions and Warnings

Men with unusually high blood levels of calcium, known or suspected cancer of the prostate, or prostate destruction or disease, cancer of the breast or with liver, heart, or kidney disease should not use this medication. Women who are pregnant should not use Fluoxymesterone since it may affect the unborn child.

Possible Side Effects

In males: inhibition of testicle function, impotence, chronic erection of the penis, enlargement of the breast.

In females: unusual hairiness, baldness in a pattern similar to that seen in men, deepening of the voice, enlargement of the clitoris. These changes are usually irreversible once they have occurred. Females may also experience increases in blood calcium and menstrual irregularities.

In both sexes: changes in libido, flushing of the skin, acne, habituation, excitation, chills, sleeplessness, nausea, vomiting, and diarrhea. Symptoms resembling stomach ulcer may develop. Fluoxymesterone may affect levels of blood cholesterol.

Drug Interactions

Fluoxymesterone may increase the effect of oral anticoagulants; dosage of the anticoagulant may have to be decreased. Fluoxymesterone may have an effect on the glucose tolerance test, a blood test used to screen people for diabetes mellitus.

Usual Dose

2 to 30 milligrams per day, depending upon the disease being treated and patient response.

Special Information

Fluoxymesterone and other androgens are potent drugs. They must be taken only under the close supervision of your doctor and never used casually. The dosage and clinical effects of the drug vary widely and require constant monitoring.

Generic Name

Flurandrenolide

Brand Name

Cordran Ointment/Lotion/Tape
Cordran SP Cream

Type of Drug

Corticosteroid.

Prescribed for

Relief of inflammation in a local skin area, itching, or other skin problems.

General Information

Flurandrenolide is used to relieve the symptom of any itching, rash, or inflammation of the skin. It does not treat the underlying cause of the skin problem, only the symptom. It exerts this effect by interfering with natural body mechanisms that produced the rash, itching, etc., in the first place. If you use this drug without finding the cause of the problem, the problem may return after you stop using the drug. Flurandrenolide should not be used without your doctor's consent because it could cover an important reaction, one that may be valuable to him in treating you.

Cautions and Warnings

Flurandrenolide should not be used if you have viral diseases of the skin (herpes), fungal infections of the skin (athlete's foot), or tuberculosis of the skin, nor should it be used in the ear if the eardrum has been perforated. Don't use this medicine if you are allergic to any of the components of the ointment, cream, lotion, or tape.

Possible Side Effects

Burning sensations, itching, irritation, dryness of the skin, secondary infection.

Special Information

Clean the skin before applying Flurandrenolide in a very thin film (effectiveness is based on contact area and not on the thickness of the layer applied).

Generic Name

Flurazepam

Brand Name

Dalmane

Type of Drug

Sedative-sleeping medicine.

Prescribed for

Insomnia or sleeplessness, frequent nighttime awakening, or waking up too early in the morning.

General Information

Flurazepam is a member of the chemical group of drugs known as benzodiazepines. These drugs are used as either antianxiety agents, anticonvulsants, or sedatives (sleeping pills). These drugs exert their effects by relaxing the large skeletal muscles and by a direct effect on the brain. In doing so, they can relax you and make you either more tranquil or sleepier, depending on the drug and how much you use. Many doctors prefer Flurazepam and the other members of this class to other drugs that can be used for the same effect. Their reason is that the benzodiazepines tend to be safer, have fewer side effects, and are usually as, if not more, effective.

These drugs are generally used in any situation where they can be a useful adjunct.

Benzodiazepine tranquilizing drugs can be abused if taken for long periods of time and it is possible to develop withdrawal symptoms if you discontinue the therapy abruptly. Withdrawal symptoms include convulsions, tremor, muscle cramps, stomach cramps, vomiting, and sweating.

Cautions and Warnings

Do not take Flurazepam if you know you are sensitive or allergic to this drug or other benzodiazepines such as Diazepam, Chlordiazepozide, Oxazepam, Chlorazepate, Lorazepam, Prazepam, and Clonazepam.

Flurazepam and other members of this drug group may aggravate narrow angle glaucoma, but if you have open angle glaucoma you may take the drugs. In any case, check this information with your physician. Flurazepam can cause tiredness, drowsiness, inability to concentrate, or similar symptoms. Be careful when driving, operating machinery, or performing other activities which require concentration. Avoid taking this drug during the first 3 months of pregnancy except under strict supervision of your doctor.

Possible Side Effects

Most common: mild drowsiness during the first few days of therapy, especially in the elderly or debilitated. If drowsiness persists, contact your doctor.

Possible Adverse Drug Effects

Major adverse reactions: confusion, depression, lethargy, disorientation, headache, lack of activity, slurred speech, stupor, dizziness, tremor, constipation, dry mouth, nausea, inability to control urination, changes in sex drive, menstrual irregularity, changes in heart rhythm, lowered blood pressure, retention of fluids, blurred or double vision, itching, rash, hiccups, nervousness, inability to fall asleep, and (occasionally) liver dysfunction. Occasionally some people have reported a paradoxical stimulatory effect, which may be secondary to relief of anxiety, and usually is seen during the first 2 weeks of therapy. If you experience this type of effect, you should stop taking the drug and contact your doctor.

Drug Interactions

Flurazepam is a central nervous system depressant. Avoid alcohol, tranquilizers, narcotics, sleeping pills, barbiturates, MAO inhibitors, antihistamines, and other medicine used to relieve depression.

Usual Dose

15 to 30 milligrams at bedtime. Must be individualized to give the patient maximum benefit.

Overdosage

Symptoms are confusion, sleep or sleepiness, lack of response to pain such as a pin stick, shallow breathing, lowered blood pressure, and coma. The patient should be taken to a hospital emergency room immediately. ALWAYS bring the medicine bottle.

Generic Name

Furosemide

Brand Name

Lasix

Type of Drug

Diuretic.

Prescribed for

Congestive heart failure, cirrhosis of the liver, kidney dysfunction, high blood pressure, and other conditions where it may be desirable to rid the body of excess fluid.

General Information

Furosemide causes the production of urine by affecting the kidneys. It may also cause lowered blood pressure. Furosemide is particularly useful, as a very strong drug with great diuretic potential, when a drug with less diuretic potential would fail to produce the desired therapeutic effect.

Cautions and Warnings

Furosemide if given in excessive quantities will cause depletion of water and electrolytes. It should not be taken unless there is constant medical supervision and the dose has been adjusted to your particular needs. You should not take this drug if your production of urine has been decreased abnormally by some type of kidney disease, or if you feel you may be allergic to it or if you have experienced an allergic reaction to it in the past. Although Furosemide has been used to treat specific conditions in pregnancy, it should generally not be used to treat a pregnant woman because of the potential effects it may have on the unborn child. If your doctor feels that your case warrants the use of Furosemide, the decision to use this drug must be made by you and your doctor based on the potential benefits derived from this drug as opposed to the potential problems that may be associated with using it. If you must take this drug during the period that you are nursing a newborn baby, you should stop nursing the baby with breast milk and give the baby prepared formulas which are available over the counter. Excessive use of Furosemide will result in dehydration or reduction in blood volume, and may cause circulatory collapse and other related problems, particularly in the elderly. In addition, because of the potent effect that this drug has on the electrolytes in the blood—potassium, sodium, carbon dioxide, and others—frequent laboratory evaluations of these electrolytes should be performed during the few months of therapy, and periodically afterward.

Possible Side Effects

If you are taking Furosemide you should be aware that changes may develop in potassium and other electrolyte concentrations in your body. In the case of lower potassium produced by Furosemide (hypokalemia), you may observe these warning signs: dryness of the mouth, thirst, weakness, lethargy, drowsiness, restlessness, muscle pains or cramps, muscular tiredness, low blood pressure, decreased frequency of urination and decreased amount of urine produced, abnormal heart rate, stomach upset including nausea and vomiting. To treat this, potassium supplements are given in the form of tablets, liquids, or powders or by increased consumption of potassium-rich foods such as bananas, citrus fruits, melons, and tomatoes.

Furosemide may alter the metabolism of sugar in

your body. If you have diabetes mellitus, you may develop high blood sugar or sugar in the urine while you are taking the drug. To treat this problem, the dose of drugs that you are taking to treat your diabetes will have to be altered.

In addition, people taking Furosemide have experienced one or more of the following side effects: abdominal discomfort, nausea, vomiting, diarrhea, skin rash, dizziness, light-headedness, weakness, headache, blurred vision, fatigue, jaundice or yellowing of the skin or whites of the eyes, acute attacks of gout, ringing in the ears, reversible periodic impairment in hearing. There have also been some reported cases of irreversible hearing loss.

Possible Adverse Drug Effects

Dermatitis, unusual skin reactions, tingling in the extremities, postural hypotension (or dizziness on rising quickly from a sitting or lying position), anemia of various types. Rare: production of a sweet taste in the mouth, burning feeling in the stomach and/or mouth, thirst, increased perspiration, frequent urination.

Drug Interactions

Furosemide will add to (potentiate) the action of other blood-pressure-lowering drugs. This is beneficial, and is frequently used to help lower blood pressure in patients with hypertension.

The possibility of developing electrolyte imbalances in body fluids is increased if you take other medications such as Digitalis and adrenal corticosteroids while you are taking Furosemide.

If you are taking Furosemide because of congestive heart failure and are also taking Digitalis, loss of potassium may significantly affect the toxicity of Digitalis. For this reason, foods which are high in potassium, including bananas, citrus fruits, melons, and tomatoes, should be given high priority in your daily diet.

If you are taking an oral antidiabetic drug and begin taking Furosemide, the antidiabetic dose may have to be altered.

If you are taking Lithium Carbonate, you should probably not take a diuretic, which by reducing the elimination of lithium from the blood adds a high risk of lithium toxicity.

Interaction with aminoglycoside antibiotics may cause periodic hearing losses: make sure your doctor knows you are taking Furosemide before he gives you an injection of an aminoglycoside.

If you are taking high doses of Aspirin to treat arthritis or similar diseases, and you begin to take Furosemide, you may have to lower the dose of Aspirin because of the effect Furosemide has on passage of Aspirin through the kidneys.

If you are taking Furosemide for the treatment of high blood pressure or congestive heart failure, avoid over-the-counter drug products for the treatment of coughs, colds, and allergies which may contain stimulant drugs. Check with your pharmacist, who can give you accurate information about any over-the-counter drug and its potential interactions with Furosemide.

Usual Dose

Adult: 20 to 80 milligrams per day, depending on disease and patient's response. Doses of 600 milligrams a day or even more have been prescribed.

Infant or child: 4 to 5 milligrams per pound of body weight daily in a single dose. If therapy is not successful, the dose may be increased by steps of 2 to 5 milligrams, but not to more than 14 to 15 milligrams per day.

Maintenance doses are adjusted to the minimum effective level.

Special Information

If the amount of urine you produce each day is dropping or if you suffer from significant loss of appetite, muscle weakness, tiredness, or nausea while taking this drug, contact your doctor immediately.

Generic Name

Gamma Benzene Hexachloride

Brand Names

Gamene
Kwell

Type of Drug

Parasiticide.

Prescribed for

Topical treatment of head lice, crab lice, and scabies.

General Information

Gamma Benzene Hexachloride is considered to be the most effective agent for lice and scabies by many authorities. It should only be used when prescribed by a physician because it cannot prevent infestation, it can only treat it. Also, this medication is extremely irritating, particularly when applied to the eyelids and genital areas. If allowed to remain in contact with the skin for too long, Gamma Benzene Hexachloride will be absorbed directly into the bloodstream, causing signs of drug overdose.

Possible Side Effects

Skin rash.

Usual Dose

For head lice, pour 1 ounce of shampoo on the affected area; rub vigorously; be sure to wet all hairy areas. Wet hair with warm water and work into a full lather for at least 4 minutes. Rinse hair thoroughly and rub with a dry towel. Comb with a fine-tooth comb to remove any remaining nit shells. A second application is usually not needed, but may be made after 24 hours if necessary. The drug should not be used more than twice in 1 week. The shampoo may also be used for crab lice.

For crab lice, after a bath or shower, apply a thin layer of lotion to hairy areas and over the skin of adjacent areas. Leave on for 12 to 24 hours, then wash thoroughly and put on freshly laundered or dry-cleaned clothing. Repeat after 4 days if necessary.

For scabies, after a bath or shower, apply a thin layer of the lotion over the entire skin surface. Leave on for 24 hours, then wash thoroughly. If necessary, a second and third weekly application may be made.

Overdosage

Anyone who ingests this drug accidentally should be

taken to a hospital emergency room immediately. When taken internally, Gamma Benzene Hexachloride is a stimulant; the patient may require Phenobarbital or a similar depressant to neutralize the effect.

If contact with your eyes occurs during shampoo or other use, flush the eyes and surrounding area with water. If irritation or sensitization occurs, discontinue use and call a doctor.

Brand Name

Gaviscon

Ingredients

Alginic Acid
Aluminum Hydroxide Dried Gel
Magnesium Trisilicate
Sodium Bicarbonate

Type of Drug

Antacid.

Prescribed for

Heartburn, acid indigestion, or sour stomach.

General Information

Gaviscon is one of many commercial antacid products on the market. Antacids are used by many people for the relief of temporary symptoms associated with indigestion caused by drugs, food, or disease.

Cautions and Warnings

Do not use this antacid if you are on a sodium-restricted diet.

Possible Side Effects

Occasional constipation or diarrhea if taken in large quantities.

Drug Interactions

Do not take this drug if you are taking a tetracycline

derivative, antibiotic, Digoxin, Phenytoin, Quinidine, Warfarin, or oral iron supplement. The antacid may interfere with the effective absorption of these drugs.

Usual Dose

Chew 2 to 4 tablets 4 times per day, as needed. Do not take more than 16 tablets per day.

Overdosage

Take the patient to an emergency facility. Bring the medication!

Storage

Store the medication at room temperature in a dry place.

Special Information

Do not swallow these tablets whole—they must be chewed.

Generic Name

Glutethimide

Brand Name

Doriden

Type of Drug

Sedative-hypnotic.

Prescribed for

Inability to sleep.

General Information

Sleep is produced within 30 minutes and lasts 4 to 8 hours.

Cautions and Warnings

Glutethimide should not be used if you are sensitive or allergic to it. It can be addictive.

Possible Side Effects

Skin rash.

Possible Adverse Drug Effects

There have been reports of nausea, morning hangover, excitation, and blurring of vision.

Drug Interactions

Do not take this drug with alcohol and/or other depressants such as sedatives, hypnotics, and antihistamines which may produce drowsiness or sleepiness.

Doses of anticoagulant (blood-thinning) drugs such as Warfarin may require adjustment because of increased effects. Dosage adjustment will also be required when you stop taking Glutethimide.

Usual Dose

One tablet at bedtime; if necessary, repeat after 4 hours.

Overdosage

Large amounts of Glutethimide can be fatal, and the drug is frequently used in suicide attempts. Symptoms are coma, lowered body temperature followed by fever, absence of normal reflexes and pain responses after pinches and needle or pin sticks, and shallow breathing. The patient should be taken to a hospital emergency room immediately.

People who have taken Glutethimide for a long time may show signs of chronic overdosage: loss of memory, inability to concentrate, shakes, tremors, loss of reflexes, slurring of speech, and general sense of depression. Abrupt discontinuation of Glutethimide often causes withdrawal reactions of nervousness, anxiety, seizures, cramping, chills, numbness of the extremities, and general behavior changes. Chronic overdosage is best treated by withdrawing the drug over a period of days or weeks.

Generic Name
Guanethidine Sulfate

Brand Name
Ismelin

Type of Drug
Antihypertensive.

Prescribed for
High blood pressure.

General Information
Guanethidine Sulfate affects the section of the nervous system which controls pressure in the major blood vessels. Its blood-pressure-lowering effect is enhanced when taken along with other medicines, such as diuretics.

Cautions and Warnings
Patients who may be allergic to this drug, are taking an MAO inhibitor, or who also have a tumor called a pheochromocytoma should not take Guanethidine Sulfate.

Possible Side Effects
Dizziness, weakness, especially on rising quickly from a sitting or prone position, slowed heartbeat, increased bowel movements, possibly severe diarrhea, male impotence (difficult ejaculation), retention of fluid in the body.

Possible Adverse Drug Effects
Difficulty in breathing, fatigue, nausea, vomiting, increased frequency of nighttime urination, difficulty in controlling urinary function, itching, rash, loss of scalp hair, dry mouth, involuntary lowering of eyelids, blurred vision, muscle aches and spasms, mental depression, chest pains (angina pectoris), tingling in the chest, stuffed nose, weight gain, asthma in some patients. This drug may affect kidney function.

Drug Interactions

Guanethidine Sulfate may interact with digitalis drugs to excessively slow heart rates. When taken with other blood-pressure-lowering drugs it can excessively lower pressure. This is a useful interaction that is sometimes used in treating hypertension (high blood pressure).

Drugs with stimulant properties (antidepressants, decongestants), oral contraceptives, and some antipsychotic drugs (phenothiazines, etc.) may reduce the effectiveness of Guanethidine Sulfate. The drug should not be taken together with MAO inhibitors. MAO's should be stopped *at least* 1 week before taking Guanethidine Sulfate.

Avoid over-the-counter cough, cold, or allergy medicines which may contain stimulants. Check with your doctor or pharmacist before combining these medicines.

Usual Dose

10 milligrams per day to start. Dose is adjusted according to patient need. Average daily requirement is between 25 and 50 milligrams.

Overdosage

Symptoms are basically exaggerated or prolonged side effects, including dizziness, weakness, slowed heartbeat, and possible diarrhea. Call your doctor immediately if the symptoms appear or if you think you have these symptoms.

Special Information

Do not stop taking this medication unless specifically directed to. Call your doctor if you develop frequent diarrhea, are often dizzy or faint. Alcoholic beverages, heat, and strenuous exercise may increase the chances of dizziness or faintness developing.

Generic Name

Haloperidol

Brand Name

Haldol

Type of Drug

Butyrophenone antipsychotic.

Prescribed for

Psychotic disorders and to help control an unusual disorder: Gilles de la Tourette's syndrome.

General Information

Haloperidol is one of many nonphenothiazine agents used in the treatment of psychosis. The drugs in this group are usually about equally effective when given in therapeutically equivalent doses. The major differences are in type and severity of side effects. Some patients may respond well to one and not at all to another: this variability is not easily explained and is thought to result from inborn biochemical differences.

Cautions and Warnings

Haloperidol should not be used by patients who are allergic to it. Patients with blood, liver, kidney, or heart disease, very low blood pressure, or Parkinson's disease should avoid this drug.

Possible Side Effects

Most common: drowsiness, especially during the first or second week of therapy. If the drowsiness becomes troublesome contact your doctor.

Possible Adverse Drug Effects

Haloperidol can cause jaundice (yellowing of the whites of the eyes or skin), usually in 2 to 4 weeks. The jaundice usually goes away when the drug is discontinued, but there have been cases when it did not. If you notice this effect or if you develop fever and generally do not feel well, contact your doctor immediately. Less frequent: changes in components of the blood including anemias, raised or lowered blood pressure, abnormal heartbeat, heart attack, feeling faint or dizzy.

Butyrophenone drugs can produce extrapyramidal effects such as spasms of the neck muscles, severe stiffness of the back muscles, rolling back of the eyes, convulsions, difficulty in swallowing, and symptoms associated with Parkinson's disease. These effects look very serious but go away after the drug has been withdrawn; however, symptoms of the face, tongue and jaw may persist for several years, especially in the elderly with a long history of brain disease. If you experience these extrapyramidal effects contact your doctor immediately.

Haloperidol may cause an unusual increase in psychotic symptoms or may cause paranoid reactions, tiredness, lethargy, restlessness, hyperactivity, confusion at night, bizarre dreams, inability to sleep, depression, or euphoria. Other reactions are itching, swelling, unusual sensitivity to bright lights, red skin, and rash. There have been cases of breast enlargement, false positive pregnancy tests, changes in menstrual flow in females, impotence and changes in sex drive in males.

Haloperidol may also cause dry mouth, stuffy nose, headache, nausea, vomiting, loss of appetite, change in body temperature, loss of facial color, salivation, perspiration, constipation, diarrhea, changes in urine and stool habits, worsening of glaucoma, blurred vision, weakening of eyelid muscles, and spasms in bronchial and other muscles, as well as increased appetite, fatigue, excessive thirst, and changes in the coloration of skin, particularly in exposed areas.

Drug Interactions

Haloperidol should be taken with caution in combination with barbiturates, sleeping pills, narcotics, or any other medication which produces a depressive effect. Avoid alcohol.

Haloperidol may increase the need for anticonvulsant medicine in patients who must take both drugs. It may interfere with oral anticoagulant drugs. Any dosage adjustment necessary can easily be accomplished by your doctor.

Usual Dose

Adult: ½ to 2 milligrams 2 to 3 times per pay. Dose may be increased according to patient need up to 100 milligrams per day.

Child: Not recommended.

Overdosage

Symptoms are depression, extreme weakness, tiredness, desire to go to sleep, coma, lowered blood pressure, uncontrolled muscle spasms, agitation, restlessness, convulsions, fever, dry mouth, and abnormal heart rhythms. The patient should be taken to a hospital emergency room immediately. ALWAYS bring the medicine bottle.

Special Information

Haloperidol has been associated with birth defects but this fact has not definitely been established. Pregnant women should only use this drug when absolutely necessary.

Generic Name

Hydralazine Hydrochloride

Brand Names

Apresoline
Dralzine
Rolazine

Type of Drug

Antihypertensive.

Prescribed for

Essential hypertension (high blood pressure).

General Information

Although the mechanism of action is not completely understood, it is felt that Hydralazine Hydrochloride lowers blood pressure by enlarging the blood vessels throughout the body.

Cautions and Warnings

Long-term administration of large doses of Hydralazine Hydrochloride may produce an arthritislike syndrome in some people, although symptoms and signs of this problem usually disappear when the drug is discontinued. Fever, chest pain, not feeling well, or other unexplained symptoms should be reported to your doctor.

Possible Side Effects

Common: headache, loss of appetite, nausea, vomiting, diarrhea, rapid heartbeat, chest pain.

Possible Adverse Drug Effects

Most frequent: stuffy nose, flushing, tearing in the eyes, itching and redness of the eyes, numbness and tingling of the hands and feet, dizziness, tremors, muscle cramps, depression, disorientation, anxiety. Less frequent: itching, rash, fever, chills, (occasional) hepatitis, constipation, difficulty in urination, adverse effects effecting the normal composition of blood.

Drug Interactions

Hydralazine Hydrochloride should be used with caution in patients who are taking MAO inhibitors.

Usual Dose

Tailored to your needs, like other antihypertensive drugs. Most people begin with 40 milligrams per day for the first several days, then increase to 100 milligrams per day for the rest of the first week. Dose increases until the maximum effect is seen.

Overdosage

If symptoms of extreme lowering of blood pressure, rapid heartbeat, headache, generalized skin flushing, chest pains, and poor heart rhythms appear, contact your doctor immediately.

Special Information

Take this medicine exactly as prescribed.

Do not self-medicate with over-the-counter cough, cold, or allergy remedies whose stimulant ingredients will increase blood pressure.

Generic Name

Hydrochlorothiazide

Brand Names

Delco-Retic	Jen-Diril
Diaqua	Lexor
Esidrix	Oretic
HydroDIURIL	Ro-Hydrazide
Hydro-Z-50	S-Aqua-D
Hydro-Z-25	X-Aqua

Type of Drug

Diuretic.

Prescribed for

Congestive heart failure, cirrhosis of the liver, kidney malfunction, high blood pressure, and other conditions where it is necessary to rid the body of excess fluid.

General Information

This drug is a member of the class known as thiazide diuretics. Thiazides act on the kidneys to stimulate the production of large amounts of urine. They also cause you to lose bicarbonate, chloride, and potassium ions from the body. They are used as part of the treatment of any disease where it is desirable to eliminate large quantities of body water. These diseases include heart failure, some kidney diseases, and liver disease.

Cautions and Warnings

Do not take Hydrochlorothiazide if you are allergic or sensitive to this drug, similar drugs of this group, or sulfa drugs. If you have a history of allergy or bronchial asthma, you may also have a sensitivity or allergy to Hydrochlorothiazide. Although this drug has been used to treat specific conditions in pregnancy, unsupervised use by pregnant patients should be avoided. Hydrochlorothiazide will cross the placenta and pass into the unborn child, possibly causing problems. The drug will pass into the breast milk of nursing mothers.

Possible Side Effects

Hydrochlorothiazide will cause a lowering of potassium in the body. Signs of low potassium levels are dryness of the mouth, thirst, weakness, lethargy, drowsiness, restlessness, muscle pains or cramps, muscular tiredness, low blood pressure, decreased frequency of urination and decreased amount of urine produced, abnormal heart rate, stomach upset including nausea and vomiting.

To treat this, potassium supplements are given in the form of tablets, liquids, or powders, or by increased consumption of foods such as bananas, citrus fruits, melons, and tomatoes.

Possible Adverse Drug Effects

Loss of appetite, stomach upset, nausea, vomiting, cramping, diarrhea, constipation, dizziness, headache, tingling of the toes and fingers, restlessness, changes in blood composition, sensitivity to sunlight, rash, itching, fever, difficulty in breathing, allergic reactions, dizziness when rising quickly from a sitting or lying position, muscle spasms, weakness, blurred vision.

Drug Interactions

Hydrochlorothiazide will add to (potentiate) the action of other blood-pressure-lowering drugs. This is beneficial, and is frequently used to help lower blood pressure in patients with hypertension.

The possibility of developing imbalances in body fluids (electrolytes) is increased if you take medications such as Digitalis and adrenal corticosteroids while you take Hydrochlorothiazide.

If you are taking an oral antidiabetic drug and begin taking Hydrochlorothiazide, the antidiabetic dose may have to be altered.

Lithium Carbonate should not be taken with Hydrochlorothiazide because the combination may increase the risk of lithium toxicity.

Usual Dose

Adult: 25 to 200 milligrams per day depending on condition treated. Maintenance dose, 25 to 100 milligrams per day; some patients may require up to 200 milligrams per day.

Child: 1 milligram per pound of body weight per day in 2 doses.

Infant (under age 6 months): 1½ milligrams per pound per day in 2 doses.

The dose, individualized to your response, must be altered until maximum therapeutic response at minimum effective dose is reached.

Overdosage

Symptoms are large amount of urination, fatigue, and coma. The patient should be taken to a hospital emergency room immediately. ALWAYS bring the medicine bottle.

Special Information

If you are taking this drug for the treatment of high blood pressure or congestive heart failure, avoid over-the-counter medicine for the treatment of coughs, colds, and allergies which may contain stimulants. If you are unsure about them, ask your pharmacist.

Brand Name
Hydropres

Ingredients
Hydrochlorothiazide
Reserpine

Other Brand Names
Hydroserpine Tablets   Hydrotensin Tablets
Hydroserp Tablets   Serpasil-Esidrix Tablets

Type of Drug
Antihypertensive.

Prescribed for
High blood pressure.

General Information

Hydropres is a good example of a drug taking advantage of a drug interaction. Each of the drug ingredients works by different mechanisms to lower your blood pressure. Hydrochlorothiazide relaxes the muscles in your veins and arteries and also helps reduce the volume of blood flowing through those blood vessels. Reserpine interferes with nervous system activity contributing to the increased pressure. These drugs complement each other so that their combined effect is better than the effect of the two individually.

It is essential that you take your medicine exactly as prescribed, for maximum benefit.

An ingredient in this drug may cause excessive loss of potassium, which may lead to a condition called hypokalemia. Warning signs are dryness of mouth, excessive thirst, weakness, drowsiness, restlessness, muscle pains or cramps, muscular fatigue, lack of urination, abnormal heart rhythms, and upset stomach. If this happens, call your doctor. You may need potassium from some outside source. This is done by taking a potassium supplement or by eating foods such as bananas, citrus fruits, melons, and tomatoes which have high concentrations of potassium.

This drug should be stopped at the first sign of despondency, early morning insomnia, loss of appetite, or sexual impotence. Drug-induced depression may persist for several months after the drug has been discontinued; it has been known to be severe enough to result in suicide attempts. This drug should be used with care by women of childbearing age.

Cautions and Warnings

Do not take this drug if you are sensitive or allergic to either of its ingredients or if you have a history of mental depression, active peptic ulcer, or ulcerative colitis.

Possible Side Effects

Loss of appetite, stomach irritation, nausea, vomiting, cramps, diarrhea, constipation, dizziness, headache, tingling in the arms and legs, restlessness, chest pains, abnormal heart rhythms, drowsiness, depression, nervousness, anxiety, nightmares, glaucoma, blood disorders, rash, itching, fever, difficulty in breathing, muscle spasms, weakness, high blood sugar, sugar in the urine, blurred vision, stuffed nose, dryness of the mouth, or rash. Occasionally, impotence or decreased sex drive occurs.

Drug Interactions

Interaction with Digitalis or Quinidine may cause abnormal heart rhythms.

Interaction with drugs containing lithium may lead to toxic effects of lithium.

Avoid over-the-counter cough, cold, or allergy remedies containing stimulant drugs which may raise your blood pressure. Ask your pharmacist for information on those over-the-counter drugs to be avoided.

Usual Dose

Must be individualized to patient's response.

Generic Name

Hydroxyzine Hydrochloride

Brand Names

Atarax
Vistaril

Type of Drug

Antihistamine with antinausea and antianxiety properties.

Prescribed for

Nausea and vomiting; the management of emotional stress such as anxiety, tension, or agitation.

General Information

Hydroxyzine Hydrochloride may be of value in relieving temporary anxiety such as stress of dental or other minor surgical procedures, acute emotional problems, and the management of anxiety associated with stomach and digestive disorders, skin problems, and behavior difficulties in children. This drug has also been used in the treatment of alcoholism.

Cautions and Warnings

Hydroxyzine Hydrochloride should not be used if you know you are sensitive or allergic to this drug, or during early pregnancy.

Possible Side Effects

The primary side effect of Hydroxyzine Hydrochloride is drowsiness, but this disappears in a few days or when the dose is reduced. At higher doses, you may experience dry mouth and occasional tremors or convulsions.

Drug Interactions

Hydroxyzine Hydrochloride has a depressive effect on the nervous system, producing drowsiness and sleepiness. It should not be used with alcohol, sedatives, tranquilizers, antihistamines, or other depressants.

Usual Dose

Adult: 25 to 100 milligrams 3 to 4 times per day.
Child (age 6 or over): 5 to 25 milligrams 3 to 4 times per day.
Child (under age 6): 5 to 10 milligrams 3 to 4 times per day.

Special Information

Be aware of the depressive effect of Hydroxyzine Hydrochloride: be careful when driving or operating heavy or dangerous machinery.

Generic Name

Ibuprofen

Brand Name

Motrin

Type of Drug

Nonsteroid anti-inflammatory.

Prescribed for

Relief of pain and inflammation of joints and muscles; arthritis.

General Information

Ibuprofen is one of several new drugs used for the treatment of various types of arthritis. All these drugs reduce inflammation, and share the same side effects, the most common of which is possible formation of ulcers and upset stomach. In general, the drugs are roughly comparable to Aspirin in controlling the signs and symptoms of arthritis, and are used by some people who cannot tolerate Aspirin.

Cautions and Warnings

Do not take Ibuprofen if you are allergic or sensitive to this drug, Aspirin, or other nonsteroid anti-inflammatory drugs. Ibuprofen may cause stomach ulcers.

Possible Side Effects

Stomach upset, blurred vision, darkening of the stool, changes in color vision, skin rash, weight gain, retention of fluids.

Possible Adverse Drug Effects

Most frequent: stomach upset, dizziness, headache, drowsiness, ringing in the ears. Others: heartburn, nausea, vomiting, bloating, gas in the stomach, stomach pain, diarrhea, constipation, dark stool, nervousness, insomnia, depression, confusion, tremor, lack of appetite, fatigue, itching, rash, double vision, abnormal heart rhythm, anemia or other changes in the composition of the blood, changes in liver function, loss of hair, tingling in the hands and feet, fever, breast enlargement, lowered blood sugar, occasional effects on the kidneys. If symptoms appear, stop taking the medicine and see your doctor immediately.

Drug Interactions

Ibuprofen increases the action of Phenytoin, sulfa drugs, drugs used to control diabetes, and drugs used to thin the blood. If you are taking any of these medicines, be sure you discuss it with your doctor, who will probably change the dose of the other drugs.

Usual Dose

900 to 1600 or even 2400 milligrams per day. Take with meals to reduce stomach upset.

Generic Name

Imipramine

Brand Names

Antipress	SK-Pramine
Imavate	Tofranil
Janimine	Tofranil-PM (long-acting
Presamine	dosage form)
Ropramine	W.D.D.

Type of Drug

Antidepressant.

Prescribed for

Depression with or without symptoms of anxiety; temporary treatment of nighttime bed-wetting in children and adolescents.

General Information

Imipramine and other members of this group are effective in treating symptoms of depression. They can elevate your mood, increase physical activity and mental alertness, improve appetite and sleep patterns. These drugs are mild sedatives and therefore useful in treating mild forms of depression asociated with anxiety. You should not expect instant results with this medicine:

results are usually seen after 1 to 4 weeks of therapy. If symptoms are not changed after 6 to 8 weeks, contact your doctor. Occasionally, this drug and other members of the group of drugs have been used in treating nighttime bed-wetting in the young child, but they do not produce long-lasting relief, and therapy with one of them for nighttime bed-wetting is of questionable value.

Cautions and Warnings

Do not take Imipramine if you are allergic or sensitive to this or other members of this class of drugs: Doxepin, Nortriptyline, Amitriptyline, Desipramine, and Protriptyline. These drugs should not be used if you are recovering from a heart attack. Imipramine may be taken with caution if you have a history of epilepsy or other convulsive disorders, difficulty in urination, glaucoma, heart disease, or thyroid disease. Imipramine can interfere with your ability to perform tasks which require concentration, such as driving or operating machinery. Imipramine will pass from mother to unborn child: consult your doctor before taking this medicine if you are pregnant.

Possible Side Effects

Changes in blood pressure (both high and low), abnormal heart rate, heart attack, confusion, especially in elderly patients, hallucinations, disorientation, delusions, anxiety, restlessness, excitement, numbness and tingling in the extremities, lack of coordination, muscle spasms or tremors, seizures and/or convulsions, dry mouth, blurred vision, constipation, inability to urinate, skin rash, itching, sensitivity to bright lights or sunlight, retention of fluids, particularly of the face, fever, allergy, changes in composition of blood, nausea, vomiting, loss of appetite, stomach upset, diarrhea, enlargement of the breasts in males and females, increased or decreased sex drive, increased or decreased blood sugar.

Possible Adverse Drug Effects

Infrequent: agitation, inability to sleep, nightmares, feeling of panic, development of a peculiar taste in the mouth, stomach cramps, black coloration of the tongue, yellowing eyes and/or skin, changes in liver function, increased or decreased weight, perspiration, flushing, frequent urination, drowsiness, dizziness, weakness, headache, loss of hair, nausea, not feeling well.

Drug Interactions

Interaction with MAO inhibitors can cause high fevers, convulsions, and occasionally death. Don't take MAO inhibitors until at least 2 weeks after Imipramine has been discontinued.

Imipramine interacts with Guanethidine, a drug used to treat high blood pressure: if your doctor prescribes Imipramine and you are taking medicine for high blood pressure, be sure to discuss this with him.

Imipramine increases the effects of barbiturates, tranquilizers, other depressive drugs, and alcohol. Don't drink alcoholic beverages if you take this medicine.

Taking Imipramine and thyroid medicine will enhance the effects of the thyroid medicine. The combination can cause abnormal heart rhythms.

Large doses of Vitamin C (Ascorbic Acid) can reduce the effect of Imipramine. Drugs such as Bicarbonate of Soda or Acetazolamide will increase the effect of Imipramine.

Usual Dose

Adult: Initial dose, about 75 milligrams per day in divided doses; then increased or decreased as judged necessary by your doctor. The individualized dose may be less than 75 or up to 200 milligrams. Long-term patients being treated for depression may be given extended-acting medicine daily at bedtime or several times per day.

Adolescent or elderly: Initial dose, 30 or 40 milligrams per day. Require less of the drug because of increased sensitivity. Maintenance dose is usually less than 100 milligrams per day.

Child: Dose for nighttime bed-wetting is 25 milligrams per day (age 6 and over), an hour before bedtime. If relief of bed-wetting does not occur within 1 week, the dose is increased to a daily 50 to 75 milligrams, depending on age; often in midafternoon and at bedtime. (A dose greater than 75 milligrams will

167

increase side effects without increasing effectiveness.) The medication should be gradually tapered off; this may reduce the probability that the bed-wetting will return.

Overdosage

Symptoms are confusion, inability to concentrate, hallucinations, drowsiness, lowered body temperature, abnormal heart rate, heart failure, large pupils of the eyes, convulsions, severely lowered blood pressure, stupor, and coma (as well as agitation, stiffening of body muscles, vomiting, and high fever). The patient should be taken to a hospital emergency room immediately. ALWAYS bring the medicine bottle.

Generic Name

Indomethacin

Brand Name

Indocin

Type of Drug

Nonsteroid anti-inflammatory.

Prescribed for

Arthritis and other forms of inflammation of joints and muscles.

General Information

Indomethacin is one of the newer nonsteroid anti-inflammatory drugs available over the last 10 years or so: it has pain-relieving, fever-lowering, and inflammation-reducing effects, but we do not know exactly how these effects are produced. It also can produce serious side effects at high doses. For this reason, the drug should be taken with caution.

Cautions and Warnings

Use Indomethacin with extra caution if you have a history of ulcers, bleeding diseases, or allergic reaction to

Aspirin. Indomethacin should be avoided by pregnant women, nursing mothers, and children under age 14. This drug is not a simple pain reliever; it should be used only under the strict supervision of your doctor.

Possible Side Effects

Indomethacin may produce severe stomach upset or other reactions. It has caused ulcers in all portions of the gastrointestinal tract, including the esophagus, stomach, small intestine, and large intestine. For this reason any unusual stomach upset, nausea, vomiting, loss of appetite, gas, gaseous feeling, or feeling of bloating must be reported immediately to your doctor. Indomethacin may cause blurred vision: this is an important drug side effect and must be reported to your doctor immediately. If you develop a persistent headache while taking Indomethacin report this to your doctor immediately and stop taking the drug.

Indomethacin may aggravate preexisting psychiatric disturbances, epilepsy, or Parkinson's disease. It may cause reduction in mental alertness and coordination and this can affect you particularly while driving, operating a machine or appliance, or engaging in any activity requiring alertness and concentration.

Possible Adverse Drug Effects

On rare occasions Indomethacin can cause effects on the liver, and anemia or other effects on components of the blood. People who are allergic to the drug can develop reactions including a rapid fall in blood pressure, difficulty in breathing, itching, and skin rashes. It has also caused ringing in the ears, retention of fluids in the body, elevation of blood pressure, passing of blood in the urine, loss of hair, (occasional) vaginal bleeding, and increased blood sugar.

Drug Interactions

Avoid alcohol, which will aggravate any problem with drowsiness or lack of alertness.

Probenecid (Benemid) increases the amount of Indomethacin in your blood by reducing its elimination from the body. This interaction will reduce the amount of Indomethacin required.

If you are taking an anticoagulant (blood-thinning) drug and start taking Indomethacin, you probably will experience no serious interaction, but your doctor should know that you are taking both drugs so he can monitor the anticoagulant during the first week or two of Indomethacin therapy, in case dosage adjustment is required.

Since Indomethacin causes stomach upset in many patients and can be a source of ulcers, it should be taken with food or antacids. Adrenal corticosteroids, Aspirin, or other drugs may aggravate this problem. Space Indomethacin and such drugs at least 2 to 3 hours apart to minimize irritating effects on the stomach.

Usual Dose

From 50 to 150 milligrams per day, individualized to patient's needs.

Special Information

If you are allergic to Aspirin, you may be allergic to Indomethacin.

Generic Name

Isosorbide Dinitrate

Brand Names

Isordil	Onset
Isordil Sublingual	Sorate
Isordil Tembids	Sorbide
Isordil Titradose	Sorbide T.D.
Isosorb	Sorbitrate
Isotrate	Sorbitrate SA
Isotrate Timecelles	Sorbitrate Sublingual
Laserdil	

Type of Drug

Antianginal agent.

Prescribed for

Relief of heart or chest pain associated with angina pectoris; also, to control or prevent recurrence of chest or heart pain.

General Information

Isosorbide Dinitrate belongs to the class of drugs known as nitrates, which are used to treat pain associated with heart problems. The exact nature of their action is not fully understood.

Cautions and Warnings

If you know that you are allergic or sensitive to this drug or other drugs for heart pain such as Nitroglycerin, do not use Isosorbide Dinitrate. Anyone who has a head injury or has recently had a head injury should use this drug with caution.

Possible Side Effects

Flushing of the skin and headache are common, but should disappear after your body has had an opportunity to get used to the drug. You may experience dizziness and weakness in the process.

Possible Adverse Drug Effects

Nausea, vomiting, weakness, sweating, skin rash with itching, redness, possible peeling. If these signs appear, discontinue the medication and consult your physician.

Drug Interactions

If you take Isosorbide Dinitrate, do not self-medicate with over-the-counter cough and cold remedies, since many of them contain ingredients which may aggravate heart disease.

Interaction with large amounts of whiskey, wine, or beer can cause rapid lowering of blood pressure resulting in weakness, dizziness, and fainting.

Usual Dose

Average daily dose, 40 milligrams. The drug may be given in doses from 5 milligrams 2 to 3 times per day to 40 milligrams 4 times per day.

Take Isosorbide Dinitrate on an empty stomach unless you get a headache which cannot be controlled by the usual means, when the medication can be taken with meals. If you take this drug sublingually (under the tongue) be sure the tablet is fully dissolved before swallowing the drug.

Generic Name

Isoxsuprine Hydrochloride

Brand Names

Isolait
Vasodilan
Vasoprine

Type of Drug

Vasodilator.

Prescribed for

Relief of symptoms arising from chronic organic brain syndrome; specifically, loss of memory and other intellectual functions. Also used to prevent the progress of this disease and at times to help reverse the disease process.

General Information

Isoxsuprine Hydrochloride works by helping to increase the amount of blood supplied to the brain, by acting on the nerves that control muscles in the major blood vessels, which relaxes the muscles and allows more blood to flow to the brain. Many studies have questioned the effectiveness of this drug. However, it continues to be widely used and prescribed.

Possible Side Effects

Isoxsuprine Hydrochloride can cause low blood pressure. In this condition blood tends to stay in the arms and legs and less is available to the brain, resulting in light-headedness or dizziness. To avoid this, if you are taking Isoxsuprine Hydrochloride or any other vasodilator do not stand for long periods and be careful not to be too quick when you get out of bed or stand up.

Possible Adverse Drug Effects

Rapid heartbeat, nausea, vomiting, dizziness, stomach distress, severe rash. If you develop a rash, stop taking the drug and consult your doctor immediately.

Drug Interactions

Alcoholic beverages increase the effect of Isoxsuprine Hydrochloride and can cause dizziness or faintness.

Usual Dose

10 to 20 milligrams, 3 to 4 times per day.

Generic Name

Levothyroxine Sodium

Brand Names

Cytolen
Letter
Levoid

Ro-Thyroxine
Synthroid

Type of Drug

Thyroid replacement.

Prescribed for

Replacement of thyroid hormone or low output of hormone from the thyroid gland.

General Information

Levothyroxine Sodium is one of several thyroid replacement products available. The major difference between these products is in effectiveness in treating certain phases of thyroid disease.

Cautions and Warnings

If you have hyperthyroid disease or high output of thyroid hormone you should not use Levothyroxine Sodium. Symptoms of hyperthyroid disease include headache, nervousness, sweating, rapid heartbeat, chest pains, and other signs of central nervous system stimulation. If you have heart disease or high blood pressure, thyroid replacement therapy should not be used unless it is clearly indicated and supervised by your physician. If you develop chest pains or other signs of heart disease while you are taking thyroid medication, contact your doctor immediately.

Possible Side Effects

Most common: palpitations of the heart, rapid heartbeat, abnormal heart rhythms, weight loss, chest pains, shaking of the hands, headache, diarrhea, nervousness, inability to sleep, sweating, inability to stand heat. These symptoms may be controlled by adjusting the dose of the medication. If you are suffering from one or more side effects, you must contact your doctor immediately so that the proper dose adjustment can be made.

Drug Interactions

Interaction of Levothyroxine Sodium with Questran can be avoided by spacing the two doses at least 4 hours apart.

Avoid over-the-counter products containing stimulant drugs, such as many drugs used to treat coughs, colds, or allergies, which will affect your heart and may cause symptoms of overdosage.

Thyroid replacement therapy may increase the effect of anticoagulant (blood-thinning) drugs such as Warfarin or Bishydroxycoumarin. Be sure you report this to your physician as it will be necessary to reduce the dose of your anticoagulant drug by approximately one-third at the beginning of thyroid therapy (to avoid hemorrhage). Further adjustments may be made later after your doctor reviews your blood tests.

Diabetics may have to increase their dose of Insulin or oral antidiabetic drugs. Changes in dose must be made by a doctor.

Usual Dose

Initial dose, as little as 25 micrograms per day; then increased in steps of 25 micrograms once every 3 to 4 weeks depending upon response, with final dose of 100 to 200 micrograms per day, or even 300 to 400 micrograms if needed to achieve normal function.

Overdosage

Symptoms are headache, irritability, nervousness, sweating, rapid heartbeat with unusual stomach rumbling and with or without cramps, chest pains, heart failure, and shock. The patient should be taken to a hospital emergency room immediately. ALWAYS bring the medicine bottle.

Brand Name

Librax

Ingredients

Chlordiazepoxide
Clidinium Bromide

Type of Drug

Anticholinergic combination.

Prescribed for

Anxiety and spasms associated with gastrointestinal disease. Librax may be specifically prescribed as an adjunct in the treatment of organic or functional gastrointestinal disorders and in the management of peptic ulcers, gastritis, irritable bowel syndrome, spastic colon, and mild ulcerative colitis.

General Information

Librax is one of many combinations of this class containing an anticholinergic or antispasmodic drug and a tranquilizer such as Chlordiazepoxide. All the drugs in this class will provide symptomatic relief only, and will not treat an underlying disease: it is important that you realize while taking this medication that you should actively pursue the treatment of the underlying cause of this problem if one is present and can be found.

Cautions and Warnings

Librax should not be used if you have glaucoma or if you have a history of prostatic hypertrophy and bladder-neck obstruction. You should not take this drug if you are allergic or think that you may be allergic to either of its ingredients, Chlordiazepoxide (Librium) and Clidinium Bromide (Quarzan), as well as Diazepam (Valium), which is related to Chlordiazepoxide.

Possible Side Effects

Most common: mild drowsiness (usually experienced during the first few days of therapy), dry mouth, difficulty in urination, constipation. These side effects may be accentuated in the elderly or debilitated person. If they persist, you should contact your doctor and discuss these problems with him, since it is possible that you may be taking too much of the drug for your system—or the side effects may be so bothersome as to suggest the possibility of using a different medication.

Possible Adverse Drug Effects

Infrequent: confusion, depression, lethargy, disorientation, headache, lack of activity, slurring of speech, stupor, dizziness, tremor, constipation, nausea, difficulty in urination, changes in sex drive, menstrual irregularity, changes in heart rhythm, stuffed nose, fever, heartburn, suppression of lactation in females, bloated feeling, drug allergy or allergic reaction to the drug including itching, rash, and less usual manifestations. Most people taking Librax experience few truly bothersome effects and although the effects listed may be a problem, in most patients they do not constitute a severe difficulty.

Drug Interactions

The central nervous system depressant (tranquilizer) or the Atropinelike drug (anticholinergic) in Librax may interact with alcoholic beverages or depressant drugs such as other tranquilizers, narcotics, barbiturates, or even antihistamines, causing excessive tiredness or sleepiness.

Both Librax ingredients may be potentiated (increased in effect) by MAO inhibitors: you may wish to discuss with your doctor the possibility of avoiding the combination.

The anticholinergic ingredient in Librax may be inhibited by certain drugs used to treat high blood pressure, including Guanethidine (Ismelin) and Reserpine. Discuss this with your doctor.

Usual Dose

One to 2 capsules 3 to 4 times per day, usually before meals and at bedtime. Amount and scheduling of medication may vary according to disease and patient's response.

Overdosage

Symptoms are dry mouth, difficulty in swallowing, thirst, blurred vision, inability to tolerate bright lights, flushed, hot dry skin, rash, high temperatures, palpitations and other unusual heart rhythms, feeling that you must urinate but difficulty in doing so, restlessness or depression, confusion, delirium, and possible coma and/or lack of reflexes, and lowered respiration (breathing) and blood pressure. The patient should be taken to a hospital emergency room immediately. ALWAYS bring the medicine bottle.

Brand Name

Lomotil

Ingredients

Atropine Sulfate
Diphenoxylate

Type of Drug

Antidiarrheal.

Prescribed for

Symptomatic treatment of diarrhea.

General Information

Lomotil and other antidiarrheal agents should only be used for short periods: they will relieve the diarrhea, but not its underlying causes. Sometimes these drugs should not be used even though there is diarrhea present: people with some kinds of bowel, stomach, or other disease may be harmed by taking antidiarrheal drugs. Obviously, the decision to use Lomotil must be made by your doctor. Do not use Lomotil without his advice.

Cautions and Warnings

Do not take Lomotil if you are allergic to this medication or any other medication containing Atropine, or if you are jaundiced (yellowing of the whites of the eyes and/or skin) or are suffering from diarrhea caused by antibiotics such as Clindamycin or Lincomycin. Do not use Lomotil if you are pregnant, because the ingredients in this medication will cross into the blood system of the unborn child. If you are nursing a newborn baby, Lomotil will appear in breast milk and can affect the newborn infant.

Possible Side Effects

Most common: dryness of the skin inside the nose or mouth, flushing or redness of the face, fever, unusual heart rates, inability to urinate.

Possible Adverse Drug Effects

People taking Lomotil for extended periods may experience abdominal discomforts, swelling of the gums, interference with normal breathing, feeling of numbness in the extremities, drowsiness, restlessness, rashes, nausea, sedation, vomiting, headache, dizziness, depression, feeling unwell, lethargy, loss of appetite, euphoria, itching, and coma.

Drug Interactions

Lomotil, a depressant on the central nervous system, may cause tiredness or inability to concentrate, and may thus increase the effect of sleeping pills, tranquilizers, and alcoholic beverages. Avoid large amounts of alcohol while taking Lomotil. .

Usual Dose

Adult: 4 tablets per day until diarrhea has stopped; then reduce to the lowest level that will control diarrhea (usually 2 tablets per day or less).

For children ages 2 to 12, the liquid form, supplied with a dropper calibrated to deliver medication as desired in milliliters, is used.

Child (ages 8 to 12, or about 60 to 80 pounds): 2 milliliters 5 times per day.

Child (ages 5 to 8, or about 45 to 60 pounds): 2 milliliters 4 times per day.

Child (ages 2 to 5, or about 26 to 45 pounds): 2 milliliters 3 times per day.

Child (under age 2): Not recommended.

Overdosage

Lomotil overdose is generally accidental: patients, feeling that the prescribed amount has not cured their diarrhea, will take more medication on their own. Symptoms of overdosage (particularly effects on breathing) may not be evident until 12 to 30 hours after the medication has been taken. Symptoms are dryness of skin, mouth, and/or nose, flushing, fever, and abnormal heart rates, with possible lethargy, coma, or depression of breathing. The patient should be taken to a hospital emergency room immediately. ALWAYS bring the medicine bottle.

Special Information

Lomotil may cause drowsiness and difficulty concentrating: be careful while driving or operating any appliance or equipment.

Loperamide

Brand Name

Imodium

Type of Drug

Antidiarrheal.

Prescribed for

Symptomatic treatment of diarrhea.

General Information

Loperamide and other antidiarrheal agents should only be used for short periods: they will relieve the diarrhea, but not its underlying causes. Sometimes these drugs should not be used even though there is diarrhea present: people with some kinds of bowel, stomach, or other disease may be harmed by taking antidiarrheal drugs. Obviously, the decision to use the drug must be made by your doctor; do not use it without his advice.

Cautions and Warnings

Do not use Loperamide if you are allergic or sensitive to it or if you suffer from diarrhea associated with colitis or with certain drugs such as Clindamycin. Pregnant women and nursing mothers should avoid taking this drug. Loperamide is not known to be addictive.

Possible Side Effects

The incidence of side effects from Loperamide is low. Stomach and abdominal pain, bloating or other discomfort, constipation, dryness of the mouth, dizziness, tiredness, nausea and vomiting, and skin rash are possible.

Drug Interactions

Loperamide, a depressant on the central nervous system, may cause tiredness, inability to concentrate, and may thus increase the effect of sleeping pills, tranquilizers, and alcoholic beverages. Avoid large amounts of alcohol while taking Loperamide.

Usual Dose

Adult or child (age 12 and over): 2 capsules to start, followed by 1 capsule after each loose stool, up to 8 capsules per day maximum. Improvement should be seen in 2 days. People with long-term (chronic) diarrhea usually need 2 to 4 capsules per day. This drug is usually effective within 10 days or not at all.

Child (under age 12): Not recommended.

Overdosage

Symptoms are constipation, central depression, and irritation of the stomach. Large doses cause vomiting. The patient should be taken to a hospital emergency room immediately. ALWAYS bring the medicine bottle.

Special Information

Loperamide may cause drowsiness and difficulty concentrating: be careful while driving or operating any appliance or equipment.

Brand Name

Marax

Ingredients

Ephedrine Sulfate
Hydroxyzine Hydrochloride
Theophylline

Type of Drug

Antiasthmatic combination product.

Prescribed for

Relief of asthma symptoms or other upper respiratory disorders.

General Information

Marax is one of several antiasthmatic combination

products prescribed for the relief of asthmatic symptoms and other breathing problems. These products contain drugs which help relax the bronchial muscles, drugs which increase the diameter of the breathing passages, and a mild tranquilizer to help relax the patient. Other products in this class may contain similar ingredients along with other medicine to help eliminate mucus from the breathing passages.

Cautions and Warnings

Take the drug with food to help prevent stomach upset.

Possible Side Effects

Large doses of Marax can produce excitation, shakiness, sleeplessness, nervousness, rapid heartbeat, chest pains, irregular heartbeat, dizziness, dryness of the nose and throat, headache, and sweating. Occasionally, people have been known to develop hesitation or difficulty in urination. Marax may also cause stomach upset, so you are advised to take this drug with food.

Possible Adverse Drug Effects

Excessive urination, heart stimulation, drowsiness, muscle weakness, muscle twitching, unsteady walk. These effects are usually controlled by having your doctor adjust the dose.

Drug Interactions

Marax may cause sleeplessness and/or drowsiness. Do not take this drug with alcoholic beverages.

Taking Marax or similar medicines with an MAO inhibitor can produce severe interaction. Consult your doctor first.

Usual Dose

Adult: 1 tablet 2 to 4 times per day.
Child (over 5 years): ½ tablet 2 to 4 times per day. Syrup, 1 teaspoon 3 to 4 times per day.
Child (ages 2 to 5): Syrup, ½ teaspoon 3 to 4 times per day.
Take doses at least 4 hours apart. The dose is adjusted to severity of disease and patient's ability to tolerate side effects.

Generic Name

Meclizine

Brand Names

Antivert	Roclizine
Bonine	Vertrol
Eldezine	Wehvert

Type of Drug

Antiemetic, antivertigo agent.

Prescribed for

Relief of nausea, vomiting, and dizziness associated with motion sickness or disease affecting the middle ear.

General Information

Meclizine is an antihistamine used to treat or prevent nausea, vomiting, and motion sickness. It takes a little longer to start working than most other drugs of this type but lasts longer (1 to 2 days). The specific method by which Meclizine acts on the brain to prevent dizziness and the nausea associated with it is not fully understood. In general, Meclizine does a better job preventing motion sickness than treating the symptoms once they are present.

Use with caution in children as a treatment for vomiting or nausea. This drug may obscure symptoms important in reaching the diagnosis of underlying disease. Meclizine is one of several drugs prescribed for the relief of nausea, vomiting, or dizziness and does not cure any underlying problems.

Cautions and Warnings

Do not take this medication if you think you are allergic to it. Women who are pregnant or who feel they may become pregnant while they are taking this medication should not take Meclizine. Meclizine has been associated with birth defects when taken by pregnant women.

Possible Side Effects

Most common: drowsiness, dry mouth, blurred vision.

Possible Adverse Drug Effects

Infrequent: difficulty in urination, constipation. Adverse effects are usually not a cause for great concern. If they become serious, discuss them with your doctor.

Drug Interactions

Meclizine may cause sleepiness, tiredness, or inability to concentrate. Avoid tranquilizers, sleeping pills, alcoholic beverages, barbiturates, narcotics, and antihistamines, which can add to these effects.

Usual Dose

25 to 50 milligrams 1 hour before travel; repeat every 24 hours for duration of journey. For control of dizziness (diseases affecting middle ear, etc.), 25 to 100 milligrams per day in divided doses.

Special Information

Meclizine may cause tiredness, sleepiness, and inability to concentrate. Be extremely careful while driving or operating any machinery, appliances, or delicate equipment.

Generic Name

Medroxyprogesterone Acetate

Brand Name

Provera

Type of Drug

Progestogen.

Prescribed for

Irregular menstrual bleeding.

General Information

Because of the potential development of secondary disease after a long period of taking Medroxyprogesterone Acetate, the decision to take this medication chronically should be made cautiously by you and your doctor together. Your continued need for chronic therapy with Medroxyprogesterone Acetate should be evaluated at least every 6 months to be sure that this therapy is absolutely necessary.

Cautions and Warnings

Do not take this drug if you have a history of blood clots or similar disorders, a history of convulsions, liver disease, known or suspected breast cancer, undiagnosed vaginal bleeding, or miscarriage. You should not be taking the drug if you are pregnant, since Medroxy-progesterone Acetate has been known to produce masculinization in the female unborn child.

Possible Side Effects

Breakthrough bleeding, spotting, changes in or loss of menstrual flow, retention of water, increase or decrease in weight, jaundice, rash (with or without itching), mental depression.

Possible Adverse Drug Effects

A significant association has been demonstrated between the use of progestogen drugs and the following serious adverse effect: development of blood clots in the veins, lungs, or brain. Other possible adverse effects: changes in libido or sex drive, changes in appetite, headache, nervousness, dizziness, tiredness, backache, loss of scalp hair, growth of hair in unusual quantities or places, itching, symptoms similar to urinary infections, unusual skin rashes.

Usual Dose

Five to 10 milligrams per day for 5 to 10 days beginning on what is assumed to be the 16th to 21st day of the menstrual cycle.

Special Information

At the first sign of sudden, partial, or complete loss of vision, leg cramps, water retention, unusual vaginal bleeding, migraine headache, or depression, or if you think you have become pregnant, stop the drug immediately and call your doctor.

Megestrol Acetate

Brand Name

Megace

Type of Drug

Progestational hormone.

Prescribed for

Cancer of the breast or endometrium.

General Information

Megestrol Acetate has been used quite successfully in the treatment of the cancers cited. It exerts its effect by acting as a hormonal counterbalance in areas rich in estrogen (breast and endometrium).

Cautions and Warnings

This drug should only be used for its two specifically approved indications. The use of this drug should be accompanied by close, continued contact with your doctor.

Possible Side Effects

None.

Possible Adverse Drug Effects

Should be used with caution if you have a history of blood clots in the veins.

Usual Dose

40 to 320 milligrams per day.

Generic Name
Meprobamate

Brand Names

Equanil
Mepriam
Meprospan
Miltown

Saronil
Sedabamate
SK-Bamate
Tranmep

Type of Drug

Tranquilizer.

Prescribed for

Relief of anxiety and tension, and to promote sleep in anxious or tense patients.

General Information

Meprobamate and the other drugs in its chemical group are used as either antianxiety agents, anticonvulsants, or sedatives (sleeping pills). This drug exerts effects by relaxing the large skeletal muscles and by a direct effect on the brain. In doing so, it can relax you and make you either more tranquil or sleepier, depending on the drug and how much you use.

Meprobamate is generally used in any situation where it can be a useful adjunct.

Meprobamate can be abused if taken for long periods of time and it is possible to develop withdrawal symptoms if you discontinue the therapy abruptly. Withdrawal symptoms include convulsions, tremor, muscle cramps, stomach cramps, vomiting, and sweating.

Cautions and Warnings

You should not take Meprobamate if you are allergic to it or if you feel that you may be allergic to a related drug such as Carisoprodol, Mebutamate, Tybamate, or Carbromal. Severe physical and psychological dependence has been experienced by people taking Meprobamate for long periods of time. The drug can produce chronic intoxication after prolonged use or if used in greater than recommended doses, leading to adverse effects such as slurred speech, dizziness, and general sleepiness or depression. If this is true of a friend of yours who is taking this drug, you should discuss this matter with him/her and urge the friend to see a doctor. Or if it is true of you, see your doctor. Sudden withdrawal of Meprobamate after prolonged and excessive use may result in drug withdrawal symptoms including severe anxiety, loss of appetite, sleeplessness, vomiting, tremors, muscle twitching, severe sleepiness, confusion, hallucinations, and possibly convulsions. Such withdrawal symptoms usually begin 12 to 48 hours after Meprobamate has been stopped and may last 1 to 4 days. When someone has taken this medication in excessive quantities for weeks, months, or longer, the medication must be gradually reduced over a period of 1 or 2 weeks in order to avoid these withdrawal symptoms. If you are taking Meprobamate you should be aware that this drug may cause inability to perform usual tasks which require coordination, such as driving or operating machinery, and you must be extremely careful when performing such tasks. Use with extreme caution if you are in the first 3 months of pregnancy or if you suspect that you may be pregnant: minor tranquilizers such as this drug and the benzodiazepine tranquilizers have been associated with a small incidence of birth defects. If you are pregnant and are taking this medication, you should discuss it with your doctor.

Possible Side Effects

Most common: drowsiness, sleepiness, dizziness, slurred speech, headache, weakness, tingling in the arms and legs, euphoria, and possibly excitement or paradoxical reactions such as overstimulation.

Possible Adverse Drug Effects

Infrequent: nausea, vomiting, diarrhea, abnormal heart rhythms, low blood pressure, itching, rash, effects on various components of the blood. Quite rarely there has been severe hypersensitivity or allergic reactions which have produced high fever, chills, closing of the throat (bronchospasm), loss of urinary function, and other severe symptoms.

Drug Interactions

Interactions with other drugs that produce depression of the central nervous system can cause sleepiness, tiredness, and tranquilization. Interaction with other tranquilizers, alcoholic beverages in excessive quantities, narcotics, barbiturates and other sleeping pills, or antihistamines can cause excessive depression, sleepiness, and fatigue.

Usual Dose

Adult (when used as a tranquilizer): 1200 to 1600 milligrams per day in divided doses; maximum permissible, 2400 milligrams per day.

Child (ages 6 to 12): 100 to 200 milligrams 2 to 3 times per day.

Should not be given to children who are under age 6.

Overdosage

In attempted suicide or accidental overdose symptoms are extreme drowsiness, lethargy, stupor, and coma, with possible shock and respiratory collapse (breathing stops).

The overdosed patient must be taken to a hospital emergency room immediately. ALWAYS bring the medicine bottle. Some people have died after taking 30 tablets; others have survived after taking 100.

The overdose is much worse if there is interaction with a large quantity of alcohol or another depressant: a much smaller dose of Meprobamate can produce fatal results.

After a large overdose, the patient will go to sleep very quickly and blood pressure, pulse, and breathing levels will be greatly reduced. After the patient is taken to the hospital his stomach should be pumped and respiratory assistance and other supportive therapy given.

Special Information

Elderly or debilitated (physically below par) people are especially sensitive to Meprobamate and should take it with care. The same dose as taken in the past may produce excessive depression and be uncomfortable or dangerous.

Methaqualone Hydrochloride

Brand Names

Parest
Quāālude
Sopor

Type of Drug

Sedative-hypnotic.

Prescribed for

Inability to sleep.

General Information

Methaqualone Hydrochloride begins to produce drowsiness within 10 to 20 minutes and sleep lasts for several hours. This drug has been implicated in suicides and accidental deaths. Particular attention should be paid to the drug interactions of Methaqualone Hydrochloride. Aged, highly agitated, or very ill people may be more sensitive than usual to this drug and require smaller doses to produce sleep.

Cautions and Warnings

Do not take Methaqualone Hydrochloride if you are allergic or sensitive to it. It can be addictive.

Possible Side Effects

Headache, hallucinations, hangover, fatigue, nausea, dizziness, rash.

Possible Adverse Drug Effects

Infrequent: tingling in the extremities, restlessness and anxiety, anemias, dry mouth, loss of appetite, vomiting, diarrhea, stomach upset, sweating, itching.

Drug Interactions

Avoid interaction with alcohol, other sleeping medicine, tranquilizers, or other depressants, which can lead to profound depression of respiration (breathing) and, eventually, death.

Usual Dose

Adult: Up to 400 milligrams at bedtime.
Child: Do not use.

Overdosage

Large amounts of Methaqualone Hydrochloride can be fatal, and the drug is frequently used in suicide attempts. Symptoms are coma, lowered body temperature followed by fever, absence of normal reflexes and pain responses after pinches or needle or pin sticks, and shallow breathing. The patient should be taken to a hospital emergency room immediately. ALWAYS bring the medicine bottle.

People who have taken Methaqualone Hydrochloride for a long time may show signs of chronic overdosage: loss of memory, inability to concentrate, shakes, tremors, loss of reflexes, slurring of speech, and general sense of depression. Abrupt discontinuation of Methaqualone Hydrochloride often causes withdrawal reactions of nervousness, anxiety, seizures, cramping, chills, numbness of the extremities, and general behavior changes. Chronic overdosage is best treated by withdrawing the drug over a period of days or weeks.

Special Information

Do not attempt to drive or operate any equipment, appliances, or machinery while under the influence of Methaqualone Hydrochloride.

Generic Name

Methocarbamol

Brand Names

Metho-500
Robaxin
Romethocarb

Type of Drug

Skeletal muscle relaxant.

Prescribed for

Partial treatment for the relief of pain and other discomforts associated with acute conditions such as sprains, strains, or bad backs.

General Information

Methocarbamol is one of several drugs available for the relief of pain caused by spasms of large skeletal muscles. These drugs give symptomatic relief only. They should not be the only form of therapy used. If you are taking Methocarbamol, follow any other instruction given by your doctor with regard to rest, physical therapy, or other measures to help to relieve your problem.

Cautions and Warnings

The effect of Methocarbamol on the pregnant female has not been studied. Methocarbamol may have an effect on the unborn child: if you are pregnant, you should not use this medicine unless it is absolutely necessary and this problem has been considered by your physician.

Possible Side Effects

Most common: light-headedness, dizziness, drowsiness, nausea, drug allergy (itching and rash), conjunctivitis with nasal congestion, blurred vision, headache, fever.

Drug Interactions

Other drugs which, like Methocarbamol, may cause drowsiness, sleepiness, or lack of ability to concentrate must be taken with extreme caution: sleeping pills, tranquilizers, barbiturates, narcotics, and alcoholic beverages.

Usual Dose

Adult: Initial dose, 1500 milligrams 4 times per day for 48 to 72 hours; then 1500 milligrams 3 times per day, 1000 milligrams 4 times per day, or 750 milligrams every 4 hours.

Overdosage

Symptoms are central nervous system depression, desire to sleep, weakness, lassitude, and difficulty in breathing. The patient should be taken to a hospital emergency room immediately. ALWAYS bring the medicine bottle.

Special Information

Methocarbamol may cause drowsiness, sleepiness, and inability to concentrate: this can affect you if you drive or operate any sort of appliance, equipment, or machinery.

Generic Name

Methyclothiazide

Brand Names

Aquatensen
Enduron

Type of Drug

Diuretic.

Prescribed for

Congestive heart failure, cirrhosis of the liver, kidney malfunction, high blood pressure, and other conditions where it is necessary to rid the body of excess fluid.

General Information

This drug is a member of the class known as thiazide diuretics. Thiazides act on the kidney to stimulate the production of large amounts of urine. They also cause you to lose bicarbonate, chloride, and potassium ions from the body. They are used as part of the treatment of any disease where it is desirable to eliminate large quantities of body water. These diseases include heart failure, some kidney diseases, and liver disease.

Cautions and Warnings

Do not take Methyclothiazide if you are allergic or sensitive to this drug, similar drugs of this group, or sulfa drugs. If you have a history of allergy or bronchial asthma, you may also have a sensitivity or allergy to

Methyclothiazide. Although this drug has been used to treat specific conditions in pregnancy, unsupervised use by pregnant patients should be avoided. Methyclothiazide will cross the placenta and pass into the unborn child, possibly causing problems. The drug will pass into the breast milk of nursing mothers.

Possible Side Effects

Methyclothiazide will cause a lowering of potassium in the body. Signs of low potassium levels are dryness of the mouth, thirst, weakness, lethargy, drowsiness, restlessness, muscle pains or cramps, muscular tiredness, low blood pressure, decreased frequency of urination and decreased amount of urine produced, abnormal heart rate, and stomach upset including nausea and vomiting.

To treat this, potassium supplements are given in the form of tablets, liquids, or powders, or by increased consumption of foods such as bananas, citrus fruits, melons, and tomatoes.

Possible Adverse Drug Effects

Loss of appetite, stomach upset, nausea, vomiting, cramping, diarrhea, constipation, dizziness, headache, tingling of the toes and fingers, restlessness, changes in blood composition, sensitivity to sunlight, rash, itching, fever, difficulty in breathing, allergic reactions, dizziness when rising quickly from a sitting or lying position, muscle spasms, weakness, blurred vision.

Drug Interactions

Methyclothiazide will add to (potentiate) the action of other blood-pressure-lowering drugs. This is beneficial, and is frequently used to help lower blood pressure in patients with hypertension.

The possibility of developing imbalances in body fluids (electrolytes) is increased if you take medications such as Digitalis and adrenal corticosteroids while you take Methyclothiazide.

If you are taking an oral antidiabetic drug and begin taking Methyclothiazide, the antidiabetic drug dose may have to be altered.

Lithium Carbonate should not be taken with Methyclothiazide because the combination may increase the risk of lithium toxicity.

If you are taking this drug for the treatment of high blood pressure or congestive heart failure, avoid over-the-counter medicine for the treatment of coughs, colds, and allergies which may contain stimulants. If you are unsure about them, ask your pharmacist.

Usual Dose

Adult: 2½ to 10 milligrams per day. Thiazide diuretic doses must be adjusted toward maximum effect with minimum medication. Eventual dose is often 5 milligrams or less.

Overdosage

Symptoms are large amount of urination, fatigue, and coma. The patient should be taken to a hospital emergency room. ALWAYS bring the medicine bottle.

Generic Name

Methyldopa

Brand Name

Aldomet

Type of Drug

Antihypertensive.

Prescribed for

High blood pressure.

General Information

Methyldopa is usually prescribed with one or more of the other high blood pressure medications or a diuretic.

Cautions and Warnings

You should not take Methyldopa if you have hepatitis or active cirrhosis or if you have ever developed a sign or symptom of reaction to Methyldopa. No unusual effects have been noted in patients using the drug while they are pregnant, but the possibility of damage to the unborn child should be kept in mind.

Possible Side Effects

Most people have little trouble with Methyldopa, but it can cause transient sedation during the first few weeks of therapy or when the dose is increased. Transient headache or weakness are other possible early symptoms.

Possible Adverse Drug Effects

Dizziness, light-headedness, tingling in the extremities, unusual muscle spasms, decreased mental acuity, and psychic disturbances including nightmares, mild psychosis, or depression; also changes in heart rate, increase of pain associated with angina pectoris, retention of water, resulting weight gain, and orthostatic hypotension (dizziness when rising suddenly from a sitting or lying position), as well as nausea, vomiting, constipation, diarrhea, mild dryness of the mouth, and sore and/or black tongue. The drug may cause liver disorders: you may develop jaundice (yellowing of the skin and/or whites of the eyes), with or without fever, in the first 2 to 3 months of therapy. If you are taking Methyldopa for the first time, be sure your doctor checks your liver function, especially during the first 6 to 12 weeks of therapy. If you develop fever or jaundice, stop taking the drug and contact your physician immediately: if the reactions are due to Methyldopa, your temperature and/or liver abnormalities will reverse toward normal as soon as the drug is discontinued. Still other adverse effects are stuffed nose, breast enlargement, lactation (in females), impotence or decreased sex drive, mild symptoms of arthritis, and skin reactions.

Drug Interactions

Methyldopa will increase the effect of other blood-pressure-lowering drugs. This is a desirable interaction which benefits patients with high blood pressure.

Avoid over-the-counter cough, cold, and allergy preparations containing stimulant drugs that can aggravate your high blood pressure. Information on over-the-counter drugs that are safe for you can be obtained from your pharmacist.

Usual Dose

Adult: Starting dose, 250-milligram tablet 2 to 3 times per day for first 2 days. Dosage may be increased or decreased until blood pressure control is achieved. Maintenance dose, 500 milligrams to 3000 milligrams per day in 2 to 4 divided doses, per patient's needs.

Child: 5 milligrams per pound of body weight per day in 2 to 4 divided doses per patient's needs. Maximum dose, 30 milligrams per pound of body weight per day, up to 3 grams per day.

Special Information

Take this drug exactly as prescribed by your doctor so you can maintain maximum control over your high blood pressure.

A mild sedative effect is to be expected from Methyldopa and will resolve within several days.

Generic Name

Methylphenidate

Brand Name

Ritalin

Type of Drug

Central nervous system stimulant.

Prescribed for

Minimal brain dysfunction in children; psychological, educational, or social disorders; narcolepsy and mild depression.

General Information

Chronic or abusive use of Methylphenidate can cause the development of drug dependence or addiction; also, the drug can cause severe psychotic episodes. The primary use for Methylphenidate is the treatment of minimal brain dysfunction in children. Common signs of this disease are short attention span, easy distractibility, emotional instability, impulsiveness, and moderate to severe hyperactivity. Children who suffer from this disorder will find it difficult to learn. There are many who feel that Methylphenidate is a temporary solution because it does not permanently change patterns of behavior. When Methylphenidate is used, it must be used with other special measures.

Cautions and Warnings

Do not take Methylphenidate if you are extremely tense or agitated, have glaucoma, are allergic to this drug, have high blood pressure, or have a history of epilepsy or other seizures.

Possible Side Effects

Most common in adults: nervousness and inability to sleep, which are generally controlled by reducing or eliminating the afternoon or evening dose. Most common in children: loss of appetite, stomach pains, weight loss (especially during prolonged periods of therapy), difficulty sleeping, and abnormal heart rhythms.

Possible Adverse Drug Effects

Infrequent in adults: skin rash, itching, fever, symptoms similar to arthritis, loss of appetite, nausea, dizziness, abnormal heart rhythms, headache, drowsiness, changes in blood pressure or pulse, chest pains, stomach pains, psychotic reactions, effects on components of the blood, loss of some scalp hair.

Drug Interactions

Methylphenidate will decrease the effectiveness of Guanethidine, a drug used to treat high blood pressure.

Interaction with MAO inhibitors may vastly increase the effect of Methylphenidate and cause problems.

Interaction with anticoagulants (blood-thinning drugs), some drugs used to treat epilepsy or other kinds of convulsions, Phenylbutazone and Oxyphenbutazone, and antidepressant drugs will slow the rate at which these drugs are broken down by the body, making more of them available in the bloodstream. Thus it may be necessary to lower the dose of them.

Usual Dose

Adult: 10 or 20 to 30 or even 60 milligrams per day in divided doses 2 to 3 times per day, preferably 30 to 45 minutes before meals.

Child (over age 6): Initial dose, 5 milligrams before breakfast and lunch; then increase in steps of 5 to 10 milligrams each week as required, but not to exceed 60 milligrams per day.

Doses should be tailored to individual needs; the doses listed here are only guidelines.

Overdosage

Symptoms are stimulation of the nervous system such as vomiting, agitation, tremors (uncontrollable twitching of the muscles), convulsions followed by coma, euphoria, confusion, hallucinations, delirium, sweating, flushing (face, hands, and extremities will be red), headache, high fever, abnormal heart rate, high blood pressure, and dryness of the mouth and nose. The patient should be taken to a hospital emergency room. ALWAYS bring the medicine bottle.

Special Information

Methylphenidate can cause temporary drowsiness: be careful while driving or operating an automobile, machine, or appliance. If you take Methylphenidate regularly, avoid alcoholic beverages; they will add to the drowsiness problem.

Generic Name

Methylprednisolone

Brand Name

Medrol

Type of Drug

Adrenal cortical steroid.

Prescribed for

Reduction of inflammation. The variety of disorders which Methylprednisolone is prescribed for is almost endless, from skin rash to cancer. The drug may be used as a treatment for adrenal gland disease, since one of the hormones produced by the adrenal gland is very similar to Methylprednisolone. If patients are not producing sufficient adrenal hormones, Methylprednisolone may be used as replacement therapy. It may also be prescribed for the treatment of bursitis, arthritis, severe skin reactions such as psoriasis or other rashes, severe allergic conditions, asthma, drug or serum sickness, severe, acute, or chronic allergic inflammation of the eye and surrounding areas such as conjunctivitis, respiratory diseases including pneumonitis, blood disorders, gastrointestinal diseases including ulcerative colitis, and inflammation of the nerves, heart, or other organs.

General Information

Methylprednisolone is one of many adrenal cortical steroids used in medical practice today. The major differences between Methylprednisolone and other adrenal cortical steroids are potency of medication and variation in some secondary effects. In most cases the choice of adrenal cortical steroids to be used in a specific disease is a matter of doctor preference and past experience. Other adrenal cortical steroids are Cortisone, Hydrocortisone, Prednisone, Prednisolone, Triamcinolone, Meprednisone, Paramethasone, Fluprednisolone, Dexamethasone, Betamethasone, and Fludrocortisone.

Cautions and Warnings

Because of the effect of Methylprednisolone on your adrenal gland, it is essential that the dose be tapered from a large dose down to a small dose over a period of time. Do not stop taking this medication suddenly and/or without the advice of your doctor. If you do, you may cause a failure of the adrenal gland with extremely serious consequences. Methylprednisolone has a strong anti-inflammatory effect, and may mask some signs of infections. If new infections appear during the use of

Methylprednisolone therapy, they may be difficult to discover and may grow more rapidly due to your decreased resistance. If you think you are getting any kind of infection during the time that you are taking Methylprednisolone, you should contact your doctor, who will prescribe appropriate therapy. If you are taking Methylprednisolone, you should not be vaccinated against infectious disease because of inability of the body to produce the normal reaction to the vaccination. Discuss this with your doctor before he administers any vaccination. If you suspect that you have become pregnant and are taking Methylprednisolone, report it immediately to your doctor. If you are taking Methylprednisolone and have just given birth, do not nurse; use prepared formulas instead.

Possible Side Effects

Stomach upset is one of the more common side effects of Methylprednisolone, which may in some cases cause gastric or duodenal ulcers. If you notice a slight stomach upset when you take your dose of Methylprednisolone, you should take this medication with food or with a small amount of antacid. If stomach upset continues or bothers you, notify your doctor. Other side effects: retention of water, heart failure, potassium loss, muscle weakness, loss of muscle mass, loss of calcium from bones which may result in bone fractures and a condition known as aseptic necrosis of the femoral and humoral heads (this means the ends of the large bones in the hip may degenerate from loss of calcium), slowing down of wound healing, black-and-blue marks on the skin, increased sweating, allergic skin rash, itching, convulsions, dizziness, headache.

Possible Adverse Drug Effects

May cause irregular menstrual cycles, slowing down of growth in children, particularly after the medication has been taken for long periods of time, depression of the adrenal and/or pituitary glands, development of diabetes, increased pressure of the fluid inside the eye, hypersensitivity or allergic reactions, blood clots, insomnia, weight gain, increased appetite, nausea, and feeling of ill health. Psychic derangements may appear which range from euphoria to mood swings, personality changes, and severe depression. Methylprednisolone may also aggravate existing emotional instability.

Drug Interactions

Methylprednisolone and other adrenal corticosteroids may interact with Insulin or oral antidiabetic drugs, causing an increased requirement of the antidiabetic drugs.

Interaction with Phenobarbital, Ephedrine, and Phenytoin may reduce the effect of Methylprednisolone by increasing its removal from the body.

If a doctor prescribes Methylprednisolone you should discuss any oral anticoagulant (blood-thinning) drugs you are taking; the dose of them may have to be changed.

Interaction with diuretics such as Hydrochlorothiazide may cause you to lose blood potassium. Be aware of signs of lowered potassium level such as weakness, muscle cramps and tiredness, and report them to your physician. It recommended that you eat high potassium foods as bananas, citrus fruits, melons, and tomatoes.

Usual Dose

Initial dose, 4 to 48 milligrams; maintenance dose, as determined by your doctor based on your response.

Overdosage

There is no specific treatment for overdosage of adrenal cortical steroids. Symptoms are anxiety, depression and/or stimulation, stomach bleeding, increased blood sugar, high blood pressure, and retention of fluid. The patient should be taken to a hospital emergency room immediately, where stomach pumping, oxygen, intravenous fluids, and other supportive treatment are available.

Generic Name

Metronidazole

Brand Name

Flagyl

Type of Drug

Amoebicide.

Prescribed for

Acute amoebic dysentery; vaginal infections (trichomonas); and diseases caused by some parasites.

General Information

Metronidazole may be prescribed for asymptomatic disease when the doctor feels that the use of this drug is indicated: specifically, asymptomatic females may be treated with this drug when vaginal examination shows evidence of trichomonas. Because trichomonas infection of the vaginal area is a venereal disease, asymptomatic sexual partners of treated patients should be treated simultaneously if the organism has been found to be present in the woman's genital tract, in order to prevent reinfection of the partner. The decision to treat an asymptomatic male partner who does not have the organism present is an individual one and must be made by the doctor.

Cautions and Warnings

If you have a history of blood disease or if you know that you are sensitive or allergic to Metronidazole you should not use this drug. It should not be used during the first 3 months of pregnancy.

Metronidazole has been shown to be carcinogenic (cancer-inducing) in mice and possibly in rats. This drug should not be used unnecessarily and should only be used in specific conditions for which it is normally prescribed.

Possible Side Effects

Most common: symptoms in the gastrointestinal tract, including nausea (sometimes accompanied by headache), loss of appetite, occasional vomiting, diarrhea, stomach upset, abdominal cramping, and constipation. A sharp, unpleasant metallic taste is also associated with the use of this drug. Dizziness and, rarely, incoordination have been reported. Numbness or tingling in the extremities and occasional joint pains have been associated with Metronidazole therapy as have confusion, irritability, depression, inability to sleep, and weakness. Itching and a sense of pelvic pressure have been reported.

Possible Adverse Drug Effects

Rarely: fever, increased urination, incontinence, decrease of libido.

Drug Interactions

Avoid alcoholic beverages: interaction with Metronidazole may cause abdominal cramps, nausea, vomiting, headaches, and flushing. Modification of the taste of alcoholic beverages has also been reported.

People taking oral anticoagulant (blood-thinning) drugs such as Warfarin will have to have their dose of Warfarin changed, because Metronidazole increases the effect of anticoagulants.

Usual Dose

Adult: For the treatment of amoebic dysentery, 3 tablets 3 times per day for 5 to 10 days.

Child: Amoebic dysentery, 16 to 23 milligrams per pound of body weight daily divided in 3 equal doses, for 10 days.

For trichomonal infections, 1 tablet 3 times per day for 7 days.

Special Information

Follow your doctor's dosage instructions faithfully and don't stop until the full course of therapy has been taken.

The occasional darkening of urine of patients taking Metronidazole is of uncertain clinical significance and is probably not important.

Generic Name

Miconazole Nitrate

Brand Name

Monistat

MULTICOLOR

Achromycin 250 mg **p. 328**	**Achromycin V** 250 mg **p. 328**	**Adapin** 25 mg **p. 114**	**Amoxil** 250 mg **p. 19**
Amoxil 500 mg **p. 19**	**Benadryl** 25 mg **p. 105**	**Benadryl** 50 mg **p. 105**	**Bentyl** w/Phenobarbital **p. 33**
Butazolidin Alka **p. 272**	**Cleocin** 150 mg **p. 62**	**Combid** **p. 73**	**Compazine Spansule** 10 mg **p. 290**
Dalmane 15 mg **p. 142**	**Darvon Compound-65** **p. 86**	**Dilantin** 100 mg **p. 274**	**Donnatal** **p. 112**
Dyazide **p. 121**	**Dynapen** **p. 93**	**Equagesic** **p. 123**	**Feosol Spansule** **p. 131**

A

MULTICOLOR

Fiorinal w/Codeine# 2 p. 135	**Fiorinal w/Codeine# 3** p. 135	**Histaspan** 12 mg p. 52	**Histaspan** 8 mg p. 52
Ilosone 250 mg p. 126	**Indocin** 50 mg p. 168	**Indocin** 25 mg p. 168	**Isordil Tembid Caps** 40 mg p. 170
Keflex 250 mg p. 43	**Keflex** 500 mg p. 43	**Librium** 5 mg p. 47	**Librium** 10 mg p. 47
Librium 25 mg p. 47	**Macrodantin** 50 mg p. 220	**Meprospan** 400 mg p. 187	**Minocin** 100 mg p. 205
Mysteclin-F 250 mg p. 209	**Navane** 1mg p. 337	**Nembutal** 50 mg p. 256	**Nicobid** 250 mg p. 218

B

Nicobid 125 mg **p. 218**	**Nitro-Bid** 2.5 mg **p. 222**	**Nitro-Bid** 6.5 mg **p. 222**	**Nitrospan** **p. 222**
Norgesic **p. 224**	**Norgesic Forte** **p. 224**	**Norlestrin-28** **p. 230**	**Omnipen** 250 mg **p. 21**
Ornade Spansule **p. 233**	**Panmycin** 250 mg **p. 328**	**Pavabid** 150 mg **p. 246**	**Peri-Colace** **p. 260**
Phenaphen# 2 **p. 3**	**Phenaphen# 3** **p. 3**	**Polycillin** 250 mg **p. 21**	**Polycillin** 500 mg **p. 21**
Polymox 250 mg **p. 19**	**Polymox** 500 mg **p. 19**	**Proloid** **p. 339**	**Pronestyl** 375 mg **p. 289**

C

MULTICOLOR

Pronestyl 500 mg **p. 289**	**Serax** 10 mg **p. 237**	**Serax** 15 mg **p. 237**	**Serax** 30 mg **p. 237**
Sinequan 25 mg **p. 114**	**Sinequan** 100 mg **p. 114**	**SK-65** **p. 295**	**SK-Lygen** 10 mg **p. 47**
Sumycin 500 mg **p. 328**	**Synalgos-DC** **p. 322**	**Synthroid** 50 mcg (white) **p. 173**	**Synthroid** 100 mcg (yellow) **p. 173**
Synthroid 150 mcg (blue) **p. 173**	**Synthroid** 200 mcg (pink) **p. 173**	**Synthroid** 300 mcg (green) **p. 173**	**Tedral S.A.** **p. 324**
Teldrin Spansule 8 mg **p. 52**	**Teldrin Spansule** 12 mg **p. 52**	**Tetracycline** 250 mg **p. 328**	**Tetracyn** 250 mg **p. 328**

D

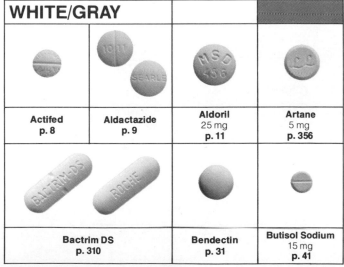

MULTICOLOR

Tetrex 250 mg **p. 328**	**Thorazine Spansule** **p. 54**	**Tigan** 100 mg **p. 357**	**Tranxene** 7.5 mg **p. 68**
Tuss-Ornade Spansule **p. 362**	**Vibramycin** 50 mg **p. 117**	**Vistaril** 50 mg **p. 162**	

WHITE/GRAY

Actifed **p. 8**	**Aldactazide** **p. 9**	**Aldoril** 25 mg **p. 11**	**Artane** 5 mg **p. 356**
Bactrim DS **p. 310**		**Bendectin** **p. 31**	**Butisol Sodium** 15 mg **p. 41**

E

WHITE/GRAY

Cogentin 1 mg **p. 36**	**Coumadin Sodium** 10 mg **p. 368**	**Deltasone** **p. 282**	**Demulen** **p. 230**
Diamox 125 mg **p. 5**	**Diamox** 250 mg **p. 5**	**Digoxin** 0.25 mg **p. 100**	**Dimetane** **Extentab** **p. 39**
Dimetane **p. 39**	**Diuril** 500 mg **p. 49**	**Donnatal** **p. 112**	**Doriden** 250 mg **p. 150**
Doriden 500 mg **p. 150**	**DES** 1 mg **p. 98**	**Empirin** w/Codeine# 2 **p. 25**	**Empirin** w/Codeine# 3 **p. 25**
Equanil 200 mg **p. 187**	**Equanil** 400 mg **p. 187**	**Fiorinal** **p. 133**	

F

WHITE/GRAY

Flagyl p. 202	**Gantrisin** 500 mg p. 320	**Gaviscon** p. 149	
Haldol 2 mg p. 153	**Hydergine** 0.5 mg p. 125	**Hydergine** 1 mg p. 125	**HydroDIURIL** 25 mg p. 158
HydroDIURIL 50 mg p. 158	**Hygroton** 100mg p. 59	**Ismelin** 10 mg p. 152	**Isordil Sublingual** 5 mg p. 170
Lanoxin 0.25 mg p. 100	**Lasix** 20 mg p. 144	**Lasix** 40 mg p. 144	**Lomotil** 2.5 mg p. 177
Lo/Ovral p. 230	**Macrodantin** 25 mg p. 220	**Marax** p. 181	**Medrol** 4 mg p. 199

G

Medrol 16 mg **p. 199**	**Medrol** 32 mg **p. 199**	**Mellaril** 50 mg **p. 334**	**Meprobamate** 200 mg **p. 187**
Meprobamate 400 mg **p. 187**	**Miltown** 400mg **p. 187**	**Motrin** 300 mg **p. 163**	**Nicotinic Acid** 50 mg **p. 218**
Norinyl 1+50 21 day **p. 230**	**Nitroglycerin Tabs** 1/150 gr. **p. 222**	**Nitrostat** 1/150 mg **p. 222**	**Oretic** 25 mg **p. 158**
Oretic 50 mg **p. 158**	**Orinase** 500 mg **p. 345**		**Os-Cal Tabs** **p. 234**
Ovral **p. 230**	**Ovulen** 25 mg **p. 230**	**Penicillin V** 500 mg **p. 252**	**Pen-Vee-K** 250 mg **p. 252**

H

Pen-Vee-K 500 mg **p. 252**	**Pentids** 500 mg **p. 250**	**Periactin** 4 mg **p. 80**	**Phenobarbital** 15 mg **p. 268**
Phenobarbital 30 mg **p. 268**	**Prednisone** 5 mg **p. 282**	**Pro-Banthine** 15 mg **p. 293**	**Pro-Banthine P.A.** **p. 293**
Principen 250 mg **p. 21**	**Principen** 500 mg **p. 21**	**Prolold** **p. 339**	**Provera** 2.5 mg **p. 184**
Provera 10 mg **p. 184**	**Quinidine Sulfate** **p. 304**	**Ritalin** 5 mg **p. 197**	**Ritalin** 10 mg **p. 197**
Robaxin 500 mg **p. 191**	**Robaxin** 750 mg **p. 191**	**Sorbitrate Sublingual Tabs** 5 mg **p. 170**	**Sudafed** 60mg **p. 299**

I

WHITE/GRAY

Synthroid 50 mcg **p. 173**	Tagamet 300 mg **p. 61**	Tedral **p. 324**	Tenuate Dospan **p. 96**
Tepanil **p. 96**	Tepanil Ten-Tab **p. 96**	Thioguanine **p. 333**	Thyroid 30 mg **p. 341**
Thyroid 60 mg **p. 341**	Tolinase 100 mg **p. 343**	Tolinase 250 mg **p. 343**	Tranxene 3.75 mg **p. 68**
Tranxene 15 mg **p. 68**	Tylenol 325 mg **p. 3**	Tylenol #3 **p. 3**	Tylenol #2 **p. 3**
Tylenol Extra Strength 500 mg **p. 3**	Valium 2 mg **p. 91**	Vasodilan 10 mg **p. 172**	Vasodilan 20 mg **p. 172**

J

WHITE/GRAY

V-Cillin K 250 mg **p. 252**	**V-Cillin K** 500 mg **p. 252**	**Zyloprim** 100 mg **p. 13**	

RED/PINK

Atarax 10 mg **p. 162**	**Azo Gantrisin** **p. 30**	**Butazolidin** **p. 272**	**Darvocet-N** 50 mg **p. 84**
Darvocet-N 100 mg **p. 84**	**Darvon** 32 mg **p. 295**	**Darvon** 65 mg **p. 295**	**Diupres** 250 mg **p. 108**
Diupres 500 mg **p. 108**	**Dolene** **p. 295**	**DES** 5 mg **p. 98**	**Elavil** 100 mg **p. 17**

K

RED/PINK

Endep 150 mg **p. 17**	**Enduron** **p. 193**	**Erythrocin** **p. 126**	**Erythromycin** **p. 126**
Esidrix 25 mg **p. 158**	**Etrafon 2/25** **p. 351**	**Hydrochloro-** **thiazide** 50 mg **p. 158**	**Ilotycin** 250 mg **p. 126**
Isordil 5 mg **p. 170**	**Medrol** 8 mg **p. 199**	**Mellaril** 15 mg **p. 334**	**Mol-Iron** **p. 131**
Mol-Iron **Chronosules** **p. 131**	**Motrin** 400 mg **p. 163**	**Naldecon** **p. 212**	**Natalins** **p. 216**
Norlestrin 2.5 mg **p. 230**	**Ovral-28 Inactive** **p. 230**	**Persantine** 25 mg **p. 107**	**Placidyl** 500 mg **p. 128**

L

RED/PINK

Polaramine **p. 89**	**Poly-Vi-Flor Chewable** **p. 279**		**Premarin** 0.625mg **p. 75**
Prostaphlin 500 mg **p. 235**	**Septra** **p. 310**	**Septra DS** **p. 310**	**Ser-Ap-Es** **p. 311**
Singlet **p. 314**	**Sudafed** 30 mg **p. 299**	**Synthroid** 200 mcg **p. 173**	

YELLOW

Aldactone **p. 315**	**Aldomet** 250 mg **p. 195**	**Antivert** 25 mg **p. 183**	**Apresoline** 10 mg **p. 156**

M

YELLOW

Apresoline 10mg **p. 156**	**Chlor-Trimeton** 4 mg **p. 52**	**Chlor-Trimeton** 8 mg **p. 52**	**Choledyl** 200 mg **p. 239**
Compazine 5 mg **p. 290**	**Compazine** 10 mg **p. 290**	**Coumadin Sodium** 7½ mg **p. 368**	**Digoxin** 0.125mg **p. 100**
Digoxin 0.25 mg **p. 100**	**Dilantin** 50 mg **p. 274**	**Elavil** 25 mg **p. 17**	**Endep** 75 mg **p. 17**
Esidrix 50mg **p. 158**		**Etrafon** 2-10 **p. 351**	**Furadantin** 100 mg **p. 220**
Furadantin 50 mg **p. 220**	**Haldol** 1 mg **p. 153**	**Inderal** 80 mg **p. 297**	**Ionamin** 30 mg **p. 270**

N

YELLOW

Isordil 10 mg **p. 170**	**Isordil Tembid** 40mg **p. 170**	**Lanoxin** 0.125mg **p. 100**	**Macrodantin** 100 mg **p. 220**
Mellaril 100 mg **p. 334**	**Mellaril** 10 mg **p. 334**	**Nembutal** 100 mg **p. 256**	**Ortho-Novum** **p. 230**
Percodan **p. 258**	**Premarin** 1.25 **p. 75**	**Pronestyl** 250 mg **p. 289**	**Quibron** **p. 301**
Salutensin **p. 308**	**Sorbitrate** 10 mg/oral tabs **p. 170**	**Synthroid** 100 mcg **p. 173**	**Triavil** 4-25 **p. 350**
Valium 5 mg **p. 91**			

BLUE/PURPLE

Antivert 12.5 mg **p. 183**	**Apresoline** 25 mg **p. 156**	**Apresoline** 50 mg **p. 156**	**Bentyl** **p. 95**
Butisol Sodium 15 mg **p. 41**	**Cyclospasmol** 200 mg **p. 78**	**Diabinese** 100 mg **p. 57**	**Diabinese** 250 mg **p. 57**
Dimetapp **p. 103**	**Elavil** 10 mg **p. 17**	**Felsules** 500 mg **p. 45**	**Gantanol** **p. 316**
Hydropres—50 **p. 160**	**Hydropres—25** **p. 160**	**Hygroton-50 mg** **p. 59**	**Librax** **p. 175**
Megace 20 mg **p. 186**	**Mysoline** 250 mg **p. 285**	**Poly-Vi-Flor Chewable** **p. 279**	

BLUE/PURPLE

Premarin 2.5 mg **p. 75**	**Pro-Banthine** 15 mg **p. 293**	**Pyribenzamine** 25 mg **p. 369**	**Pyridium** 200 mg **p. 261**
SK-Pramine 25 mg **p. 165**	**SK-Pramine** 50 mg **p. 165**	**Sorbitrate** 5 mg **p. 170**	
Stelazine 1 mg **p.353**	**Stelazine** 2 mg **p. 353**	**Stelazine** 5 mg **p. 353**	**Stelazine** 10 mg **p. 353**
Synthroid 150 mcg **p. 173**	**Tigan** 250 mg **p. 357**	**Tranxene-SD** 11.25 mg **p. 68**	**Triavil** 2-10 **p. 350**
Valium 10 mg **p. 91**	**Vibramycin** 100 mg **p. 117**		

ORANGE

Atromid-S 500 mg **p. 64**	**Bonine** 25 mg **p. 183**	**Chlor-Trimeton** 12 mg **p. 183**	**Coumadin Sodium** 2.5 mg **p. 368**
Coumadin Sodium 5 mg **p. 368**	**Diamox Sequel** **p. 5**	**E-Mycin** 250 mg **p. 126**	**Endep** 10 mg **p. 17**
Endep 50 mg **p. 17**	**Endep** 100 mg **p. 17**	**Enovid-E** **p.230**	**Ilotycin** 250 mg **p.126**
Inderal 10 mg **p. 297**	**Minocin** 50 mg **p. 205**	**Noctec** 250 mg **p. 45**	**Penicillin VK** 250 mg **p. 252**
Poly-Vi-Flor Chewable **p. 279**		**Pro-Banthine** 7.5mg **p. 293**	**Pronestyl** 500 mg **p. 289**

B

ORANGE

SK-Lygen 25 mg **p. 47**	Slow-K **p. 280**	Tandearil **p. 243**	Thorazine 10 mg **p. 54**
Thorazine 150 mg **p. 54**	Tofranil 10 mg **p. 165**	Tofranil 25 mg **p. 165**	Triavil 4-10 **p. 350**
Triavil 2-25 **p. 350**	Veetids **p. 252**	Zyloprim 300 mg **p. 13**	

GREEN

Adapin 50 mg **p. 114**	Bactrim **p. 310**	Butisol Sodium 30 mg **p. 41**	Drixoral **p. 119**

GREEN			
Feosol **p. 131**	**Haldol** 5 mg **p. 153**	**Halotestin** **p. 139**	**Imodium** **p. 180**
Imuran 50 mg **p. 28**	**Inderal** 40 mg **p. 297**	**Librax** **p. 175**	**Medrol** **p. 199**
Parafon Forte **p. 247**	**Pensyn** 250 mg **p. 21**	**Premarin** 0.3 mg **p. 75**	**Sorbitrate** 5 mg **p. 170**
Synthroid 300 mcg **p. 173**	**Vistaril** 25 mg **p. 162**		

T

BROWN

Azulfidine 500 mg **p. 318**	**Catapres** 0.1mg **p. 66**	**Catapres** 0.2mg **p. 66**
Elavil 50 mg **p. 17**	**Mellaril** 25 mg **p. 334**	**Nystatin** **p. 229**	**Pavabid** **p. 246**
Peri-Colace **p. 260**	**Thorazine** 25 mg **p. 54**	**Thorazine** 100 mg **p. 54**	**Thyroid** 30 mg **p. 341**
Thyroid 60 mg **p. 341**	**Tranxene-SD** 22.5 mg **p. 68**		

11

DRUG INTERACTIONS

Drug interactions have been studied intensively only during the past two decades. Most people are not seriously affected by drug interactions. In fact, only 0.3 to 3 percent of the population are affected.

Then why worry about drug interactions? Because there are documented reports of serious, even life-threatening interactions from some drug, or drug and food, combinations. It is in your best interest to avoid the known interactions and resultant adverse effects.

We can use this basic definition: *A drug interaction occurs when the effect of a drug is altered by another drug, a food, a chemical, or the environment.*

Who May Suffer a Drug Interaction:

1. *People taking several medications.* The more drugs you take, the greater the likelihood of an interaction. Many potent drugs are available without a prescription and may not even be bought at a pharmacy. Commonly used products such as laxatives, antacids, and cough and cold remedies have the potential for interacting.

2. *People taking combinations of drugs known to have interacted in the past.* This may seem an obvious point; however, drug interactions are not completely predictable. A friend may have taken a suspect combination with no ill effects, but that doesn't necessarily mean you will be able to tolerate the same combination.

3. *People with certain diseases.* Patients with diabetes, thyroid disease, liver disease, alcoholism or kidney disease may break down drugs differently resulting in a changed or increased susceptibility to drug interactions.

4. *Elderly people.* As people get older their ability to handle drugs changes. They are more likely to experience interactions.

Other Factors

Your susceptibility to drug interactions is also affected by:

1. *Diet.*

2. *Environmental factors*:
   - Air pollution
   - Smoking
   - Presence of chemicals in the environment resistant to being broken down (insecticides, pesticides, etc.)

3. *General susceptibility.* Some people are genetically more susceptible to interactions. There is no way to take this factor into account yet, though we know it exists.

4. *How the drug is given.* Some interactions occur only when the drug is taken by mouth, others are affected by the order in which drugs are taken or by when they are taken.

5. *How much of the drug is taken.* The more of the drug you take and the longer you take it, the greater the likelihood of interactions.

6. *Sex.* There is little information to substantiate sex differences, but it appears that women are more susceptible than men to interactions. This may be due to basic hormonal differences or to differences in psychological makeup.

What to Do

If you experience what you think may be a drug interaction, notify your doctor immediately. Generally, he will do one of the following:

1. Discontinue one of the offending drugs or alter your diet to avoid interaction.

2. Alter the dose of an interactant to compensate for the interaction.

3. Treat the interaction effect with another medication.

4. Evaluate the interaction, decide it is not significant, and ignore it.

5. Evaluate the alleged interaction and determine that it is not, in fact, an interaction but a usual side effect of one of the drugs.

The drug interaction table lists the more important potential interactions. This table is *not* meant to be a complete listing of all interactions and does not contain every possible problem. It is merely a reference source for the more common problems.

ALCOHOL

May Interact With:	To Produce:	
Anticoagulants (blood-thinning drugs)	May affect blood coagulation in people who are chronic, heavy drinkers	
Antidiabetic drugs (including Insulin)	Severe lowering of blood sugar. Can also cause stomach cramps, nausea, vomiting	
Antihistamines, sleeping pills, sedatives, tranquilizers, narcotics, Propoxyphene (in large amounts)	Excessive sedation, sleepiness, lack of coordination, difficulty in concentrating. Has been associated with serious accidents and severe breathing difficulty leading to coma and death. People with heart disease are particularly prone to this interaction. Avoid driving or operating machinery	
Aspirin	May increase amount of blood lost due to stomach bleeding normally caused by Aspirin. People with gastrointestinal disease and those taking large doses of Aspirin are most affected	
Isoniazid (tuberculosis drug)	Intoxication after taking unusually small amounts of alcohol. Avoid driving. Small amount may make Isoniazid less effective	
Lithium drugs, antidepressants, Phenylbutazone, Oxyphenbutazone; rare with Griseofulvin, Atropine (in many OTC drugs)	Lack of coordination, difficulty in concentrating, sedation. Avoid driving	
Metronidazole	May cause stomach cramps, nausea, vomiting, general aversion to alcohol	
Phenytoin	May decrease the effectiveness of Phenytoin. Usually seen only in chronic, heavy drinkers	

ANTIBIOTICS

	May Interact With:	To Produce:	
Chloramphenicol	Antidiabetics	Low blood sugar	
Chloramphenicol	Anticoagulants	Bleeding	
Chloramphenicol	Phenytoin	Increased toxic effects from Phenytoin	
Griseofulvin	Anticoagulants	Less anticoagulant effect. More anticoagulant may be needed	
Isoniazid	Alcohol	Intoxication may make Isoniazid less effective and more toxic	
Isoniazid	Antacids containing aluminum	Decreased Isoniazid effectiveness	
Isoniazid	Disulfiram (Antabuse)	Psychotic reaction	
Isoniazid	Phenytoin	Increased Phenytoin side effects	
Lincomycin	Kaolin, Pectin	Decreased antibiotic effect	
Nalidixic Acid	Anticoagulants	Bleeding	
Rifampin	Adrenal corticosteroids	Less steroid effect	
Rifampin	Anticoagulants	Less anticoagulant effect	
Rifampin	Antidiabetics	Raised blood sugar	
Rifampin	Methadone	Narcotic withdrawal symptoms	
Rifampin	Oral contraceptives	Less contraceptive effect	
Sulfa drugs	Anticoagulants	Bleeding	
Sulfa drugs	Antidiabetics	Low blood sugar	
Tetracycline drugs	Antacids	Decreased antibiotic effect	
Tetracycline drugs	Barbiturates	Decreased antibiotic effect (especially Doxycycline)	
Tetracycline drugs	Carbamazepine (Tegretol)	Decreased antibiotic effect (especially Doxycycline)	
Tetracycline drugs	Iron-containing drugs	Decreased antibiotic effect (especially Doxycycline)	

ANTICOAGULANTS (Warfarin, etc.)

May Interact With:	To Produce:	
Alcohol (chronic abuse)	Need for more anticoagulant. Bleeding	
Allopurinol	Need for more anticoagulant. Bleeding	
Antidiabetics	Low blood sugar	
Aspirin	Bleeding	
Barbiturates	Need for more anticoagulant	
Chloral Hydrate	Bleeding	
Chloramphenicol	Bleeding	
Cholestyramine (Questran)	Need for more anticoagulant	
Clofibrate (Atromid-S)	Bleeding	
Disulfiram (Antabuse)	Bleeding	
D-Thyroxine (Choloxin)	Bleeding	
Glutethimide	Need for more anticoagulant	
Griseofulvin	Need for more anticoagulant	
Indomethacin	Bleeding (possible)	
Metronidazole	Bleeding (possible)	
Nalidixic Acid	Bleeding (possible)	
Oral contraceptives	Need for more anticoagulant	
Oxyphenbutazone	Bleeding (possible)	
Phenylbutazone	Bleeding (possible)	
Phenytoin	Increased Phenytoin side effects	
Rifampin (Rifadin, Rimactane)	Need for more anticoagulant	
Sulfa drugs	Bleeding	
Thyroid Hormone	Bleeding	
Vitamin E	Bleeding	

ANTIHYPERTENSIVES

	May Interact With:	To Produce:	
Clonidine	Antidepressants	Increased blood pressure	
Clonidine	Tolazoline (Priscoline)	Increased blood pressure	
Guanethidine	Antidepressants	Increased blood pressure	
Guanethidine	Antidiabetics	Low blood sugar	
Guanethidine	Phenothiazines (Thioridazine, Chlorpromazine, Prochlorperazine, etc.)	Increased blood pressure	
Methyldopa	Haloperidol	Increase in Haloperidol side effects	
Methyldopa	Lithium drugs	Increase in side effects of lithium drugs	
All blood-pressure-lowering drugs	Stimulants*	Increased blood pressure	
	*Often found in nose drops and sprays, and in over-the-counter cold and allergy remedies.		

DIURETICS

	May Interact With:	To Produce:	
Spironolactone	Aspirin	Loss of body sodium	
Spironolactone	Potassium drugs	Unusually high blood levels of potassium	
Thiazide diuretics	Adrenal corticosteroids (Prednisone, Hydrocortisone, etc.)	Low blood level of potassium	
Thiazide diuretics, Furosemide	Digitalis drugs (including Digoxin)	Increased Digitalis side effects (due to potassium loss)	
Triamterene	Potassium drugs	Unusually high blood levels of potassium	

ORAL ANTIDIABETICS (Tolbutamide, etc.)

May Interact With:	To Produce:	
Alcoholic Beverages	Minor stomach cramps and nausea; low blood sugar (acute intoxication); high blood sugar (chronic alcohol abuse)	
Anticoagulants	Low blood sugar	
Aspirin	Low blood sugar	
Chloramphenicol	Low blood sugar	
Guanethidine	Low blood sugar	
MAO Inhibitors	Low blood sugar	
Oxyphenbutazone	Low blood sugar	
Phenylbutazone	Low blood sugar	
Propranolol	Low blood sugar	
Rifampin (Rifadin, Rimactane)	High blood sugar (possible)	
Sulfa drugs	Low blood sugar	

PSYCHOTROPIC DRUGS

	May Interact With:	To Produce:	
Antidepressants	Barbiturates	Less antidepressant effect	
Antidepressants	Clonidine	Increased blood pressure	
Antidepressants	Guanethidine	Increased blood pressure	
Antidepressants	MAO inhibitors*	Fever, convulsions (possible)	
Antidepressants	Stimulants	High blood pressure	
Diazepam, Oxazepam, Flurazepam, Chlordiazepoxide	Alcoholic beverages	Sleepiness; sedation; loss of coordination and difficulty in concentrating. Don't use this combination and drive	
Haloperidol	Lithium drugs	Increased Haloperidol side effects	
Haloperidol	Methyldopa	Increased Haloperidol side effects	
Lithium drugs	Haloperidol	Increased Haloperidol side effects	
Lithium drugs	Thiazide diuretics, Furosemide, Ethacrynic Acid, Methyldopa	Increased side effects of lithium drugs	
MAO inhibitors* (Furoxone, Marplan, Eutonyl, Nardil, Matulane, Parnate)	Antidepressants	Fever, convulsions	
	Antidiabetics	Low blood sugar	
	L-Dopa	Rapid rise in blood pressure	
	Meperidine	Changes in blood pressure	
MAO inhibitors	Stimulants*	Rapid rise in blood pressure	
MAO inhibitors	Certain foods	Rapid rise in blood pressure	
Phenothiazines (Chlorpromazine, Thioridazine, etc.)	Guanethidine	Increased blood pressure	
Phenothiazines	L-Dopa	Decrease in L-Dopa effect	
*Often found in nose drops and sprays, and in over-the-counter cold and allergy remedies.			

OTHER DRUGS

		May Interact With:	To Produce:	
	Adrenal corticosteroids (Prednisone, Hydrocortisone, etc.)	Barbiturates	Decreased steroid effect	
	Adrenal corticosteroids	Phenytoin	Decreased steroid effect	
	Adrenal corticosteroids	Rifampin (Rifadin, Rimactane)	Decreased steroid effect	
	Adrenal corticosteroids	Thiazide diuretics, Furosemide, Ethacrynic Acid	Increased potassium loss	
	Allopurinol	Anticoagulants	Bleeding	
	Allopurinol	Cytoxan	Increased Cytoxan side effects	
	Allopurinol	6-MP (Purinethol)	Increased 6-MP side effects	
	Allopurinol	Imuran	Increased Imuran side effects	
	Antacids	Digitalis drugs (including Digoxin)	Decreased Digitalis effect	
	Antacids	Isoniazid	Decreased Isoniazid effect (with antacids containing aluminum only)	
	Antacids	Tetracycline antibiotics	Decreased antibiotic effect	
	Aspirin	Alcohol	Increase in stomach bleeding normally associated with Aspirin	
	Aspirin	Anticoagulants	Bleeding	
	Aspirin	Antidiabetics	Low blood sugar	
	Aspirin	Methotrexate	Increase in Methotrexate side effects	
	Aspirin	Probenecid (Benemid)	Decrease in Probenecid effect	
	Barbiturates	Adrenal corticosteroids (e.g., Prednisone)	Decreased steroid effect	
	Barbiturates	Alcohol (chronic abuse)	Decreased barbiturate effectiveness	

OTHER DRUGS

	May Interact With:	To Produce:	
Barbiturates	Alcohol (acute intoxication), tranquilizers, sleeping pills	Increased sedation; sleepiness; loss of concentration and coordination. This interaction has led to accidental and other deaths and should be avoided	
Barbiturates	Anticoagulants	Decreased anticoagulant effect	
Barbiturates	Antidepressants	Decreased antidepressant effect	
Barbiturates	Quinidine	Decreased Quinidine effect	
Barbiturates	Tetracycline drugs	Decreased antibiotic effect	
Chloral Hydrate	Alcohol	Oversedation; loss of concentration and coordination. This interaction has led to accidental and other deaths	
Chloral Hydrate	Anticoagulants	Bleeding	
Cholestyramine	Anticoagulants	Decreased anticoagulant effect	
Cholestyramine	Digitalis drugs (e.g., Digoxin)	Decreased Digitalis effect	
Cholestyramine	Thyroid Hormone	Decreased Thyroid Hormone effect	
Digitalis drugs (Digoxin, Digitoxin, etc.)	Amphotericin-B	Increased Digitalis side effect	
Digitalis drugs	Antacids	Decreased Digitalis effectiveness	
Digitalis drugs	Cholestyramine (Questran)	Decreased Digitalis effectiveness	
Digitalis drugs	Kaolin, Pectin (Kaopectate)	Decreased Digitalis effectiveness	
Digitalis drugs	Stimulants*	Possible abnormal heart rhythms	
Digitalis drugs	Thiazide diuretics, Ethacrynic Acid, Furosemide	Increased Digitalis side effect	
L-Dopa	MAO inhibitors	Rapid rise in blood pressure	

OTHER DRUGS

		May Interact With:	To Produce:	
	L-Dopa	Papaverine, Phenothiazine drugs, Phenytoin, Pyridoxine	Decreased L-Dopa effect	
	Oral contraceptives	Anticoagulants	Less anticoagulant effect	
	Oral contraceptives	Rifampin (Rifadin, Rimactane)	Decreased contraceptive effect (could lead to pregnancy)	
	Phenytoin	Adrenal corticosteroids	Decreased steroid effect	
	Phenytoin	Alcohol (acute intoxication)	Increased Phenytoin side effect	
	Phenytoin	Alcohol (chronic abuse)	Decreased Phenytoin effect	
	Phenytoin	Anticoagulants, Chloramphenicol	Increased Phenytoin side effect	
	Phenytoin	Isoniazid	Increased Phenytoin side effect	
	Phenytoin	Quinidine	Decreased Quinidine effect	
	Quinidine	Barbiturates	Decreased Quinidine effect	
	Quinidine	Phenytoin	Decreased Quinidine effect	
	Stimulants*	Antidepressants	Increased blood pressure	
	Stimulants*	Digitalis drugs	May cause unusual heart rhythms	
	Stimulants*	Drugs for high blood pressure	Increased blood pressure	
	Stimulants*	MAO inhibitors	Rapid increase in blood pressure	
	Thyroid Hormone	Anticoagulants	Bleeding	
	Thyroid Hormone	Cholestyramine (Questran)	Decreased Thyroid Hormone effect	
			*Often found in nose drops and sprays, and in over-the-counter cold and allergy remedies	

Type of Drug

Vaginal anti-infective.

Prescribed for

Treatment of vaginal infections.

General Information

Miconazole Nitrate is a synthetic antifungal drug which is effective against a wide variety of organisms. In this form it is used mostly for candida infections of the vagina. It is effective against many other fungi and has been experimentally given by injection to some patients. It may be prescribed for nonspecific vaginal infections on the theory that it will cover most organisms likely to be present.

Cautions and Warnings

Do not use Miconazole Nitrate if you know you are allergic to it.

Possible Side Effects

Women complain mostly of vaginal burning, itching, or irritation. Other side effects have included cramps, hives, skin rash, and headache.

Usual Dose

One full applicator is inserted into the vagina once a day at bedtime for 14 days.

Special Information

The safety of Miconazole Nitrate in pregnancy has not been established. It should not be used at all during the first 3 months of pregnancy and only used in the next 6 months if absolutely necessary.

Generic Name

Minocycline

Brand Names

Minocin
Vectrin

Type of Drug

Broad-spectrum antibiotic effective against gram-positive and gram-negative organisms.

Prescribed for

Bacterial infections such as gonorrhea, infections of the mouth, gums, and teeth, Rocky Mountain spotted fever and other fevers caused by ticks and lice from a variety of carriers, urinary tract infections, and respiratory system infections such as pneumonia and bronchitis.

These diseases may be produced by gram-positive or gram-negative organisms such as diplococci, staphylococci, streptococci, gonococci, *E. coli*, and *Shigella*.

Minocycline has also been successfully used to treat some skin infections, but is not considered the first-choice antibiotic for the treatment of general skin infections or wounds.

General Information

Minocycline works by interfering with the normal growth cycle of the invading bacteria, preventing them from reproducing and thus allowing the body's normal defenses to fight off the infection. This process is referred to as bacteriostatic action. Minocycline has also been used along with other medicines to treat amoebic infections of the intestinal tract, known as amoebic dysentery. It is also prescribed for diseases caused by ticks, fleas, and lice.

Minocycline has been successfully used in the treatment of adolescent acne, using small doses over a long period of time. Adverse effects or toxicity in this type of therapy are almost unheard of.

Since the action of this antibiotic depends on its concentration within the invading bacteria, it is imperative that you, the patient, completely follow the doctor's directions.

Cautions and Warnings

You should not use Minocycline if you are pregnant. Minocycline, when used in children, has been shown to interfere with the development of the long bones and may retard growth.

Exceptions would be when Minocycline is the only effective antibiotic available and all risk factors have been made known to the patient.

Minocycline should not be given to people with known liver disease or to people with kidney or urine excretion problems. You should avoid taking high doses of Minocycline or undergoing extended Minocycline therapy if you will be exposed to sunlight for a long period because this antibiotic can interfere with your body's normal sun-screening mechanism, possibly causing a severe sunburn. If you have a known history of allergy to Minocycline you should avoid taking this drug or other drugs within this category such as Aureomycin, Terramycin, Rondomycin, Vibramycin, and Declomycin.

Possible Side Effects

As with other antibiotics, the common side effects of Minocycline are stomach upset, nausea, vomiting, diarrhea, and skin rash. Less common side effects include hairy tongue, itching and irritation of the anal and/or vaginal region. If these symptoms appear, consult your physician immediately. Periodic physical examinations and laboratory tests should be given to patients who are on long-term Minocycline.

Possible Adverse Drug Effects

Loss of appetite, peeling of the skin, sensitivity to the sun, fever, chills, anemia, possible brown spotting of the skin, decrease in kidney function, and damage to the liver.

Drug Interactions

Minocycline (a bacteriostatic drug) may interfere with the action of bactericidal agents such as Penicillin. It is not advisable to take both.

Don't take multivitamin products containing iron at the same time as Minocycline, or you may reduce the antibiotic's effectiveness. Space the taking of these two medicines at least 2 hours apart.

People receiving anticoagulation therapy (blood-thinning agents) should consult their doctor, since Minocycline will interfere with this form of therapy. An adjustment in the anticoagulation dosage may be required.

Usual Dose

Adult: First day, 200 milligrams, followed by 100 milligrams every 12 hours. Or 100 to 200 milligrams may be given to start, followed by 50 milligrams 4 times per day.

Child (age 9 and over): Approximately 2 milligrams per pound of body weight initially, followed by 1 milligram per pound every 12 hours.

Child (up to age 8): Not recommended, as it has been shown to produce serious discoloration of the permanent teeth.

Storage

Minocycline can be stored at room temperature.

Special Information

Do *not* take after the expiration date on the label. The decomposition of Minocycline produces a highly toxic substance which can cause serious kidney damage.

Brand Name

Mycolog Cream/Ointment

Ingredients

Gramicidin
Neomycin
Nystatin
Triamcinolone Acetonide

Type of Drug

Topical adrenal corticosteroid combination.

Prescribed for

Relief of infected rash or inflammation.

General Information

Mycolog is used to relieve the symptoms of itching, rash, or inflammation of the skin. It does not treat the underlying cause of the skin problem, but only the symptoms. It exerts this effect by interfering with natural body mechanisms that produced the rash, itching, etc., in the first place. If you use this drug without finding the cause of the problem, you may find that the problem returns after you stop using it. Mycolog should not be used without your doctor's consent because it could cover an important reaction, one that may be of value to him in treating you.

Cautions and Warnings

Do not use Mycolog if you are allergic to any of its ingredients. This drug should not be used in the eyes, or the external ear if the eardrum is perforated, unless specifically directed by your doctor. Severe local infections require antibiotic therapy to treat them. If you have some Mycolog left over from an old prescription, do not use it without first contacting your doctor. If this medication fails to help you or a new infection develops on your skin while you are using it, contact your doctor so that appropriate treatment can be given.

Possible Side Effects

Most frequent: burning sensation, itching, irritation of the skin, dryness, secondary infection after prolonged use of this medication.

Usual Dose

Apply to affected areas several times daily.

Special Information

Clean the skin before applying Mycolog to prevent secondary infection. Apply in a very thin film (effectiveness is based on contact area and not on the thickness of the layer applied).

Brand Name

Mysteclin-F

Ingredients

Amphotericin-B
Tetracycline

Type of Drug

Broad-spectrum antibiotic effective against gram-positive and some gram-negative organisms.

Prescribed for

Bacterial infections such as gonorrhea, infections of the mouth, gums, and teeth, Rocky Mountain spotted fever and other fevers caused by ticks and lice from a variety of carriers, urinary tract infections, and respiratory system infections such as pneumonia and bronchitis.

These diseases may be produced by gram-positive or gram-negative organisms such as diplococci, staphylococci, streptococci, gonococci, *E. coli,* and *Shigella.*

Mysteclin-F has also been successfully used to treat some skin infections, but is not considered the first-choice antibiotic for the treatment of general skin infections or wounds.

General Information

Mysteclin-F works by interfering with the normal growth cycle of the invading bacteria, preventing them from reproducing and thus allowing the body's normal defenses to fight off the infection. This process is referred to as bacteriostatic action. Mysteclin-F has also been used along with other medicines to treat amoebic infections of the intestinal tract, known as amoebic dysentery. It is also prescribed for diseases caused by ticks, fleas, and lice.

Mysteclin-F has been successfully used in the treatment of adolescent acne, using small doses over a long period of time. Adverse effects or toxicity in this type of therapy are almost unheard of.

Since the action of this antibiotic depends on its concentration within the invading bacteria, it is imperative that you, the patient, completely follow the doctor's directions.

Cautions and Warnings

You should not use Mysteclin-F if you are pregnant. Mysteclin-F, when used in children, has been shown to interfere with the development of the long bones and may retard growth.

Exceptions would be when Mysteclin-F is the only effective antibiotic available and all risk factors have been made known to the patient.

Mysteclin-F should not be given to people with known liver disease or to people with kidney or urine excretion problems. You should avoid taking high doses of Mysteclin-F or undergoing extended Mysteclin-F therapy if you will be exposed to sunlight for a long period because this antibiotic can interfere with your body's normal sun-screening mechanism, possibly causing a severe sunburn. If you have a known history of allergy to Mysteclin-F you should avoid taking this drug or other drugs within this category such as Aureomycin, Terramycin, Rondomycin, Vibramycin, Declomycin, and Minocin.

Possible Side Effects

Amphotericin-B, when given by mouth, is not absorbed into the blood system. For this reason, there are few side effects associated with Amphotericin-B in this combination.

As with other antibiotics, the common side effects of Mysteclin-F are stomach upset, nausea, vomiting, diarrhea, and skin rash. Less common side effects include hairy tongue, itching and irritation of the anal and/or vaginal region. If these symptoms appear, consult your physician immediately. Periodic physical examinations and laboratory tests should be given to patients who are on long-term Mysteclin-F.

Possible Adverse Drug Effects

Loss of appetite, peeling of the skin, sensitivity to the sun, fever, chills, anemia, possible brown spotting of the skin, decrease in kidney function, damage to the liver.

Drug Interactions

Mysteclin-F (a bacteriostatic drug) may interfere with the action of bactericidal agents such as Penicillin. It is not advisable to take both together.

The antibacterial effect of Mysteclin-F is neutralized when taken with food, some dairy products (such as milk and cheese), and antacids.

Don't take multivitamin products containing minerals at the same time as Mysteclin-F, or you will reduce the antibiotic's effectiveness. Space the taking of these two medicines at least 2 hours apart.

People receiving anticoagulation therapy (blood-thinning agents) should consult their doctor, since Mysteclin-F will interfere with this form of therapy. An adjustment in the anticoagulation dosage may be required.

Usual Dose

Adult: 250 to 500 milligrams 4 times per day.

Child (age 9 and over): 10 to 20 milligrams per pound of body weight per day in divided doses taken 1 hour before or 2 hours after meals.

Child (up to age 8): Should avoid Mysteclin-F, as it has been shown to produce serious discoloration of the permanent teeth.

Special Information

Do not take outdated Mysteclin-F under any circumstances. Its decomposition produces a highly toxic substance which can cause serious kidney damage. The only difference between Mysteclin-F and Tetracycline is that Mysteclin-F contains a small amount of Amphotericin-B to prevent the growth of fungal organisms in the intestine. Since the Amphotericin-B in Mysteclin-F is often ineffective in reducing the incidence of fungal infections, you may be better off taking plain Tetracycline. Discuss it with your doctor.

Brand Name

Naldecon Tablets

Ingredients

Chlorpheniramine Maleate
Phenylephrine Hydrochloride
Phenylpropanolamine Hydrochloride
Phenyltoloxamine Citrate

Type of Drug

Long-acting combination antihistamine-decongestant.

Prescribed for

Relief of sneezing, runny nose, and other symptoms of nasal congestion associated with the common cold, allergy, or other upper respiratory condition.

General Information

Naldecon Tablets are one of many products marketed to relieve the symptoms of the common cold. Most of these products contain ingredients to relieve nasal congestion or dry up runny noses or relieve a scratchy throat, and several of them may contain ingredients to suppress cough, or to help eliminate unwanted mucus. All these products are good only for the relief of symptoms and do not treat the underlying problem such as the cold virus or other infections.

Cautions and Warnings

Naldecon Tablets should not be given to pregnant women.

Possible Side Effects

Mild drowsiness.

Possible Adverse Drug Effects

Infrequent: restlessness, tension, nervousness, tremor, weakness, inability to sleep, headache, palpitations, elevation of blood pressure, sweating, sleeplessness, loss of appetite, nausea, vomiting, dizziness, constipation.

Drug Interactions

Interaction with alcoholic beverages, sedatives, tranquilizers, antihistamines, and sleeping pills may produce excessive drowsiness and/or sleepiness, or inability to concentrate.

Do not self-medicate with additional over-the-counter drugs for the relief of cold symptoms; taking Naldecon Tablets with such drugs may result in the aggravation of high blood pressure, heart disease, diabetes, or thyroid disease.

Do not take Naldecon Tablets if you are taking or suspect you may be taking a monoamine oxidase inhibitor: severe elevation in blood pressure may result.

Usual Dose

Adult and child (age 12 or over): 1 tablet 3 times per day.

Child (under age 12): Not recommended.

Special Information

Since drowsiness may occur during use of Naldecon Tablets, be cautious while performing mechanical tasks requiring alertness.

Generic Name

Naproxen

Brand Name

Naprosyn

Type of Drug

Nonsteroid anti-inflammatory.

Prescribed for

Relief of pain and inflammation of joints and muscles; arthritis.

General Information

Naproxen is one of several new drugs used to treat various types of arthritis. These drugs reduce inflammation and share side effects, the most common of which is possible formation of ulcers and upset stomach. The drugs are roughly comparable to Aspirin in controlling the symptoms of arthritis, and are used by some people who cannot tolerate Aspirin.

Cautions and Warnings

Do not take Naproxen if you are allergic or sensitive to this drug, Aspirin, or other nonsteroid anti-inflammatory drugs. Naproxen may cause stomach ulcers.

Possible Side Effects

Stomach upset, blurred vision, darkening of stool, changes in color vision, skin rash, weight gain, retention of fluids.

Possible Adverse Drug Effects

Most frequent: stomach upset, dizziness, headache, drowsiness, ringing in the ears. Other: heartburn, nausea, vomiting, bloating, gas in the stomach, stomach pain, diarrhea, constipation, dark stool, nervousness, insomnia, depression, confusion, tremor, lack of appetite, fatigue, itching, rash, double vision, abnormal heart rhythm, anemia or other changes in the composition of the blood, changes in liver function, loss of hair, tingling in the hands and feet, fever, breast enlargement, lowered blood sugar, occasional effects on the kidneys. If symptoms appear, stop taking the medicine and see your doctor immediately.

Drug Interactions

Naproxen increases the action of Phenytoin, sulfa drugs, drugs used to control diabetes, and drugs used to thin the blood. If you are taking any of these medicines, be sure you discuss it with your doctor, who will probably change the dose of the other drug.

Usual Dose

Adult: 250 milligrams morning and night, to start. Dose may be adjusted up to 750 milligrams per day, if needed.
Child: Not recommended.

Natalins

Ingredients

Calcium
Folic Acid
Iodine
Iron
Magnesium
Vitamin A
Vitamin B$_1$
Vitamin B$_2$
Vitamin B$_3$
Vitamin B$_6$
Vitamin B$_{12}$
Vitamin C
Vitamin D
Vitamin E

Type of Drug

Vitamin (with minerals).

Prescribed for

Prenatal vitamin supplement.

General Information

Natalins is one of many prenatal vitamin formulas offered for sale without prescription. The rationale for using prenatal vitamins is to see that the expectant mother receives sufficient vitamins and minerals to keep her healthy and support the growth of the baby she is carrying. Some people state that what vitamin pills provide can be obtained by eating the right foods. They are right; however, practical experience has told us that not all pregnant women eat everything they should. Therefore, most obstetricians prescribe a prenatal vitamin supplement for pregnant patients.

Cautions and Warnings

Do not take Natalins if you are allergic or sensitive to any of its ingredients.

Possible Side Effects

Indigestion, gastrointestinal intolerance.

Possible Adverse Drug Effects

Serious adverse effects are rare.

Usual Dose

1 tablet per day.

Brand Name

Neosporin Ophthalmic Solution

Ingredients

Gramicidin
Neomycin Sulfate
Polymyxin-B Sulfate

Other Brand Name

Neo-Polycin Ophthalmic Solution

Type of Drug

Topical antibiotic for use in the eye.

Prescribed for

Superficial infections of the eye.

General Information

Neosporin Ophthalmic Solution is a combination of antibiotics which are effective against the most common
eye infections. It is most useful when the infecting
organism is one known to be sensitive to one of the
three antibiotics contained in Neosporin Ophthalmic
Solution. It is also useful when the infecting organism
is not known, because of the drug's broad range of
coverage.

Prolonged use of any antibiotic product in the eye
should be avoided because of the possibility of developing sensitivity to the antibiotic. Frequent or prolonged

use of antibiotics in the eye may result in the growth of other organisms such as fungus. If the infection does not clear up within a few days, contact your doctor.

Cautions and Warnings

Neosporin Ophthalmic Solution should not be used if you know you are sensitive to or have an allergy to this product or to any of the ingredients in this product.

Possible Side Effects

Occasional local irritation after application to the eye.

Usual Dose

From 1 to 2 drops in the affected eye or eyes 2 to 4 times per day; more frequently if the infection is severe.

Generic Name

Nicotinic Acid (Niacin)

Brand Names

Diacin	Nicolar
Niac	nico-Span
Niacels	Nicotinex
Nicalex	SK-Niacin
NICL	Tega-Span
Nicobid	Vasotherm
Nicocap	Wampocap
Nico-400 Plateau Caps	

Type of Drug

Vitamin.

Prescribed for

Treatment of Nicotinic Acid deficiency (pellagra). Also prescribed to help lower high blood levels of lipids or fats, and to help dilate or enlarge certain blood vessels.

General Information

Nicotinic Acid or Niacin, also known as Vitamin B_3, is essential to normal body function through the part it plays in enzyme activity. It is effective in lowering blood levels of fats and can help enlarge or dilate certain blood vessels, but we do not know exactly how it does these things. Normally, individual requirements of Nicotinic Acid are easily supplied in a well-rounded diet.

Cautions and Warnings

Do not take this drug if you are sensitive or allergic to it or to any related drugs or if you have liver disease, stomach ulcer, severely low blood pressure, or hemorrhage (bleeding). When used in normal doses, Nicotinic Acid can be taken by pregnant women but if it is used in high doses (to help lower blood levels of fats) there may be some problems.

Possible Side Effects

Most common: flushing (redness and a warm sensation in the face and hands).

Possible Adverse Drug Effects

Decreased sugar tolerance in diabetics, activation of stomach ulcers, jaundice (yellowing of the whites of the eyes and skin), stomach upset, oily skin, dry skin, possible aggravation of skin conditions such as acne, itching, high blood levels of uric acid, low blood pressure, temporary headache, tingling feeling, skin rash, abnormal heartbeats, dizziness.

Drug Interactions

Nicotinic Acid, which can enlarge blood vessels, can intensify the effect of antihypertensive (blood-pressure-lowering) drugs, causing postural hypotension (getting dizzy when you rise quickly from a sitting or lying position).

If you are diabetic, large doses of Nicotinic Acid can throw your blood sugar slightly out of control; then your doctor may have to adjust either your diet or your drug therapy.

Usual Dose

Supplementary vitamin product, 25 milligrams per day. Treatment of high blood levels of lipids or fats, initial dose, 500 milligrams to 3 grams per day with or after

meals. (Take with cold water to assist in swallowing.)
If 3 grams does not prove effective the dose may be increased slowly to a maximum of 6 grams per day.

The dose should be built up slowly so you can watch carefully for common side effects: flushing or redness of the face and extremities, itching, and stomach upset.

Generic Name

Nitrofurantoin

Brand Names

Cyantin	J-Dantin
Furadantin	Macrodantin
Furalan	Nitrex
Furatoin	Sarodant

Type of Drug

Urinary anti-infective.

Prescribed for

Urinary tract infections by organisms susceptible to Nitrofurantoin. These organisms cause pyelonephritis, pyelitis, and cystitis.

General Information

Nitrofurantoin, like several other drugs, is of value in treating urinary tract infections because it appears in large amounts in the urine. It should not be used to treat infections in other parts of the body.

Cautions and Warnings

Do not take Nitrofurantoin if you have kidney disease, if you are allergic to this agent, or if you are pregnant and near term. Infants under age 3 months should not be given this medication.

Possible Side Effects

Loss of appetite, nausea, vomiting, stomach pain, and diarrhea. Some people develop hepatitislike symptoms.

Side effects are less prominent when Macrodantin (large crystal form of Nitrofurantoin) is used rather than Furadantin (regular crystal size).

Possible Adverse Drug Effects

Fever, chills, cough, chest pain, difficulty in breathing, development of fluid in the lungs: if these occur in the first week of therapy they can generally be resolved by stopping the medication. If they develop after a longer time they can be more serious because they develop more slowly and are more difficult to associate with the drug. If you develop chest pains or difficulty in breathing while taking Nitrofurantoin, report the effects to your physician immediately. Other adverse effects: rashes, itching, asthmatic attacks in patients with a history of asthma, drug fever, symptoms similar to arthritis, jaundice (yellowing of the whites of the eyes and/or skin), effects on components of the blood, headache, dizziness, drowsiness, temporary loss of hair. The oral liquid form of Nitrofurantoin can stain your teeth if you don't swallow the medicine rapidly.

Usual Dose

Adult: 50 to 100 milligrams 4 times per day.

Child (over age 3 months): 2 to 3 milligrams per pound of body weight in 4 divided doses.

Child (under age 3 months): Not recommended.

Nitrofurantoin may be used in lower doses over a long period by people with chronic urinary infections.

Nitrofurantoin may be given with food or milk to help decrease stomach upset, loss of appetite, nausea, or other gastrointestinal symptoms. Continue to take this medicine at least 3 days after you stop experiencing symptoms of urinary tract infection.

Special Information

Nitrofurantoin may give your urine a brownish color: this is not dangerous.

Generic Name

Nitroglycerin

Brand Names

Cardabid
Cardabid-Forte
Gly-Trate Meta-Kaps
Niglycon
Nitora
Nitrine-TDC
Nitro-Bid
Nitro-Bid Plateau Caps
Nitrobon
Nitrodyl
Nitroglyn
Nitrol

Nitro-Lor
Nitrong
Nitro-SA
Nitrospan
Nitrostat
Nitro-T.D.
Nitrovas
Nitrozem
Ro-Nitro
Trates Granucaps
Vasoglyn Unicelles

Type of Drug

Antianginal agent.

Prescribed for

Prevention and treatment of chest pains associated with angina pectoris.

General Information

Nitroglycerin is available in several different dosage forms, including sublingual tablets (which are taken under the tongue and are allowed to dissolve), capsules (which are swallowed), and ointment (which is usually spread over the chest wall, although it can be spread on any area of the body). Frequently patients may take one or more different dosage forms of Nitroglycerin to prevent and/or treat the attack of chest pain associated with angina.

Cautions and Warnings

You should not take Nitroglycerin if you are known to be allergic to it. Also, because Nitroglycerin will increase the pressure of fluid inside your head, it should be taken with great caution if head trauma or bleeding in the head is present.

Possible Side Effects

The most frequent side effect of Nitroglycerin is flushing of the skin. Headache is common and may be severe or persistent. Once in a while, episodes of dizziness and weakness have been associated with the use of Nitroglycerin.

Possible Adverse Drug Effects

Occasionally an individual exhibits a marked sensitivity to the blood-pressure-lowering effect of Nitroglycerin, causing severe responses of nausea, vomiting, weakness, restlessness, loss of facial color or pallor, perspiration, and collapse even with the usual therapeutic dose. Drug rash occasionally occurs.

Drug Interactions

If you are taking Nitroglycerin continuously, avoid excessive alcohol intake, which may cause lowering of blood pressure and resulting faintness and dizziness.

Avoid over-the-counter drugs containing stimulants, which may aggravate your heart disease. Such drugs are used to treat coughs, colds, and allergies, and as appetite suppressants.

Usual Dose

Only as much as is necessary to control chest pains. Since the sublingual dosage form (tablet taken under the tongue) acts within 10 to 15 seconds of being taken, the drug is only taken when necessary. The sublingual tablet causes a local burning sensation when the tablet is dissolving and the drug is being absorbed, which is good because it indicates that the tablet is potent.

Long-acting (sustained-release) capsules or tablets are generally used to prevent chest pains associated with angina, with dose of 1 capsule or tablet every 8 to 12 hours.

One to 2 inches of Nitroglycerin ointment are squeezed from the tube onto a prepared piece of paper with markings on it. (Some patients may require as much as 4 to 5 inches.) The ointment is spread on the skin every 3 to 4 hours as needed for control of chest pains. The drug is absorbed through the skin. Application sites should be rotated to prevent skin inflammation and rash.

Special Information

The sublingual form (tablets which are dissolved under the tongue) should be acquired from your pharmacist only in the original, unopened bottle, and the tablets must not be transferred to a secondary bottle or container, otherwise the tablets may lose potency. Close the bottle tightly after each use or the drug may evaporate from the tablets.

The sublingual form should produce a burning sensation under the tongue, which indicates that the drug is potent and will produce the desired effect. If there is no such sensation you must have the tablets replaced immediately.

Orthostatic hypotension, where more blood stays in the extremities and less becomes available to the brain, resulting in light-headedness or faintness if you rise suddenly from the prone position, can be a problem if you take Nitroglycerin over a long period of time. Avoid prolonged standing and be careful to stand up slowly.

Brand Name

Norgesic

Ingredients

Aspirin
Caffeine
Orphenadrine Citrate
Phenacetin

Type of Drug

Muscle relaxant combination.

Prescribed for

Muscle spasms.

General Information

The primary ingredient in Norgesic is Orphenadrine Citrate, a derivative of the antihistamine Diphenhydramine Hydrochloride (Benadryl). It is a moderately effective muscle relaxant which works by exerting a general sedative effect. The Aspirin and Phenacetin in Norgesic are there only for pain relief. Norgesic cannot solve the problems of pain due to muscle spasm: it can only temporarily relieve the pain. You must follow any additional advice given regarding exercise, diet, or immobilization to help solve the underlying problem.

Cautions and Warnings

Norgesic should not be used if you have a history of glaucoma, stomach ulcer, intestinal obstruction, difficulty in passing urine, or known sensitivity or allergy to this drug or any of its ingredients. It should not be used by pregnant women or children.

Be aware of the potential depressive effects of Norgesic: drowsiness, sleepiness, and inability to concentrate. These may affect your ability to drive or operate machinery or equipment.

Possible Side Effects

Dryness of the mouth is usually the first side effect to appear. As the daily dose increases, other possible side effects include rapid heartbeat, palpitations, difficulty in urination, blurred vision, enlarged pupils, weakness, nausea, vomiting, headache, dizziness, constipation, drowsiness, skin rash, itching, running or stuffy nose, hallucinations, agitation, tremor, stomach upset. Elderly patients taking this drug may occasionally experience some degree of mental confusion. Large doses or prolonged therapy may result in Aspirin intoxication, with symptoms of ringing in the ears, headache, dizziness, fever, confusion, sweating, thirst, drowsiness, dimness of vision, rapid breathing, increased pulse rate, or diarrhea.

Drug Interactions

One of the ingredients in Norgesic is Aspirin, which may significantly affect the effectiveness of oral anticoagulant (blood-thinning) drugs, may increase the effect of Probenecid, and may increase the blood-sugar-lowering effects of oral antidiabetic drugs such as Chlorpropamide and Tolbutamide.

Interaction with Propoxyphene may cause confusion, anxiety, tremors, or shaking.

Long-term users should avoid excessive alcohol intake, which may aggravate stomach upset and bleeding.

Usual Dose

From 1 to 2 tablets 3 to 4 times per day.

Special Information

Take with food or at least ½ glass of water to prevent stomach upset.

Brand Name

Novahistine DH

Ingredients

Chlorpheniramine Maleate
Codeine Phosphate
Phenylpropanolamine Hydrochloride

Type of Drug

Decongestant; antitussive.

Prescribed for

Relief of cough, nasal congestion, runny nose, and other symptoms associated with the common cold, viruses, or other upper respiratory diseases. May also be used to treat allergies, asthma, ear infections, or sinus infections.

General Information

Novahistine DH is one of almost 100 products marketed to relieve the symptoms of the common cold and other upper respiratory infections. These products contain medicine to relieve congestion, act as an antihistamine, relieve or suppress cough, and help cough up mucus. They may contain medicine for each purpose, or may contain a combination of medicines. Some combinations leave out the antihistamine, the decongestant, or the expectorant. You must realize while taking Novahistine DH or similar products that these drugs are good only for the relief of symptoms and will not treat the underlying problem, such as a cold virus or other infections.

Cautions and Warnings

Can cause excessive tiredness or drowsiness.

Possible Side Effects

Dry mouth, blurred vision, difficulty in passing urine, (possibly) constipation, nervousness, restlessness, or even inability to sleep.

Drug Interactions

Taking Novahistine DH with an MAO inhibitor can produce severe interaction. Consult your doctor first.

Novahistine DH contains Codeine. Drinking alcoholic beverages while taking this drug may produce excessive drowsiness and/or sleepiness, or inability to concentrate.

Usual Dose

Adult: 1 to 2 teaspoons 4 times per day.
Child: Not recommended for children.

Special Information

Take with a full glass of water to reduce stomach upset and help remove excessive mucus from the throat.

Brand Name

Novahistine Expectorant

Ingredients

Chlorpheniramine
Phenylpropanolamine Hydrochloride

Type of Drug

Decongestant combination.

Prescribed for

Relief of cough, nasal congestion, runny nose, and other symptoms associated with the common cold, viruses, or other upper respiratory diseases. It may also be used to treat allergies, asthma, ear infections, or sinus infections.

General Information

Novahistine Expectorant is one of almost 100 products marketed to relieve the symptoms of the common cold and other upper respiratory infections. These products contain medicine to relieve congestion, act as an antihistamine, relieve or suppress cough, and help cough up mucus. They may contain medicine for each purpose, or may contain a combination of medicines. Some combinations leave out the antihistamine, the decongestant or the expectorant. You must realize while taking Novahistine Expectorant or similar products that these drugs are only good for relief of symptoms and will not treat the underlying problem, such as a cold virus or other infections.

Cautions and Warnings

Can cause excessive tiredness or drowsiness.

Possible Side Effects

Dry mouth, blurred vision, difficulty passing urine, (possibly) constipation, nervousness, restlessness, or even inability to sleep.

Drug Interactions

Taking Novahistine Expectorant with MAO inhibitors like Isocarboxazid (Marplan), Tranylcypromine Sulfate (Parnate), or Phenelzine Sulfate (Nardil) can produce severe interaction. Consult your doctor first.

Novahistine Expectorant contains Chlorpheniramine. Drinking alcoholic beverages while taking this drug may produce excessive drowsiness and/or sleepiness, or inability to concentrate.

Usual Dose

1 to 2 teaspoons 4 times per day.

Special Information

Take with a full glass of water to reduce stomach upset and help remove excessive mucus from the throat.

Generic Name

Nystatin Vaginal Tablets

Brand Names

Korostatin   Nilstat
Mycostatin   O-V Statin

Type of Drug

Vaginal anti-infective.

Prescribed for

Fungal infection of the vagina.

General Information

Generally you will have relief of symptoms in 1 to 3 days. Nystatin Vaginal Tablets effectively control troublesome and unpleasant symptoms such as itching, inflammation, and discharge. In most cases, 2 weeks of therapy is sufficient for treatment, but prolonged treatment may be necessary. It is important that you continue using this medicine during menstruation. This drug has been used to prevent thrush or candida infection in the newborn infant by treating the mother for 3 to 6 weeks before her due date. At times the vaginal tablet has been used to treat candida infections of the mouth: the vaginal tablet is used as a lozenge and is allowed to be dissolved in the mouth and then swallowed.

Cautions and Warnings

Do not take this drug if you know you may be sensitive or allergic to Nystatin Vaginal Tablets.

Possible Side Effects

Nystatin Vaginal Tablets is virtually nontoxic, and is generally well tolerated. The only side effect reported has been intravaginal irritation: if this occurs, discontinue the drug and contact your doctor.

Usual Dose

One or 2 tablets inserted high in the vagina daily.

Special Information

Do not stop taking the medication just because you begin to feel better. All the medication prescribed must be taken for at least 2 days after the relief of symptoms.

Generic Name

Oral Contraceptives (Combination)

Brand Names

Brevicon	Norlestrin
Demulen	Norlestrin-FE
Enovid	Ortho-Novum
Enovid-E	Ovcon
Loestrin	Ovral
Lo/Ovral	Ovulen
Modicon	Zorane
Norinyl	

Note:
Brand names may appear with a number (i.e. Loestrin 28) that represents the number of tablets in each package, or with FE which indicates that iron pills are included.

Type of Drug

Oral contraceptive.

Prescribed for

Prevention of pregnancy.

General Information

These oral contraceptives (the Pill) are a combination of two natural female hormones, Estrogen and Progestin. These hormones control the menstrual cycle and prepare the woman's body to accept a fertilized egg: once the fertilized egg is implanted, no more eggs can be produced. The Pill works by preventing the production of eggs. Other products (Micronor, Nor Q-I, Ovrette) contain Progestin only.

Any woman taking the Pill should be fully aware of all the problems associated with this type of contraception and should discuss them fully with her doctor.

Cautions and Warnings

You should not use oral contraceptives if you have a history of blood clots of the veins or arteries, have a disease affecting blood coagulation, have known or suspected breast cancer, have undiagnosed or abnormal bleeding, or suspect you are pregnant.

Women with hepatitis or any other liver dysfunction should avoid taking the Pill.

Possible Side Effects

Nausea, abdominal cramps, bloating, vaginal bleeding, change in menstrual flow, possible infertility after coming off the Pill, breast tenderness, weight change, headaches, skin rash, vaginal itching and burning, general vaginal infection, nervousness, dizziness, formation of eye cataract, changes in sex drive, changes in appetite, loss of hair.

Possible Adverse Drug Effects

Women who take oral contraceptives are more likely to develop several serious conditions including the formation of blood clots in the deep veins, stroke, heart attack, liver cancer, gallbladder disease, and high blood pressure. Women who smoke cigarettes are much more likely to develop some of these adverse effects.

Drug Interactions

Interaction with Rifampin decreases the effectiveness of oral contraceptives. The same may be true of barbiturates, Phenylbutazone, Phenytoin, and Ampicillin.

Another interaction reduces the effect of anticoagulant (blood-thinning) drugs. Discuss this with your doctor.

The Pill can also increase blood cholesterol (fat), and can interfere with blood tests for thyroid function and blood sugar.

Usual Dose

The first day of bleeding is the first day of the menstrual cycle. To start, 1 tablet, beginning on the fifth day of the menstrual cycle, is taken every day for 20 or 21 days according to the number of contraceptive tablets supplied by the manufacturer. If 7 days after taking the last tablet menstrual flow has not begun, begin the next month's cycle of pills.

Overdosage

Overdosage may cause nausea and withdrawal bleeding in adult females. Accidental overdosage in children who take their mother's pills has not shown serious adverse effects.

Special Information

Some manufacturers have included 7 blank or 7 iron pills in their packages, to be taken on days when the Pill is not taken. These pills have the number 28 as part of their brand name and a pill should be taken every day.

If you forget to take the Pill for 1 day, take 2 pills the following day. If you miss 2 consecutive days, take 2 pills for the next 2 days. Then continue to take 1 pill daily. If you miss 3 consecutive days, don't take any more pills for the next 7 days; then start a new cycle.

Forgetting to take the Pill reduces your protection: if you keep forgetting to take it you should consider other means of birth control.

All oral contraceptive prescriptions must come with a "patient package insert" for you to read. It gives detailed information about the drug and is required by federal law.

Brand Name

Ornade

Ingredients

Chlorpheniramine Maleate
Isopropamide Iodide
Phenylpropanolamine

Type of Drug

Long-acting combination antihistamine-decongestant.

Prescribed for

Relief of sneezing, runny nose, and nasal congestion associated with the common cold, allergy, or other upper respiratory condition.

General Information

Ornade is one of many products marketed to relieve the symptoms of the common cold. Most of these products contain ingredients to relieve nasal congestion or to dry up runny noses or relieve a scratchy throat; and several of them may contain ingredients to suppress cough, or to help eliminate unwanted mucus. All these products are good only for the relief of symptoms and do not treat the underlying problem such as the cold virus or other infections.

Cautions and Warnings

If you are pregnant you should not take this drug.

Possible Side Effects

Mild drowsiness has been seen in patients taking Ornade.

Possible Adverse Drug Effects

Infrequent: restlessness, tension, nervousness, tremor, weakness, inability to sleep, headache, palpitations, elevation of blood pressure, sweating, sleeplessness, loss of appetite, nausea, vomiting, dizziness, constipation.

Drug Interactions

One of the ingredients in Ornade may cause drowsiness and/or sleepiness and other signs of central nervous system depression. Do not take this drug with alcohol, sedatives, tranquilizers, antihistamines, or sleeping pills.

Do not take additional over-the-counter drugs for the relief of cold symptoms along with Ornade as this may aggravate high blood pressure.

Usual Dose

Adult and child (age 12 and over): 1 capsule every 12 hours.

Child (under age 12): Not recommended.

Special Information

Since drowsiness may occur during use of Ornade, be cautious while performing mechanical tasks requiring alertness.

Brand Name

Os-Cal

Ingredients

Calcium
Copper
Iron
Magnesium
Manganese
Silica
Vitamin D
Zinc

Type of Drug

Calcium and mineral supplement.

Prescribed for

Calcium deficiency.

General Information

This drug is used as an aid in the treatment of any disorder associated with calcium deficiency. The Vitamin D helps promote more efficient absorption of the calcium.

Usual Dose

1 tablet 3 times per day with meals.

Generic Name

Oxacillin Sodium

Brand Names

Bactocil
Prostaphlin

Type of Drug

Broad-spectrum antibiotic.

Prescribed for

Gram-positive bacterial Infections. Gram-positive bacteria (pneumococci, streptococci, and staphylococci) are organisms which usually cause diseases such as pneumonia, infections of the tonsils and throat, venereal disease, meningitis (infection of the spinal column), and septicemia (infection of the bloodstream). This drug is best used to treat infections resistant to Penicillin, although it may be used as initial treatment for some patients.

General Information

Oxacillin Sodium is manufactured in the laboratory by fermentation and by general chemical reaction, and is classified as a semisynthetic antibiotic. Because the effectiveness of the antibiotic is determined by the drug's ability to affect the cell wall of the invading bacteria, it is very important that the patient completely follow the doctor's prescribing directions. These directions include spacing of doses as well as the number of days the patient should continue taking the medicine. If they are not followed, the effect of the antibiotic is severely reduced. To ensure the maximum effect, you should take the medication on an empty stomach, either 1 hour before or 2 hours after meals.

Cautions and Warnings

If you have a known history of allergy to Penicillin you should avoid taking Oxacillin Sodium, since the drugs are chemically similar. The most common allergic reaction to Oxacillin Sodium, as well as to the other penicillins, is a hivelike rash over the body with itching and redness. It is important to tell your doctor if you have ever taken Oxacillin Sodium or penicillins before and if you have experienced any adverse reaction to the drug such as skin rash, itching, or difficulty in breathing.

Possible Side Effects

Common: stomach upset, nausea, vomiting, diarrhea, possible skin rash. Less common: hairy tongue, itching or irritation around the anus and/or vagina. If these symptoms occur, contact your doctor immediately.

Drug Interactions

The effect of Oxacillin Sodium can be significantly reduced when taken with other antibiotics. Consult your doctor if you are taking both during the same course of therapy. Otherwise, Oxacillin Sodium is generally free of interactions with other medications.

Usual Dose

Adult (and child weighing 88 pounds or more): 500 to 1000 milligrams every 4 to 6 hours.

Child (less than 88 pounds): 20 to 40 milligrams per pound of body weight per day, in divided doses.

This drug is frequently used in higher doses when given by the intravenous route. It must be used intravenously for serious infections because of the unusually high doses required.

Storage

Oxacillin Sodium can be stored at room temperature.

Special Information

Do not take Oxacillin Sodium after the expiration date on the label. Its safety in pregnancy has not been established.

Generic Name

Oxazepam

Brand Name

Serax

Type of Drug

Tranquilizer.

Prescribed for

Relief of symptoms of anxiety, tension, fatigue, or agitation.

General Information

Oxazepam is a member of the chemical group of drugs known as benzodiazepines. These drugs are used as either antianxiety agents, anticonvulsants, or sedatives (sleeping pills). They exert their effects by relaxing the large skeletal muscles and by a direct effect on the brain. In doing so, they can relax you and make you either more tranquil or sleepier, depending on the drug and how much you use. Many doctors prefer Oxazepam and the other members of this class to other drugs that can be used for the same effect. Their reason is that the benzodiazepines tend to be safer, have fewer side effects, and are usually as, if not more, effective.

These drugs are generally used in any situation where they can be a useful adjunct.

Benzodiazepine tranquilizing drugs can be abused if taken for long periods of time and it is possible to develop withdrawal symptoms if you discontinue the therapy abruptly. Withdrawal symptoms include convulsions, tremor, muscle cramps, stomach cramps, vomiting, and sweating.

Cautions and Warnings

Do not take Oxazepam if you know you are sensitive or allergic to this drug or other benzodiazepines, such as Diazepam, Chlordiazepoxide, Clorazepate, Lorazepam, Prazepam, Flurazepam, and Clonazepam.

Oxazepam and other members of this drug group may aggravate narrow angle glaucoma, but if you have open angle glaucoma you may take the drugs. In any case, check this information with your doctor. Oxazepam can cause tiredness, drowsiness, inability to concentrate, or similar symptoms. Be careful if you are driving, operating machinery, or performing other activities which require concentration. Avoid taking this drug during the first 3 months of pregnancy except under strict supervision of your doctor.

Possible Side Effects

Most common: mild drowsiness during the first few days of therapy, especially in the elderly or debilitated. If drowsiness persists, contact your doctor.

Possible Adverse Drug Effects

Major adverse reactions: confusion, depression, lethargy, disorientation, headache, lack of activity, slurred speech, stupor, dizziness, tremor, constipation, dry mouth, nausea, inability to control urination, changes in sex drive, irregular menstrual cycle, changes in heart rhythm, lowered blood pressure, retention of fluid, blurred or double vision, itching, rash, hiccups, nervousness, inability to fall asleep, and (occasional) liver dysfunction. If you experience any of these reactions stop taking the medicine and contact your doctor immediately.

Drug Interactions

Oxazepam is a central nervous system depressant. Avoid alcohol, tranquilizers, sleeping pills, barbiturates, MAO inhibitors, antihistamines, and other medicine used to relieve depression.

Usual Dose

Adult: 10 to 120 milligrams per day, as individualized for maximum benefit, depending on symptoms and re-

238

sponse to treatment, which may call for a dose outside the range given.

Elderly: If debilitated, will usually require less of the drug to control tension and anxiety.

Overdosage

Symptoms are confusion, sleep or sleepiness, lack of response to pain such as a pin stick, shallow breathing, lowered blood pressure, and coma. The patient should be taken to a hospital emergency room immediately. ALWAYS bring the medicine bottle.

Generic Name

Oxtriphylline

Brand Name

Choledyl

Type of Drug

Xanthine bronchodilator.

Prescribed for

Relief of bronchial asthma and spasms of bronchial muscles associated with emphysema, bronchitis, and other diseases.

General Information

Oxtriphylline is one of several drugs known as xanthine derivatives which are the mainstay of therapy for bronchial asthma and similar diseases. Other members of this group are Aminophylline, Dyphylline, and Theophylline. Although the dosage for each of these drugs is different, they all work by relaxing bronchial muscles and helping reverse spasms in these muscles.

Cautions and Warnings

Do not use this drug if you are allergic or sensitive to it or to any related drug, such as Aminophylline. If you have a stomach ulcer or heart disease, you should use this drug with caution. If you are pregnant or think that you may be pregnant you should carefully discuss the use of this drug with your doctor, since Oxtriphylline may induce an adverse effect in the unborn child.

Possible Side Effects

Possible side effects from Oxtriphylline or other xanthine derivatives are nausea, vomiting, stomach pain, diarrhea, irritability, restlessness, difficulty sleeping, excitability, muscle twitching or spasms, heart palpitations, other unusual heart rates, low blood pressure, rapid breathing, and local irritation (particularly if a suppository is used).

Possible Adverse Drug Effects

Infrequent: vomiting blood, fever, headache, dehydration.

Drug Interactions

Taking Oxtriphylline at the same time as another xanthine derivative may increase side effects. Don't use together except under the direct care of a doctor.

Oxtriphylline is often given in combination with a stimulant drug such as Ephedrine. Such combinations can cause excessive stimulation and should be used only as specifically directed by your doctor.

Some reports have indicated that combining Erythromycin and Oxtriphylline will give you higher blood levels of Oxtriphylline. Remember that higher blood levels mean the possibility of more side effects.

Usual Dose

Adult: 200 milligrams 4 times per day.

Child (ages 2 to 12): 6⅔ milligrams per pound of body weight per day in 4 divided doses.

Note: Each 100 milligrams of Oxtriphylline is equal to 64 milligrams of Theophylline in potency.

Overdosage

The first symptoms are loss of appetite, nausea, vomiting, difficulty sleeping, and restlessness, followed by unusual behavior patterns, frequent vomiting, and extreme thirst, with delirium, convulsions, very high temperature, and collapse. These serious toxic symptoms are rarely experienced after overdose by mouth, which produces loss of appetite, nausea, vomiting, and stimulation. The overdosed patient should be taken to a hospital emergency room where proper treatment can be given.

Special Information

Take on an empty stomach, at least 1 hour before or 2 hours after meals; but occasional mild stomach upset can be minimized by taking the dose with some food (note if you do this a reduced amount of drug will be absorbed into your bloodstream).

Generic Name

Oxymetazoline Hydrochloride

Brand Names

Afrin (nose drops and spray)
Duration (nose drops and spray)
St. Joseph's Decongestant for Children (nose drops and spray)

Type of Drug

Nasal decongestant.

Prescribed for

Relief of stuffed nose secondary to allergy, the common cold, or any other cause.

Cautions and Warnings

Do not use Oxymetazoline Hydrochloride if you are taking an MAO inhibitor or antidepressant, if you are allergic to Oxymetazoline or any similar preparations, or if you have glaucoma, high blood pressure, heart disease, chest pains, thyroid disease, or diabetes.

Possible Side Effects

Common side effects are burning, stinging, dryness of the mucosa inside the nose, and sneezing.

Possible Adverse Drug Effects

Oxymetazoline Hydrochloride may produce abnormal heart rhythms, increase in blood pressure, headache, feeling of light-headedness, nervousness, difficulty in sleeping, blurred vision, and some drowsiness or lethargy.

Drug Interactions

Oxymetazoline Hydrochloride is a stimulant drug which will increase the effect of any other stimulant. It may block some of the effect of depressant drugs such as tranquilizers or sleeping medications, but this is unusual if recommended doses are observed.

Interaction with MAO inhibitor drugs may cause severe stimulation.

Usual Dose

Adult: 2 to 3 drops or sprays of the (generally 0.5 percent) solution in each nostril no more than twice per day.

Child (ages 2 to 5): 2 to 3 drops of half-strength solution in each nostril no more than twice per day.

Overdosage

Symptoms are sedation, desire to go to sleep, possible coma—or with extreme overdosage, high blood pressure, low heart rate, other effects on the heart, with even collapse of the cardiovascular system, and depressed breathing. The patient should be taken to a hospital emergency room immediately, where proper care can be provided. ALWAYS bring the medicine bottle.

Special Information

Use this drug exactly as directed—not more frequently. If Oxymetazoline Hydrochloride is used more than twice a day or in excessive quantities, "rebound congestion" will occur. The nose will produce excessive amounts of mucus in reaction to the medication.

Generic Name

Oxyphenbutazone

Brand Names

Oxalid
Tandearil

Type of Drug

Anti-inflammatory agent.

Prescribed for

Local inflammation related to gout, rheumatoid arthritis, osteoarthritis, painful shoulder such as bursitis or arthritis of a joint, or other inflammatory processes which cause pain that cannot be readily controlled by usual analgesics such as Aspirin, and when severe disability, because of the inflammation, is not relieved by usual treatment.

General Information

Oxyphenbutazone and its sister drug Phenylbutazone are toxic and dangerous drugs which should only be used when the situation absolutely warrants it. Because the list of potential side effects is long with these drugs, any change in habits or any unusual effect which may even be remotely connected with the use of this drug should be reported immediately to your doctor.

Cautions and Warnings

You should not take Oxyphenbutazone if you have a history of symptoms associated with gastrointestinal inflammation or ulcer, including severe, recurrent, or persistent upset stomach. This drug is not a simple pain reliever and should never be taken casually. It should not be prescribed before a careful and detailed history, plus physical and laboratory tests, have been completed by the doctor. If your problem can be treated by a less toxic drug such as Aspirin, use that first and try to stay away from Oxyphenbutazone. Never take more than the recommended dosage: this would lead to toxic effects. If you have fever, rash, sore throat, sores in the mouth, upset stomach or pain in the stomach, feeling of weakness, black or tarry stool, or a significant or sudden weight gain, report this to your doctor immediately. In addition, stop taking the drug. If the drug is not effective after 1 week, stop taking it.

Possible Side Effects

Most common: stomach upset, drowsiness, water retention.

Possible Adverse Drug Effects

Infrequent: acute gastric or duodenal ulcer, ulceration or a perforation of the large bowel, bleeding from the stomach and resultant anemia, stomach pain, vomiting of blood, nausea, vomiting, diarrhea. This drug may cause abnormal effects on various components of the blood including various types of anemias, effects on the platelets and white blood cells. It will cause water retention and will upset the normal acid base balance of the body. It has been known to cause fatal and nonfatal hepatitis, and may cause the appearance of black-and-blue marks on the skin. It has been known to cause serum sickness, drug allergy serious enough to cause shock, itching, serious rashes, fever, signs of arthritis, and a variety of kidney effects including passage of blood through the kidney, the shutdown of or permanent damage to the kidney, and kidney stones. Oxyphenbutazone has caused various types of heart disease, high blood pressure, blurred vision, bleeding on the back of the eye, detachment of the retina, hearing loss, high blood sugar, thyroid disease, agitation, confusion, and lethargy.

Drug Interactions

Oxyphenbutazone increases the effects of Insulin and oral antidiabetic agents. If you are taking antidiabetic drugs, discuss this matter with your doctor immediately.

Usual Dose

Adult: Depending upon the condition being treated, 300 to 600 milligrams per day in 3 to 4 equal doses, for 7 days. If dose is effective it can then be reduced to 100 to 400 milligrams per day, depending on the condition being treated.

Elderly: Drug to be given only for 7 days because of high risk of severe reactions. Not to be given to senile patients.

Child (under age 14): Not recommended.

Overdosage

Symptoms are convulsions, euphoria, depression, headache, hallucinations, giddiness, dizziness, coma, rapid breathing rate, and insomnia or sleeplessness. Contact your doctor immediately.

Symptoms discussed in other sections above may also appear.

Special Information

Oxyphenbutazone is a central nervous system depressant that can cause drowsiness and tiredness: be careful driving or operating other equipment, and avoid high quantities of alcoholic beverages, since they will aggravate the situation.

Oxyphenbutazone causes stomach upset In many patients; take your dose with food, and if stomach pain continues or your stool becomes bloody or black and tarry in appearance, notify your doctor.

If you experience sore throat, fever, sores in the mouth, water retention, or blurred vision, contact your physician immediately.

Generic Name

Papaverine

Brand Names

Blupav	Pavadel
Cerebid	Pavadur
Cerespan	Pavadyl
Delapav	Pavakey
Dipav	Pava-Mead
Dylate	Pava-Pav
J-Pav	Pavased
Kavrin	Pavasule
Lapav	Pavatest
Lempav	Pavatran
Myobid	Pava-2
Orapav Timecelles	Pava-Wol
Papacon	Paverolan
Pap-Kaps	Ro-Papav
Pavabid Plateau Caps	Sustaverine
Pavacap Unicelles	Vasal Granucaps
Pavacels	Vasocap-300
Pavacen Cenules	Vasospan

Type of Drug

Vasodilator.

Prescribed for

Relief of spasms of arteries in the heart, brain, arms, and legs.

General Information

Papaverine relaxes various smooth muscles: it slows their normal degree of responsiveness but does not paralyze them. Papaverine may directly widen blood vessels in the brain and other areas, increasing the flow of blood and oxygen to those areas.

Cautions and Warnings

Papaverine may aggravate glaucoma. If you develop stomach upset, yellowing of the skin and/or the whites of the eyes, call your doctor immediately.

Possible Side Effects

Most frequent: nausea, stomach upset, loss of appetite, sweating, flushing of the face, not feeling well, dizziness, drowsiness, headache, skin rash, constipation, diarrhea. In general, few side effects are experienced by people taking Papaverine.

Usual Dose

Plain tablet, 100 to 300 milligrams 3 to 5 times per day. Time-release tablets or capsules, 150 milligrams every 12 hours; if patients do not respond to this, medication may be increased to 150 milligrams every 8 hours, or 300 milligrams every 12 hours.

Brand Name

Parafon Forte

Ingredients

Acetaminophen
Chlorzoxazone

Type of Drug

Skeletal muscle relaxant.

Prescribed for

Relief of pain and spasm of muscular conditions, including lower back pain, strains, sprains, or muscle bruises.

General Information

Parafon Forte is one of several drugs used to treat the aches and pains associated with muscle aches, strains, or a bad back. It gives only temporary relief and is not a substitute for other types of therapy such as rest or surgery.

Cautions and Warnings

Do not take Parafon Forte if you are allergic to either of its ingredients. Do not take more than the exact amount of medication prescribed.

Possible Side Effects

The major side effects are stomach upset and other gastrointestinal problems. Parafon Forte has been associated with bleeding from the stomach, drowsiness, dizziness, light-headedness, not feeling well, and over-stimulation.

Possible Adverse Drug Effects

Both ingredients in Parafon Forte have been associated with liver disease: this is especially true when the medicine is taken in large doses for a long time. If you have been taking it for several weeks, your doctor should perform routine tests to be sure that your liver is functioning properly; but if you take Parafon Forte for a short time (several days or less), the problem should not bother you.

Usual Dose

2 tablets 4 times per day.

Overdosage

Symptoms of massive overdosage are sleepiness, weakness, tiredness, turning blue of lips, fingertips, or other areas, and signs of liver damage such as nausea, vomiting, diarrhea, and severe abdominal pain. Contact your doctor immediately or go to a hospital emergency room where appropriate therapy can be provided. ALWAYS bring the medicine bottle.

Special Information

Parafon Forte can make you sleepy, dull your senses, or disturb your concentration, so be extremely careful while driving or operating equipment or machinery. Drinking alcoholic beverages further complicates this problem and enhances the sedative effects of Parafon Forte.

A breakdown product of the Chlorzoxazone ingredient in Parafon Forte can turn your urine orange to purple-red: this is not dangerous.

Generic Name

Paregoric

Type of Drug

Antidiarrheal.

Prescribed for

Symptomatic treatment of diarrhea.

General Information

Paregoric and other antidiarrheal agents should only be used for short periods: they will relieve the diarrhea, but not its underlying causes. Sometimes these drugs should not be used even though there is diarrhea present: people with some kinds of bowel, stomach, or other disease may be harmed by taking antidiarrheal drugs. Obviously, the decision to use Paregoric must be made by your doctor. Do not use Paregoric without his advice.

Cautions and Warnings

Paregoric is a derivative of Morphine; the cautions and warnings that go with the use of narcotics also go with the use of Paregoric. When taken in the prescribed dose, however, there should be no serious problems.

Possible Side Effects

Most people do not experience side effects from Paregoric, but some may experience nausea, upset stomach, and other forms of gastrointestinal disturbance.

Possible Adverse Drug Effects

Most adverse drug effects associated with narcotic drugs are not experienced with Paregoric because of the limited amount of narcotic contained in the medication and the unappealing taste of the drug. Prolonged use of Paregoric may produce some of the narcotic effects such as difficulty in breathing, light-headedness, dizziness, sedation, nausea, and vomiting.

Drug Interactions

Paregoric, a depressant on the central nervous system, may cause tiredness or inability to concentrate, and may thus increase the effect of sleeping pills, tranquilizers, and alcoholic beverages. Avoid large amounts of alcohol.

Usual Dose

Adult: For diarrhea, 1 to 2 teaspoons 4 times per day.
Infant: For diarrhea, 2 to 10 drops 4 times per day.
Paregoric is only a symptomatic treatment; it should be accompanied by fluids and other therapy prescribed by your doctor.

Overdosage

A patient with paregoric overdose should be taken to a hospital emergency room immediately. ALWAYS bring the medicine bottle.

Special Information

To help mask the taste, Paregoric can be mixed with a small amount of water or juice immediately before it is taken. The milky color of the mixture is of no consequence.
Take care while driving or operating any appliance or machinery.

Generic Name

Penicillin G

Brand Names

Genecillin-400	Pentids
G-Recillin	Pfizerpen G
K-Cillin	SK-Penicillin G
K-Pen	Sugracillin
Palocillin-5	

Type of Drug

Antibiotic.

Prescribed for

Bacterial infections susceptible to this drug.

General Information

Because the effectiveness of the antibiotic is determined by the drug's ability to destroy the cell wall of the invading bacteria, it is very important that the patient completely follow the doctor's prescribing directions. These directions include spacing of doses as well as the number of days the patient should continue taking the medicine. If they are not followed, the effect of the antibiotic is severely reduced.

Cautions and Warnings

Serious and occasionally fatal hypersensitivity reaction has been reported to Penicillin G. Although this is more common following injection of the drug, it has occurred with oral use. It is more likely to occur in individuals with a history of sensitivity to this drug or sensitivity in general as indicated by multiple allergies.

Possible Side Effects

The most important side effect seen with Penicillin G is sensitivity or allergic reaction.

Possible Adverse Drug Effects

Occasional: stomach upset, nausea, vomiting, diarrhea, coating of the tongue, skin rash, itching, various types of anemia, other effects on the blood system, oral or rectal infestation with fungal diseases.

Drug Interactions

Penicillin G should not be given at the same time as one of the bacteriostatic antibiotics such as Erythromycin and Tetracycline, which may diminish the effectiveness of Penicillin G. Aspirin or Phenylbutazone will increase the level of free Penicillin G in the blood by making more of it available from blood proteins.

Usual Dose

From 200,000 to 500,000 units every 6 to 8 hours for 10 days.

Storage

Oral Penicillin G may have to be stored in a refrigerator.

Special Information

It takes 7 to 10 days for Penicillin G to be effective against most susceptible organisms; be sure to take all the medicine prescribed for the full period prescribed.

Penicillin G is best absorbed on an empty stomach. It can be taken 1 hour before or 2 hours after meals, or first thing in the morning and last thing at night with other doses spaced evenly through the day.

Generic Name

Penicillin V (Phenoxymethyl Penicillin)

Brand Names

Betapen-VK	Repen-VK
Compocillin V	Robicillin VK
Compocillin-VK	Ro-Cillin VK
Ledercillin VK	Saropen-VK
Penapar VK	SK-Penicillin VK
Penicillin V	Uticillin VK
Penicillin VK	V-Cillin
Pen-Vee-K	V-Cillin-K
Pfizerpen VK	Veetids

Type of Drug

Antibiotic.

Prescribed for

Bacterial infections susceptible to this drug.

General Information

General use of Penicillin V is identical to that of Penicillin G, the difference being that Penicillin V is not destroyed by the acids of the stomach, and thus is more effective when taken by mouth than Penicillin G.

Cautions and Warnings

Serious and occasionally fatal hypersensitivity reaction has been reported to Penicillin V. Although it is more common following injection of the drug, it has occurred with oral use. It is more likely to occur in individuals with a history of sensitivity to this drug or sensitivity in general as indicated by multiple allergies.

Possible Side Effects

The most important side effect seen with Penicillin V is sensitivity or allergic reaction.

Possible Adverse Drug Effects

Occasional: stomach upset, nausea, vomiting, diarrhea, coating of the tongue, skin rash, itching, various types of anemia, other effects on the blood system, oral or rectal infestation with fungal diseases.

Drug Interactions

Penicillin V should not be given at the same time as one of the bacteriostatic antibiotics such as Erythromycin and Tetracycline, which may diminish the effectiveness of Penicillin V.

Aspirin or Phenylbutazone will increase the level of free Penicillin V in the blood by making more of it available from blood proteins.

Usual Dose

From 125 to 250 milligrams every 6 to 8 hours for 10 days.

Storage

Oral Penicillin V may have to be stored in a refrigerator. The bottle should be labeled to that effect and the information should be available on the prescription label.

Special Information

It takes 7 to 10 days for Penicillin V to be effective against most susceptible organisms; be sure to take all the medicine prescribed for the full period prescribed.

Penicillin V is best absorbed on an empty stomach.

It can be taken 1 hour before or 2 hours after meals, or first thing in the morning and last thing at night with other doses spaced evenly through the day.

Generic Name

Pentazocine

Brand Name

Talwin

Type of Drug

Nonnarcotic analgesic.

Prescribed for

Relief of moderate to severe pain.

General Information

Pentazocine is useful for mild to moderate pain. Fifty to 100 milligrams of Pentazocine is approximately equal in pain-relieving effect to 2 Aspirin tablets (650 milligrams). Pentazocine may be less active than Aspirin for types of pain associated with inflammation, since Aspirin reduces inflammation but Pentazocine does not.

Cautions and Warnings

Do not take Pentazocine if you believe that you are allergic to it. It is possible to develop addiction to or dependence on Pentazocine, but addiction is much more likely to occur with people who have a history of abusing narcotics or other drugs. Abrupt stoppage of Pentazocine after extended periods of therapy has produced withdrawal symptoms such as stomach cramps, fever, stuffed or runny nose, restlessness, anxiety, and tearing of the eyes. The drug may cause visual hallucinations or make you disoriented and confused: if this happens, stop taking the drug immediately and contact your physician. While taking Pentazocine, be extremely careful when operating machinery or driving. If you are pregnant, seriously consider taking another analgesic, because Pentazocine can make it difficult for the newborn infant to breathe on its own. If you suffer from respiratory conditions such as bronchial asthma or emphysema, avoid taking Pentazocine, because it may make breathing more difficult for you.

Possible Side Effects

Nausea, vomiting, constipation, cramps, stomach upset, loss of appetite, diarrhea, dry mouth, alteration of taste, dizziness, light-headedness, sedation, euphoria, headache, difficulty sleeping, disturbed dreams, hallucinations, muscle spasms, irritability, excitement, nervousness, apprehension and depression, feeling of being disoriented and detached from your body.

Possible Adverse Drug Effects

Blurred vision, difficulty in focusing the eyes, double vision, sweating, flushing, chills, rash, itching, swelling of the face, flushing and reddening of the skin, changes in blood pressure, abnormal heart rate, difficulty in breathing, effects on components of the blood, difficult urination, tingling in the arms and legs.

Drug Interactions

Avoid interaction with drugs that have a sedative or depressive effect, such as alcohol, barbiturates, sleeping pills, and some pain-relieving medications. The combination will produce extreme sedation, sleepiness, and difficulty concentrating.

Pentazocine has the unusual effect of being a mild narcotic antagonist. If you must take narcotics for pain relief, do not take Pentazocine, because it will reverse the effect of the narcotic drug. This can be a special problem for patients in Methadone treatment programs. If one of these patients takes Pentazocine, he will experience narcotic withdrawal effects.

Usual Dose

50 milligrams every 3 to 4 hours. Maximum dose, 600 milligrams per day to control pain.

Overdosage

Symptoms resemble those of narcotic overdose: decreased breathing, sleepiness, lassitude, low blood pressure, and even coma. The patient should be taken to a hospital emergency room immediately. ALWAYS bring the medicine bottle.

Special Information

Pentazocine can cause euphoria or hallucinations, affecting your routine activities.

Generic Name

Pentobarbital

Brand Names

Nebralin
Nembutal Sodium

Type of Drug

Hypnotic; sedative; anticonvulsive.

Prescribed for

Daytime sedative or sleeping medication.

General Information

Pentobarbital, like the other barbiturates, appears to act by interfering with nerve impulses to the brain. When used as an anticonvulsive, Pentobarbital is not very effective by itself; but when used in combination with anticonvulsive agents such as Phenytoin, the action of both the Pentobarbital and the Phenytoin is dramatic. This combination has been used very successfully in the control of epileptic seizures.

Cautions and Warnings

Pentobarbital may slow down your physical and mental reflexes, so you must be extremely careful when operating machinery, driving an automobile, or performing other potentially dangerous tasks. Pentobarbital is classified as a barbiturate; long-term or unsupervised use may cause addiction. Elderly people on Pentobarbital may exhibit nervousness and confusion at times.

Barbiturates are neutralized in the liver and eliminated from the body through the kidneys; consequently, people who have liver or kidney disorders—namely, difficulty in forming or excreting urine—should be carefully monitored by their doctor when taking Pentobarbital.

If you have known sensitivities or allergies to barbiturates, or if you have previously been addicted to sedatives or hypnotics, or if you have a disease affecting the respiratory system, you should not take Pentobarbital.

Possible Side Effects

Difficulty in breathing, skin rash, and general allergic reaction such as running nose, watering eyes, scratchy throat.

Possible Adverse Drug Effects

Drowsiness, lethargy, dizziness, hangover, nausea, vomiting, diarrhea. More severe adverse reactions may include anemia and yellowing of the skin and eyes.

Drug Interactions

Interaction with alcohol, tranquilizers, or other sedatives increases the sedative effect of Pentobarbital.

Interaction with anticoagulants (blood-thinning agents) can reduce their effect. This is also true of muscle relaxants and painkillers.

Usual Dose

Daytime sedative, 30 milligrams 3 to 4 times per day; hypnotic for sleep, 100 milligrams at bedtime, which may be repeated once if necessary (occasionally) to induce sleep.

Overdosage

Symptoms are difficulty in breathing, decrease in size of the pupils of the eyes, lowered body temperature progressing to fever as time passes, fluid in the lungs, and eventually coma.

Anyone suspected of having taken an overdose must be taken to the hospital for immediate care. ALWAYS bring the medicine bottle to the emergency room physician so he can quickly and correctly identify the medicine and start treatment. Severe overdosage of this medication can kill; the drug has been used many times in suicide attempts.

Brand Name

Percodan

Ingredients

Aspirin
Caffeine
Oxycodone
Phenacetin

Type of Drug

Narcotic analgesic combination.

Prescribed for

Relief of mild to moderate pain.

General Information

Percodan is one of many combination products containing narcotics and analgesics. These products often also contain barbiturates or tranquilizers, and Acetaminophen may be substituted for Aspirin, or Phenacetin and/or Caffeine may be omitted. All these products are used for the relief of mild to moderate pain.

Cautions and Warnings

Do not take Percodan if you know you are allergic or sensitive to any of its components. Long-term use of this drug may cause drug dependence or addiction. The Oxycodone component of Percodan is a respiratory depressant. Use this drug with extreme caution if you suffer from asthma or other breathing problems. The Oxycodone component of Percodan affects the central nervous system, producing sleepiness, tiredness, and/or inability to concentrate. If you are pregnant or suspect that you are pregnant do not take this drug.

Possible Side Effects

Most frequent: light-headedness, dizziness, sleepiness, nausea, vomiting, loss of appetite, sweating. If these effects occur, consider calling your doctor and asking him about lowering the dose of Percodan you are taking. Usually the side effects disappear if you simply lie down.

More serious side effects of Percodan are shallow breathing or difficulty in breathing.

Possible Adverse Drug Effects

Adverse effects of Percodan include euphoria (feeling high), weakness, sleepiness, headache, agitation, uncoordinated muscle movement, minor hallucinations, disorientation and visual disturbances, dry mouth, loss of appetite, constipation, flushing of the face, rapid heartbeat, palpitations, faintness, urinary difficulties or hesitancy, reduced sex drive and/or potency, itching, skin rashes, anemia, lowered blood sugar, and a yellowing of the skin and/or whites of the eyes. Narcotic analgesics may aggravate convulsions in those who have had convulsions in the past.

Drug Interactions

Interaction with alcohol, tranquilizers, barbiturates, or sleeping pills produces tiredness, sleepiness, or inability to concentrate, and seriously increases the depressive effect of Percodan.

The Aspirin component of Percodan can affect anticoagulant (blood-thinning) therapy. Be sure to discuss this with your doctor so that the proper dosage adjustment can be made.

Interaction with adrenal cortical steroids, Phenylbutazone, or alcohol can cause severe stomach irritation with possible bleeding.

Usual Dose

One tablet every 6 hours as needed for relief of pain.

Overdosage

Symptoms are depression of respiration (breathing), extreme tiredness progressing to stupor and then coma, pinpointed pupils of the eyes, no response to stimulation such as a pin stick, cold and clammy skin, slowing down of the heartbeat, lowering of blood pressure, convulsions, and cardiac arrest. The patient should be taken to a hospital emergency room immediately. ALWAYS bring the medicine bottle.

Special Information

Drowsiness may occur: be careful when driving or operating hazardous machinery.

Take with food or ½ glass of water to prevent stomach upset.

The Phenacetin ingredient of Percodan may be toxic to your kidneys; do not take this medication for longer than 10 days unless directed by your doctor.

Brand Name

Peri-Colace

Ingredients

Casanthranol
Dicotyl Sodium Sulfosuccinate

Other Brand Names

Afko-Lube Lax	D-S-S plus
Bu-Lax Plus	Genericace
Casa-Laud	Molatoc-CST
Comfolax-plus	Peri-Conate
Constiban	Peri-Doss
Disanthrol	Stimulax
Disosol Forte	

Type of Drug

Laxative.

Prescribed for

Treatment or prevention of constipation. Also used to clear intestines prior to X-ray procedures.

General Information

This is one of many laxative combinations available

without a prescription. Composed of a stool softener and a stimulant which makes the stool easier to pass by acting directly on the intestine to move the stool through it, such laxatives should be used for short periods only when necessary. Long-term use of a stimulant laxative can produce laxative dependency, where normal bowel function is lost and the stimulant is required to pass any stool.

Cautions and Warnings

Patients with abdominal pain, nausea, vomiting, or symptoms of appendicitis should not take a laxative.

Possible Side Effects

Severely constipated patients may experience stomach cramps. Nausea, vomiting, and diarrhea may occur after excessive amounts have been taken.

Usual Dose

1 to 2 capsules at bedtime.

Special Information

If this laxative is not effective after 7 days, stop taking it and call your doctor.

Generic Name

Phenazopyridine Hydrochloride

Brand Names

Azo-Standard	Penyl-Idium
Azo-Stat	Pyridium
Di-Azo	Urodine

Type of Drug

Urinary analgesic.

Prescribed for

Relief of pain and discomfort associated with urinary tract infection.

General Information

Phenazopyridine Hydrochloride is only used to relieve the pain associated with urinary infections. It has little antibacterial action and cannot be used, therefore, to cure a urinary infection by itself. It is usually used in combination with a sulfa antibacterial drug.

Possible Side Effects

Occasional stomach upset.

Usual Dose

Two hundred milligrams 3 times per day.

Special Information

Phenazopyridine Hydrochloride may produce an orange-red color in the urine. This is normal, but the color change may interfere with urine tests to monitor diabetes.

Brand Name

Phenergan Expectorant Plain

Ingredients

Alcohol
Citric Acid
Fluid Extract of Ipecac
Potassium Guaiacolsulfonate
Promethazine Hydrochloride
Sodium Citrate

Other Brand Names

Proclan Expectorant
Promethazine Hydro-
   chloride Expectorant
   Plain

Promex Liquid
Rola-Methazine
   Expectorant Plain

Type of Drug

Expectorant combination.

Prescribed for

Relief of coughs and symptoms associated with the common cold.

General Information

Phenergan Expectorant Plain is one of many products marketed for the relief of coughs. The major active ingredient contained in Phenergan Expectorant Plain is an antihistamine. Therefore, the drug is most effective in relieving the symptoms of excess histamine production. Basically Phenergan Expectorant Plain is only able to help you feel well. It cannot help you recover more quickly, only more comfortably.

Cautions and Warnings

Phenergan Expectorant Plain may cause drowsiness or sleepiness. Do not use this product with similar products such as sedatives, tranquilizers, sleeping pills, antihistamines, or other drugs which can cause sleepiness or drowsiness.

Possible Side Effects

Dryness of the mouth, blurred vision, occasional dizziness.

Drug Interactions

Avoid alcohol, which increases central nervous system depression and leads to drowsiness, sleepiness, or similar problems.

Usual Dose

One teaspoon every 4 to 6 hours.

Special Information

Take with a full glass of water to help the expectorant effect and reduce any stomach upset caused by the drug.

Phenergan Expectorant with Codeine

Ingredients

Alcohol
Citric Acid
Codeine Phosphate
Fluid Extract of Ipecac
Potassium Guaiacolsulfonate
Promethazine Hydrochloride
Sodium Citrate

Other Brand Names

Mallergan Expectorant with Codeine
Promethazine Hydrochloride Expectorant with Codeine
Rola-Methazine Expectorant with Codeine

Type of Drug

Cough suppressant and expectorant combination.

Prescribed for

Coughs, symptoms of the common cold.

General Information

Phenergan Expectorant with Codeine is one of almost 100 products marketed to treat symptoms of the common cold or other upper respiratory problems. It is useful in helping to relieve symptoms but does not treat the basic problem.

Cautions and Warnings

Do not take this medicine if you are allergic to any of its ingredients.

Possible Side Effects

Drowsiness, dry mouth, blurred vision, difficulty in urination, constipation.

Possible Adverse Drug Effects

Palpitations—pounding of the heart.

Drug Interactions

Avoid alcohol, sedatives, tranquilizers, antihistamines, or other medication which can cause tiredness and/or drowsiness.

Taking Phenergan Expectorant with Codeine with Isocarboxazid (Marplan), Tranylcypromine Sulfate (Parnate), Phenelzine Sulfate (Nardil), or other MAO inhibitor drugs can produce a severe interaction. Consult your doctor first.

Usual Dose

Adult: 2 teaspoons 4 times per day.

Child (over age 1): ½ to 1 teaspoon 3 to 4 times per day.

Take with a full glass of water. This will help the expectorant effect of the drug and may reduce stomach upset.

Special Information

Be aware of the potential depressive effects of Phenergan Expectorant with Codeine; be careful when driving or operating heavy or dangerous machinery.

Brand Name

Phenergan VC Expectorant Plain

Ingredients

Alcohol
Citric Acid
Fluid Extract of Ipecac
Phenylephrine
Potassium Guaiacolsulfonate
Promethazine Hydrochloride
Sodium Citrate

Other Brand Names

J-Gan-V. C. Expectorant Plain
Proclan VC Expectorant Plain
Rola-Methazine VC Expectorant

Type of Drug

Expectorant combination.

Prescribed for

Coughs.

General Information

Phenergan VC Expectorant Plain is one of many products marketed to relieve the symptoms of the common cold or other upper respiratory infections. These products relieve runny nose, eliminate unwanted mucus, and unclog nasal and sinus passages.

Cautions and Warnings

Drowsiness, dry mouth, blurred vision, difficulty in urination, and/or constipation can occur.

Possible Adverse Drug Effects

The drug may cause mild stimulation and you may experience nervousness, restlessness, or even inability to sleep.

Drug Interactions

Avoid alcohol, sedatives, tranquilizers, antihistamines, or other medication which can cause tiredness and/or drowsiness. Taking Phenergan VC Expectorant Plain with MAO inhibitor drugs can produce severe interaction. Consult your doctor first.

Usual Dose

One teaspoon every 4 to 6 hours as needed for the relief of cough or the expectoration of undesired mucus.

Special Information

Be aware of the potential depressive effects of this drug: take care when driving or operating heavy or dangerous machinery.

Phenergan VC Expectorant with Codeine

Ingredients

Alcohol
Citric Acid
Codeine Phosphate
Fluid Extract of Ipecac
Phenylephrine
Potassium Guaiacolsulfonate
Promethazine Hydrochloride
Sodium Citrate

Other Brand Names

Mallergan-VC Expectorant with Codeine
Proclan VC Expectorant with Codeine
Promethazine Hydrochloride VC Expectorant with Codeine

Type of Drug

Decongestant; expectorant.

Prescribed for

Relief of cough, nasal congestion, runny nose, and other symptoms associated with the common cold, viruses, or other upper respiratory diseases. It may also be used to treat allergies, asthma, ear infections, or sinus infections.

General Information

Phenergan VC Expectorant with Codeine is one of almost 100 products marketed to relieve the symptoms of the common cold and other respiratory infections. These products contain medicine to relieve congestion, act as an antihistamine, relieve or suppress cough, and help cough up mucus. They may contain medicine for each purpose, or may contain a combination of medicines. Some combinations leave out the antihistamine, the decongestant, or the expectorant. You must realize while taking Phenergan VC Expectorant with Codeine or similar products that these drugs are good only for the relief of symptoms and will not treat the underlying problem, such as a cold virus or other infections.

Cautions and Warnings

Can cause excessive tiredness or drowsiness.

Possible Side Effects

Dry mouth, blurred vision, difficulty passing urine, (possibly) constipation, nervousness, restlessness, or even inability to sleep.

Drug Interactions

Taking Phenergan VC Expectorant with Codeine with MAO inhibitor drugs can produce severe interaction. Consult with your doctor first.

Drinking alcoholic beverages while taking Codeine may produce excessive drowsiness and/or sleepiness, or inability to concentrate.

Usual Dose

1 to 2 teaspoonfuls 4 times per day.

Special Information

Take with a full glass of water to reduce stomach upset and help remove excessive mucus.

Generic Name

Phenobarbital

Brand Names

Eskabarb	SK-Phenobarbital
Luminal	Solfoton
Pheno-Squar	

Type of Drug

Hypnotic; sedative; anticonvulsive.

Prescribed for

Epileptic seizures, convulsions; as an anticonvulsive or a daytime sedative; as a mild hypnotic (sleeping medication); and for eclampsia (toxemia in pregnancy).

General Information

Phenobarbital, like the other barbiturates, appears to act by interfering with nerve impulses to the brain. When used as an anticonvulsive Phenobarbital is not very effective by Itself, but when used in combination with anticonvulsive agents such as Phenytoin, the action of both the Phenobarbital and the Phenytoin is dramatic. This combination has been used very successfully to control epileptic seizures.

Cautions and Warnings

Phenobarbital may slow down your physical and mental reflexes, so you must be extremely careful when operating machinery, driving an automobile, or performing other potentially dangerous tasks. Phenobarbital is classified as a barbiturate; long-term or unsupervised use may cause addiction. Elderly patients on Phenobarbital exhibit nervousness and confusion at times. Barbiturates are neutralized in the liver and eliminated from the body through the kidneys; consequently, people who have liver disorders or kidney disorders—namely, difficulty in forming or excreting urine—should be carefully monitored by their doctor when taking Phenobarbital.

If you have known sensitivities or allergies to barbiturates, or have previously been addicted to sedatives or hypnotics, or if you have a disease affecting the respiratory system, you should not take Phenobarbital.

Possible Side Effects

Difficulty in breathing, skin rash, and general allergic reaction such as running nose, watering eyes, and scratchy throat.

Possible Adverse Drug Effects

Drowsiness, lethargy, dizziness, hangover, nausea, vomiting, diarrhea. More severe adverse reactions may include anemia and yellowing of the skin and eyes.

Drug Interactions

Interaction with alcohol, tranquilizers, or other sedatives increases the sedative effect of Phenobarbital.

Interaction with anticoagulants (blood-thinning agents) can reduce their effect. This is also true of muscle relaxants and painkillers.

Usual Dose

Anticonvulsant, 15 to 30 milligrams 3 times per day; hypnotic (for sleep), 30 milligrams at bedtime; sedative, 15 to 30 milligrams 3 times per day.

Specific dose is determined by patient's size, weight, and physical condition.

Overdosage

Symptoms are difficulty in breathing, decrease in size of the pupils of the eyes, lowered body temperature progressing to fever as time passes, fluid in the lungs, and eventually coma.

Anyone suspected of having taken an overdose must be taken to the hospital for immediate care. ALWAYS bring the medicine bottle to the emergency room physician so he can quickly and correctly identify the medicine and start treatment. Severe overdosage of this medication can kill; the drug has been used many times in suicide attempts.

Generic Name

Phentermine Hydrochloride

Brand Names

Adipex	Phentrol
Ambesa-LA	Phentrol-II
Anoxine-AM	Rolaphent
Fastin	Tora
Ionamin	

Type of Drug

Nonamphetamine appetite suppressant.

Prescribed for

Suppression of appetite and treatment of obesity.

General Information

Although Phentermine Hydrochloride is not an amphetamine, it can produce the same adverse effects as the amphetamine appetite suppressants.

Cautions and Warnings

Do not use Phentermine Hydrochloride if you have heart disease, high blood pressure, thyroid disease, or glaucoma, or if you are sensitive or allergic to this or similar drugs. Furthermore, do not use this medicine if you are emotionally agitated or have a history of drug abuse.

Possible Side Effects

Some people taking Phentermine Hydrochloride may experience palpitations, high blood pressure, overstimulation, nervousness, restlessness, drowsiness, sedation, weakness, dizziness, inability to sleep, tremor, headache, dry mouth, nausea, vomiting, diarrhea and other intestinal disturbances, rash, itching, changes in sex drive, hair loss, muscle pain, difficulty in passing urine, sweating, chills, blurred vision, and fever.

Usual Dose

Adult: 8 milligrams ½ hour before meals or 15 to 37 milligrams once a day before breakfast. Do not take late in the evening.

Overdosage

Symptoms are restlessness, tremor, shallow breathing, confusion, hallucinations, and fever followed by fatigue and depression, with additional symptoms such as high or possibly low blood pressure, cold and clammy skin, nausea, vomiting, diarrhea, and stomach cramps. The patient should be taken to a hospital emergency room immediately. ALWAYS bring the medicine bottle.

Special Information

Use only for a few weeks as an adjunct to diet, under strict supervision of your doctor.

Medicine alone will not take off weight. You must limit and modify your food intake, preferably under medical supervision.

Generic Name

Phenylbutazone

Brand Names

Azolid	Butazolidin
Azolid-A (Phenylbu- tazone and antacid)	Butazolidin Alka

Type of Drug

Anti-inflammatory agent.

Prescribed for

Local inflammation of bone joints such as gout, rheumatoid arthritis, osteoarthritis, painful shoulder such as bursitis or arthritis of a joint, or other inflammatory diseases which cause pain that cannot be controlled by Aspirin, and when the inflammation is not relieved by usual treatment.

General Information

Phenylbutazone should be used only for the short-term relief of pain due to inflammation of muscles, tendons, and joint area. It has anti-inflammatory, analgesic, and fever-reducing properties. This drug is quite useful but is limited by its side effects and adverse drug reactions. It must not be taken without your doctor's advice.

Phenylbutazone and its sister drug Oxyphenbutazone are toxic and dangerous and should only be used when absolutely necessary. The list of potential side effects is long. Therefore, any change in habits or unusual effect which may even be remotely connected with the use of these drugs should be reported immediately to your doctor.

Cautions and Warnings

Phenylbutazone should not be given to children or senile adults. Elderly patients should not take this drug for more than 7 days. You should not take Phenylbutazone if you have a history or symptoms associated with gastrointestinal inflammation or ulcer, including severe, recurrent, or persistent upset stomach. This drug is not a simple pain reliever and should never be taken casually. It should not be prescribed before a careful and detailed history, plus physical and laboratory tests, have been completed by the doctor. Always discuss your state of health and medical history with your doctor completely before taking this medicine. If your problem can be treated by a less toxic drug such as Aspirin, use that first and try to stay away from Phenylbutazone. Never take more than the recommended dosage: this would lead to toxic effects. If you have fever, rash, sore throat, sores in the mouth, upset stomach or pain in the stomach, feeling of weakness, black or tarry stool, or a significant or sudden weight gain, report this to the doctor immediately. In addition, stop taking the drug. If the drug is not effective after 1 week, stop taking it.

Possible Side Effects

Most common: stomach upset, drowsiness, water retention.

Possible Adverse Drug Effects

Gastric or duodenal ulcer, ulceration or perforation of the large bowel, bleeding from the stomach, anemia, stomach pain, vomiting, vomiting of blood, nausea, diarrhea, changes in the components of the blood, water retention, disruption of normal chemical balance of the body. This drug can cause fatal or nonfatal hepatitis, black-and-blue marks on the skin, serum sickness, drug allergy serious enough to cause shock, itching, serious rashes, fever, and signs of arthritis. It has been known to cause kidney effects including bleeding and kidney stones. Phenylbutazone may be a cause of heart disease, high blood pressure, blurred vision, bleeding in back of the eye, detachment of the retina, hearing loss, high

273

blood sugar, thyroid disease, agitation, confusion, or lethargy.

Drug Interactions

Phenylbutazone increases the effects of Insulin and oral antidiabetic agents. If you are taking antidiabetic drugs, discuss this matter with your doctor immediately.

Usual Dose

Adult and child (14 years or over): 300 to 600 milligrams per day in 3 to 4 equal doses for 7 days. If dose is effective it can then be reduced to 100 to 400 milligrams per day depending on the condition being treated.

Elderly: Drug to be given only for 7 days because of high risk of severe reactions. Not to be given to senile patients.

Child (under age 14): Not recommended.

To avoid stomach upset, take the dose with food.

Overdosage

If symptoms of convulsions, euphoria, depression, headache, hallucinations, giddiness, dizziness, coma, rapid breathing rate, continued stomach pain, and bloody or black stool appear, contact your doctor immediately.

Special Information

This drug can make you drowsy and/or tired: be careful when driving or operating equipment. Avoid alcoholic beverages.

Generic Name

Phenytoin

Brand Names

Dilantin
Diphenylan Sodium

Type of Drug

Anticonvulsant.

Prescribed for

Control of epileptic seizures.

General Information

Phenytoin is one of several drugs of the same chemical group used to control convulsions. All these drugs act by the same mechanism although some patients may respond to one and not another.

Cautions and Warnings

If you have been taking Phenytoin for a long time and no longer need it the dosage should be reduced gradually over a period of about a week. Abrupt stopping may bring on severe epileptic seizures. Pregnant women who use anticonvulsive medicine are said to tend to give birth to children with birth defects, but the data available are somewhat questionable. If you become pregnant and you are taking this medicine, consult your doctor immediately.

Possible Side Effects

Most common: slurred speech, mental confusion, ataxia or nystagmus, dizziness, insomnia, nervousness, uncontrollable twitching, double vision, tiredness, irritability, depression, tremors, headaches. These side effects will generally go away as therapy continues and the dosage is reduced.

Possible Adverse Drug Effects

Nausea, vomiting, diarrhea, constipation, fever, rashes, balding, weight gain, numbness of the hands and feet, chest pains, retention of water, sensitivity to bright lights, especially sunlight, conjunctivitis, changes of the blood system including anemia, swollen glands. Phenytoin can cause an abnormal growth of the gums surrounding the teeth, so good oral hygiene including gum massage, frequent brushing, and appropriate dental care is very important. Occasionally Phenytoin produces unusual hair growth over the body, and liver damage, including hepatitis.

Drug Interactions

A barbiturate taken with Phenytoin may increase the rate at which Phenytoin is excreted from the body; then if the barbiturate is discontinued, the patient may show an increased response to Phenytoin, and the dose may have to be reduced slightly.

Tricyclic antidepressant drugs, Warfarin, Isoniazid, Disulfiram, Phenylbutazone, and Oxyphenbutazone may cause Phenytoin to remain in the body for a longer time, increasing the incidence of Phenytoin side effects. The dose of Phenytoin may have to be adjusted by your doctor.

Usual Dose

Adult: Initial dose, 300 milligrams per day. If this does not result in satisfactory control, gradually increase to 600 milligrams per day. (The most frequent maintenance dose is 300 to 400 milligrams per day.) Medicine may be taken once daily or throughout the day, as convenient.

Child: Initial dose, 2½ milligrams per pound of body weight per day in 2 to 3 equally divided doses; then adjust according to needs and response of child (normal maintenance dose, 2 to 4 milligrams per pound of body weight per day). Children over age 6 may require the same dose as an adult, but no child should be given more than 300 milligrams per day.

Overdosage

Symptoms are those listed in "Possible Side Effects" and "Possible Adverse Drug Effects" above. The patient should be taken to a hospital emergency room immediately. ALWAYS bring the medicine bottle.

Special Information

If you get upset stomach after taking Phenytoin, take the medicine with meals. If you develop a rash, sore throat, fever, unusual bleeding, or bruising, contact your doctor immediately. Phenytoin sometimes produces a pink-brown color in the urine; don't worry about it.

Generic Name

Pilocarpine Hydrochloride Ophthalmic Solution

Brand Names

Almocarpine	Pilocar
Isopto Carpine	Pilocel
Mi-Pilo	Pilomiotin
Mistura P	P.V. Carpine Liquifilm

Type of Drug

Miotic agent.

Prescribed for

Management of open angle glaucoma (increased pressure in the eye).

General Information

Pilocarpine Hydrochloride Ophthalmic Solution is the drug of choice in the treatment of open angle glaucoma. It works on muscles in the eye to open passages so that fluid can flow normally out of the eye chamber, reducing fluid pressure inside the eye. Pilocarpine Hydrochloride Ophthalmic Solution may also help reduce the amount of fluid produced within the eye.

Although used as eye drops, the drug can affect other parts of the body, especially after long use. When this drug is prescribed, it is usually given for long periods of time, as long as eye pressure does not increase or eyesight does not worsen. The concentration of Pilocarpine Hydrochloride Ophthalmic Solution is determined by the physician, and is based on the severity of the disease. This drug is also marketed in a special form called Pilo-Ocusert—a thin football-shaped wafer designed to continuously release the drug for 1 week. This eliminates the need for putting drops in your eyes 3 to 4 times a day. The wafer is placed under the eyelid similarly to the way contact lenses are placed.

If you use the conventional eye drops, be very careful not to touch the eyelids or surrounding area with the dropper tip; otherwise you will contaminate the dropper and cause the medicine to become unsterile. Be sure you recap the bottle tightly in order to preserve the sterility of the medicine.

Cautions and Warnings

Pilocarpine Hydrochloride Ophthalmic Solution should only be used when prescribed by an eye specialist (ophthalmologist). This drug should not be used if you know you are allergic to it.

Possible Side Effects

This drug may produce spasms of the eye muscles resulting in an aching feeling over the brow. You may also find it hard to focus your eyes. These effects are seen in younger people and will disappear with continued use. Some people may complain of decreased vision in low light.

Possible Adverse Drug Effects

Allergy or itching and tearing of the eye may develop after prolonged use.

Usual Dose

Initial dose, 1 to 2 drops in the affected eye up to 6 times per day; then according to severity of disease.

At first Pilocarpine Hydrochloride Ophthalmic Solution is also placed in the healthy eye to keep it from becoming diseased.

The usual concentration of the drug ranges from 0.5 to 4 percent. Concentrations above 4 percent are used less often. The most frequently used concentrations are 1 and 2 percent.

Overdosage

After long-term use, small amounts of Pilocarpine Hydrochloride Ophthalmic Solution may be absorbed by the drainage systems of the eye. If symptoms of stomach upset, nausea, vomiting, diarrhea, and cramps appear, contact your doctor immediately.

Poly-Vi-Flor Chewable Tablets

Ingredients

Folic Acid
Sodium Fluoride
Vitamin A
Vitamin B$_1$
Vitamin B$_2$
Vitamin B$_3$
Vitamin B$_6$
Vitamin B$_{12}$
Vitamin C
Vitamin D
Vitamin E

Type of Drug

Multivitamin supplement with a fluoride.

Prescribed for

Vitamin deficiencies and prevention of dental cavities in infants and children.

General Information

Poly-Vi-Flor is a vitamin supplement containing a fluoride. Fluorides taken in small daily doses have been effective in preventing cavities in children by strengthening their teeth and making them resistant to cavity formation. Too much of a fluoride can cause damage to the teeth. Because of this, vitamins with a fluoride should only be used in areas where the water supply is not fluoridated.

Cautions and Warnings

Poly-Vi-Flor Chewable Tablets should not be used in areas where the fluoride content exceeds 0.7 ppm (part per million). Your pediatrician or local water company can tell you the fluoride content of the water you drink.

Possible Side Effects

Occasional skin rash, itching, stomach upset, headache, weakness.

Usual Dose

One tablet per day.

Generic Name

Potassium Chloride

Brand Names

Liquids
  Duo-K
  Kaochlor S-F
  Kaochlor 10%
  Kaon-Cl
  Klor-Con
  Kloride
  KLOR-10%
  Klorvess
  Kolyum
  K-10
  Pan-Kloride
  Pfiklor
  Rum-K

Powders
  Kato
  Kay Ciel
  K-Lor
  K-Lyte/Cl
  Kolyum
  Pfiklor

Effervescent tablets
  Kaochlor-Eff
  KEFF
  Klorvess
  K-Lyte/Cl

Oral tablets
  Kaon-Cl (wax matrix)
  Potassium Chloride
    Coated
  Slow-K (wax matrix)

Type of Drug

Potassium supplement.

Prescribed for

Replacement of potassium in the body.

General Information

Potassium Chloride is a very important component of the body which has a major effect on maintaining the proper tone of all body cells. Potassium Chloride is also important for the maintenance of normal kidney function. Potassium is required for the passage of electrical impulses in the nervous system, and has a major effect on the heart and all other muscles of the body.

Cautions and Warnings

Potassium replacement should always be monitored and controlled by your physician. Potassium Chloride tablets have produced ulceration in some patients with compression of the esophagus. Potassium Chloride supplements for these patients should be given in liquid form. Potassium Chloride tablets have been reported to cause ulcers of the small bowel, leading to hemorrhage, obstruction, and/or perforation.

Do not take Potassium Chloride supplements if you are dehydrated or experiencing muscle cramps due to excessive sun exposure. The drug should be used with caution in patients who have kidney and/or heart disease.

Possible Side Effects

Potassium Chloride toxicity, or overdose, is extremely rare. Toxicity can occur when high doses of Potassium Chloride supplements are taken in combination with foods high in Potassium Chloride. Common side effects are nausea, vomiting, diarrhea, and abdominal discomfort. Less common side effects are tingling of hands and feet, listlessness, mental confusion, weakness and heaviness of legs, decreased blood pressure, and/or heart rhythm changes.

Drug Interactions

Potassium Chloride supplements should not be taken with Spironolactone, Triamterene, or combinations of these drugs, as Potassium Chloride toxicity may occur.

Usual Dose

As regulated by physician, generally 20 to 60 milliequivalents.

Special Information

Directions for taking Potassium Chloride supplements should be followed closely. Liquid Potassium Chloride should be diluted properly. Effervescent tablets and Potassium Chloride supplement powders should be dissolved completely.

Generic Name

Prednisone

Brand Names

Deltasone	Pred-5
Fernisone	Ropred
Lisacort	Servisone
Meticorten	SK-Prednisone
Orasone	Sterapred
Paracort	

Type of Drug

Adrenal cortical steroid.

Prescribed for

Reduction of inflammation. The variety of disorders which Prednisone is prescribed for is almost endless, from skin rash to cancer. The drug may be used as a treatment for adrenal gland disease, since one of the hormones produced by the adrenal gland is very similar to Prednisone. If patients are not producing sufficient adrenal hormones, Prednisone may be used as replacement therapy. It may also be prescribed for the treatment of bursitis, arthritis, severe skin reactions such as psoriasis or other rashes, severe allergic conditions, asthma, drug or serum sickness, severe, acute, or chronic allergic inflammation of the eye and surrounding areas such as conjunctivitis, respiratory diseases including pneumonitis, blood disorders, gastrointestinal diseases including ulcerative colitis, and inflammation of the nerves, heart, or other organs.

General Information

Prednisone is one of many adrenal cortical steroids used in medical practice today. The major differences between Prednisone and other adrenal cortical steroids are potency of medication and variation in some secondary effects. Choice of an adrenal cortical steroid to be used for a specific disease is usually a matter of doctor preference and past experience. Other adrenal cortical steroids are Cortisone, Hydrocortisone, Prednisolone,

Triamcinolone, Methylprednisolone, Meprednisone, Paramethasone, Fluprednisolone, Dexamethasone, Betamethasone, and Fludrocortisone.

Cautions and Warnings

Because of the effect of Prednisone on your adrenal gland, it is essential that the dose be tapered from a large dose down to a small dose over a period of time. Do not stop taking this medication suddenly and/or without the advice of your doctor. If you do, you may cause a failure of the adrenal gland with extremely serious consequences.

Prednisone has a strong anti-inflammatory effect, and may mask some signs of infections. If new infections appear during the use of Prednisone therapy, they may be difficult to discover and may grow more rapidly due to your decreased resistance. If you think you are getting an infection during the time that you are taking Prednisone, you should contact your doctor, who will prescribe appropriate therapy.

If you are taking Prednisone, you should not be vaccinated against any infectious diseases because of inability of the body to produce the normal reaction to vaccination. Discuss this with your doctor before he administers any vaccination.

If you suspect that you are pregnant and are taking Prednisone, report it immediately to your doctor. If you are taking Prednisone and have just given birth, do not nurse; use prepared formulas instead.

Possible Side Effects

Stomach upset is one of the more common side effects of Prednisone, which may in some cases cause gastric or duodenal ulcers. If you notice a slight stomach upset when you take your dose of Prednisone, take this medication with food or a small amount of antacid. If stomach upset continues or bothers you, notify your doctor. Other side effects: retention of water, heart failure, potassium loss, muscle weakness, loss of muscle mass, loss of calcium from bones which may result in bone fractures and a condition known as aseptic necrosis of the femoral and humoral heads (this means the ends of the large bones in the hip may degenerate from loss of calcium), slowing down of wound healing, black-and-blue marks on the skin, increased sweating, allergic skin rash, itching, convulsions, dizziness, headache.

Possible Adverse Drug Effects

May cause irregular menstrual cycles, slowing down of growth in children, particularly after the medication has been taken for long periods of time, depression of the adrenal and/or pituitary glands, development of diabetes, increased pressure of the fluid inside the eye, hypersensitivity or allergic reactions, blood clots, insomnia, weight gain, increased appetite, nausea, and feeling of ill health. Psychic derangements may appear which range from euphoria to mood swings, personality changes, and severe depression. Prednisone may also aggravate existing emotional instability.

Drug Interactions

Prednisone and other adrenal corticosteroids may interact with Insulin or oral antidiabetic drugs, causing an increased requirement of the antidiabetic drugs.

Interaction with Phenobarbital, Ephedrine, and Phenytoin may reduce the effect of Prednisone by increasing its removal from the body.

If a doctor prescribes Prednisone you should discuss any oral anticoagulant (blood-thinning) drugs you are taking: the dose of them may have to be changed.

Interaction with diuretics such as Hydrochlorothiazide may cause you to lose blood potassium. Be aware of signs of lowered potassium level such as weakness, muscle cramps, and tiredness, and report them to your physician. Eat high potassium foods such as bananas, citrus fruits, melons, and tomatoes.

Usual Dose

Initial dose, 5 to 60 or even more milligrams; maintenance dose, 5 to 60 milligrams depending on patient's response. Dose also varies according to disease being treated. The lowest effective dose is desirable. Stressful situations may require a temporary increase in your Prednisone dose.

The drug must be tapered off slowly and not stopped abruptly. Prednisone may be given by alternate day therapy in which twice the usual daily dose is given every other day.

Overdosage

There is no specific treatment for overdosage of adrenal cortical steroids. Symptoms are anxiety, depression and/or stimulation, stomach bleeding, increased blood sugar, high blood pressure, and retention of fluid. The patient should be taken to a hospital emergency room immediately, where stomach pumping, oxygen, intravenous fluids, and other supportive treatments are available.

Generic Name

Primidone

Brand Names

Mysoline
Ro-Primidone

Type of Drug

Anticonvulsive.

Prescribed for

Control of epileptic and other seizures.

General Information

Although this drug is not a barbiturate, it is a close chemical cousin to the barbiturates and possesses many of their characteristics. It acts on a portion of the brain that inhibits the unusual nerve transmissions that are present in seizure disorders.

Cautions and Warnings

If you have been taking Primidone for a long time and no longer need it do not stop abruptly, but reduce the dosage gradually over a period of about a week. Abrupt stopping may bring on severe epileptic seizures. Pregnant women who use anticonvulsive medicine are said to tend to give birth to children with birth defects, but the data available are somewhat questionable. If you become pregnant and you are taking this medicine, consult your doctor immediately.

Possible Side Effects

Dizziness and some loss of muscle coordination. Side effects tend to disappear as time goes on.

Possible Adverse Drug Effects

Fatigue, loss of appetite, nystagmus (a rhythmic, uncontrolled movement of the eyeballs), irritability, emotional upset, sexual impotence, double vision, skin rash. If side effects are persistent or severe, your doctor may have to discontinue treatment or use a different medication.

Drug Interactions

This drug, because of its relation to barbiturates, may affect oral anticoagulants, Doxycycline, corticosteroids, or Griseofulvin. Special care should be taken if you need any sedative, sleeping pill, antidepressant, or strong analgesic, because of the possibility of drug interaction. Consult your physician or pharmacist for more information on this. Avoid alcoholic beverages, which may enhance the side effects of fatigue and dizziness normally experienced with Primidone.

Usual Dose

Adult (and child age 8 and over): 250 milligrams per day to start. Dose may be increased in steps of 250 milligrams per day, up to 1500 milligrams per day, according to patient need.

Child (under age 8): 125 milligrams per day to start. Dose may be increased in steps of 125 milligrams per day up to 750 milligrams per day, according to patient need.

Overdosage

The symptoms are those listed in "Possible Side Effects" and "Possible Adverse Drug Effects" above. The patient should be taken to a hospital emergency room immediately. ALWAYS bring the medicine bottle.

Special Information

If you get an upset stomach after taking Primidone, take the medicine with meals. If you develop a rash, sore throat, fever, unusual bleeding or bruising, contact your doctor immediately. Primidone sometimes produces a pink-brown color in the urine; this is normal, don't worry about it.

Brand Name

Pro-Banthine with Phenobarbital

Ingredients

Phenobarbital
Propantheline

Other Brand Name

Robantaline with Phenobarbital

Type of Drug

Gastrointestinal anticholinergic agent.

Prescribed for

Symptomatic relief of stomach upset and spasms. Often prescribed to treat morning sickness associated with the first trimester of pregnancy.

General Information

Pro-Banthine with Phenobarbital works by reducing spasms in muscles of the stomach and other parts of the gastrointestinal tract. This helps relieve some of the uncomfortable symptoms associated with peptic ulcer, irritable bowel and/or colon, spastic colon, and other gastrointestinal disorders. It only relieves symptoms. It does not cure the underlying disease.

Cautions and Warnings

Pro-Banthine with Phenobarbital should not be used if you know you are sensitive or allergic to Propantheline.

Do not use this medicine if you have glaucoma, asthma, obstructive disease of the gastrointestinal tract, or other serious gastrointestinal disease. Because this drug reduces your ability to sweat, its use in hot climates may cause heat exhaustion.

Possible Side Effects

Occasional: difficulty in urination, blurred vision, rapid heartbeat, palpitations, sensitivity to light, headache, flushing, nervousness, dizziness, weakness, drowsiness, inability to sleep, nausea, vomiting, fever, nasal congestion, heartburn, constipation, feeling of being bloated; also a drug allergy or a drug idiosyncratic reaction, which may include itching or other skin manifestations.

Possible Adverse Drug Effects

Elderly patients taking this drug may develop mental confusion or excitement.

Drug Interactions

Interaction with antihistamines, phenothiazines, tranquilizers, antidepressants, and some narcotic painkillers may cause blurred vision, dry mouth, or drowsiness.

Do not use with MAO inhibitor drugs, which will tend to prevent excretion of Pro-Banthine with Phenobarbital from the body and thus potentiate it (increase its effect).

Usual Dose

1 to 2 tablets 3 to 4 times per day.

Special Information

Dry mouth from Pro-Banthine with Phenobarbital can be relieved by chewing gum or sucking hard candy. Constipation can be treated with a stool softener (rather than a harsh cathartic).

Generic Name

Procainamide Hydrochloride

Brand Names

Pronestyl
Sub-Quin

Type of Drug

Antiarrhythmic.

Prescribed for

Abnormal heart rhythms.

General Information

Procainamide Hydrochloride is used to control unusual heart rhythms by affecting the response of heart muscle to nervous system stimulation. It also slows the rate at which nervous system impulses are carried in the heart. It may be given to patients who do not respond to or cannot tolerate other antiarrhythmic drugs. It is also frequently used as primary treatment for arrhythmias (unusual heart rhythms).

Cautions and Warnings

Tell your doctor if you have the disease myasthenia gravis. If you have had myasthenia gravis, you should be taking a drug other than Procainamide Hydrochloride. Tell your doctor if you are allergic to Procainamide Hydrochloride or to the local anesthetic Procaine.

Possible Side Effects

Large oral doses of Procainamide Hydrochloride may produce loss of appetite, nausea, or itching. A group of symptoms resembling the disease lupus erythematosus has been reported in patients taking the drug: fever and chills, nausea, vomiting, and abdominal pains. Your doctor may detect enlargement of your liver and changes in blood tests indicating a change in the liver. Soreness of the mouth or throat, unusual bleeding, skin rash, or fever may also occur. If any of these things happen while you are taking Procainamide Hydrochloride, tell your doctor immediately.

Possible Adverse Drug Effects

Bitter taste in the mouth, diarrhea, weakness, mental depression, giddiness, hallucinations, drug allergy (such as rash and drug fever).

Drug Interactions

Avoid over-the-counter cough, cold, or allergy remedies containing drugs which have a direct stimulating effect on your heart. Questions about over-the-counter remedies can be directed to your pharmacist, who can tell you what the ingredients of any medication are.

Usual Dose

Adult: Initial dose, 1000 milligrams; maintenance dose, 25 milligrams per pound per day in divided doses every 3 hours adjusted according to individual needs.

Storage

Store capsules in a place protected from excessive moisture; do not keep them in a bathroom medicine chest where they will be exposed to high concentrations of moisture.

Generic Name

Prochlorperazine

Brand Name

Compazine

Type of Drug

Phenothiazine antipsychotic, antinauseant.

Prescribed for

Severe nausea, vomiting, psychotic disorders, excessive anxiety, tension, and agitation.

General Information

Prochlorperazine and other members of the phenothiazine group act on a portion of the brain called the hypothalamus. They affect parts of the hypothalamus that control metabolism, body temperature, alertness, muscle tone, hormone balance, and vomiting, and may be used to treat problems related to any of these functions.

Cautions and Warnings

Sudden death has occurred in patients who have taken this drug because of its effect on the cough reflex. In some cases the patients choked to death because of failure of the cough reflex to protect them. Prochlorperazine, because of its effect in reducing vomiting, can obscure signs of toxicity due to overdose of other drugs or symptoms of disease.

Prochlorperazine should not be taken if you are allergic to one of the drugs in the broad classification of phenothiazine drugs. Do not take Prochlorperazine if you have any blood, liver, kidney, or heart disease, very low blood pressure, or Parkinson's disease. This medication is a tranquilizer and can have a depressive effect, especially during the first few days of therapy. Care should be taken when performing activities requiring a high degree of concentration, such as driving. If you are taking this medication and become pregnant contact your doctor immediately.

Possible Side Effects

Most common: drowsiness, especially during the first or second week of therapy. If the drowsiness becomes troublesome, contact your doctor.

Possible Adverse Drug Effects

Prochlorperazine can cause jaundice (yellowing of the whites of the eyes or skin), usually in 2 to 4 weeks. The jaundice usually goes away when the drug is discontinued, but there have been cases when it did not. If you notice this effect or if you develop symptoms such as fever and generally not feeling well, contact your doctor immediately. Less frequent: changes in components of the blood including anemias, raised or lowered blood pressure, abnormal heart rate, heart attack, feeling faint or dizzy.

Phenothiazines can produce "extrapyramidal effects," such as spasms of the neck muscles, severe stiffness of the back muscles, rolling back of the eyes, convulsions, difficulty in swallowing, and symptoms associated with Parkinson's disease. These effects look very serious but go away after the drug has been withdrawn; however, symptoms of the face, tongue, and jaw may persist for as long as several years, especially in the elderly with a history of brain disease. If you experience extrapyramidal effects contact your physician immediately.

Prochlorperazine may cause an unusual increase in psychotic symptoms or may cause paranoid reactions, tiredness, lethargy, restlessness, hyperactivity, confusion at night, bizarre dreams, inability to sleep, depression, and euphoria. Other reactions are itching, swelling, unusual sensitivity to bright lights, red skin, and rash. There have been cases of breast enlargement, false positive pregnancy tests, and changes in menstrual flow in females, and impotence and changes in sex drive in males. Prochlorperazine may also cause dry mouth, stuffy nose, headache, nausea, vomiting, loss of appetite, change in body temperature, loss of facial color, salivation, perspiration, constipation, diarrhea, changes in urine and stool habits, worsening of glaucoma, blurred vision, weakening of eyelid muscles, and spasms in bronchial and other muscles, as well as increased appetite, fatigue, excessive thirst, and changes in the coloration of skin, particularly in exposed areas.

Drug Interactions

Prochlorperazine should be taken with caution in combination with barbiturates, sleeping pills, narcotics, or any other medication which may produce a depressive effect. Avoid alcohol.

Usual Dose

Adult: 15 to 150 milligrams per day depending on disease and patient's response. For nausea and vomiting, 15 to 40 milligrams per day by mouth; 25 milligrams twice per day in rectal suppositories.

Child (40 to 85 pounds): 10 to 15 milligrams per day; (30 to 40 pounds), 2½ milligrams 2 to 3 times per day; (20 to 30 pounds), 2½ milligrams 1 to 2 times per day; not recommended for children under age 2 years or weight 20 pounds, except to save life. Usually only 1 to 2 days of therapy is needed for nausea and vomiting. For psychosis, doses of 25 milligrams or more per day may be required.

Overdosage

Symptoms are depression, extreme weakness, tiredness, desire to go to sleep, coma, lowered blood pressure, uncontrolled muscle spasms, agitation, restlessness, convulsions, fever, dry mouth, and abnormal heart rhythms. The patient should be taken to a hospital emergency room immediately. ALWAYS bring the medicine bottle.

Generic Name

Propantheline Bromide

Brand Name

Pro-Banthine
Pro-Banthine B.A.

Type of Drug

Gastrointestinal anticholinergic agent.

Prescribed for

Relief of stomach upset and spasms. This medication is sometimes prescribed to treat morning sickness during the early months of pregnancy.

General Information

Propantheline Bromide works by reducing spasms in muscles of the stomach and other parts of the gastrointestinal tract. In doing so, it helps relieve some of the uncomfortable symptoms associated with peptic ulcer, irritable bowel and/or colon, spastic colon, and other gastrointestinal disorders. It only relieves symptoms. It does not cure the underlying disease.

Cautions and Warnings

Propantheline Bromide should not be used if you know you are sensitive or allergic to it. Do not use this medicine if you have glaucoma, asthma, obstructive disease of the gastrointestinal tract, or other serious gastrointestinal disease. Because this drug reduces your ability to sweat, its use in hot climates may cause heat exhaustion.

Possible Side Effects

Difficulty in urination, blurred vision, rapid heartbeat, skin rash, sensitivity to light, headache, flushing of the skin, nervousness, dizziness, weakness, drowsiness, nausea, vomiting, fever, nasal congestion, heartburn, constipation.

Possible Adverse Drug Effects

Elderly patients taking this drug may develop mental confusion or excitement.

Drug Interactions

Interaction with antihistamines, phenothiazines, tranquilizers, antidepressants, and some narcotic pain-killers may cause blurred vision, dry mouth, or drowsiness.

Do not use with Tranylcypromine Sulfate (Parnate), Isocarboxazid (Marplan), Phenelzine Sulfate (Nardil), or other MAO inhibitor drugs, which will tend to prevent excretion of Propantheline Bromide from the body and thus potentiate it (increase its effect).

Usual Dose

30 milligrams at bedtime, or 7½ to 15 milligrams 3 times per day; or 7½ milligrams 3 times per day for mild symptoms.

Special Information

Dry mouth from Propantheline Bromide can be relieved by chewing gum or sucking hard candy; constipation can be treated by using a stool softening laxative.

Generic Name

Propoxyphene Hydrochloride

Brand Names

Darvon	Proxagesic
Dolene	SK-65
Pargesic 65	S-Pain-65
Progesic-65	

Type of Drug

Analgesic.

Prescribed for

Relief of pain.

General Information

Propoxyphene Hydrochloride is a chemical derivative of Methadone, a narcotic used for pain relief. It Is estimated that Propoxyphene Hydrochloride is about half to two-thirds as strong a pain reliever as Codeine and about as effective as Aspirin. Propoxyphene Hydrochloride is widely used for mild pain; it can produce drug dependence when used for extended periods of time.

Propoxyphene Hydrochloride may interfere with your ability to concentrate. Therefore, be extra careful when driving an automobile or operating complicated or dangerous machinery. Do not drink alcohol when taking this medicine. As there is a possibility that Propoxyphene Hydrochloride may affect the development of unborn children, do not take this medicine, except under your doctor's advice, if you are pregnant or suspect that you may be pregnant. Never take more medicine than is prescribed by your doctor.

Cautions and Warnings

Do not take Propoxyphene Hydrochloride if you are allergic to this or similar drugs. This drug can produce psychological or physical drug dependence (addiction). The major sign of dependence is anxiety when the drug

Is suddenly stopped. Propoxyphene Hydrochloride can be abused to the same degree as Codeine.

Possible Side Effects

Dizziness, sedation, nausea, vomiting. These effects usually go away if you lie down and relax for a few moments.

Possible Adverse Drug Effects

Infrequent: constipation, stomach pain, skin rashes, light-headedness, headache, weakness, euphoria, minor visual disturbances. Taking Propoxyphene Hydrochloride over long periods of time and in very high doses has caused psychotic reactions and convulsions.

Drug Interactions

Propoxyphene Hydrochloride may cause drowsiness. Therefore, avoid other drugs which also cause drowsiness, such as tranquilizers, sedatives, hypnotics, narcotics, and possibly antihistamines.

There may be an interaction between Propoxyphene Hydrochloride and Orphenadrine. However, this reaction is only a probability and only for patients who have a tendency toward low blood sugar.

Usual Dose

65 milligrams every 4 hours as needed.

Take with a full glass of water or with food to reduce the possibility of stomach upset.

Overdosage

Symptoms resemble those of a narcotic overdose: decrease in rate of breathing (in some people breathing rate is so low that the heart stops), changes in breathing pattern, extreme sleepiness leading to stupor or coma, pinpointed pupils, convulsions, abnormal heart rhythms, and development of fluid in the lungs. The patient should be taken to a hospital emergency room immediately. ALWAYS bring the medicine bottle.

Generic Name

Propranolol Hydrochloride

Brand Name

Inderal

Type of Drug

Beta-adrenergic blocking agent.

Prescribed for

High blood pressure, angina pectoris (a specific type of chest pain), abnormal heart rhythm, thyroid disease, and pheochromocytoma. In addition, Propranolol Hydrochloride has been studied for effects in migraine headaches, diarrhea, and other applications which may or may not be generally accepted by the medical profession.

General Information

Propranolol Hydrochloride was the first beta-adrenergic blocking agent available in the United States. The drug acts to block a major chemical reaction of the nervous system in our bodies. For this reason, it can exert a broad variety of effects, as is evident from the wide variety of diseases in which it can be used effectively. Because of this wide variety of effects, it is impossible to say specifically what you will be taking this drug for. Therefore, this information must be discussed specifically with your doctor.

Cautions and Warnings

Propranolol Hydrochloride should be used with care if you have a history of asthma or upper respiratory disease, which may become worsened by the effects of this drug.

Possible Side Effects

Propranolol Hydrochloride may decrease the heart rate; may aggravate or worsen a condition of congestive heart failure; and may produce lowered blood pressure, tingling in the extremities, light-headedness, mental depression including inability to sleep, weakness, and tiredness. It may also produce a mental depression which is reversible when the drug is withdrawn, visual disturbances, hallucinations, disorientation, and short-term memory loss. Patients taking Propranolol Hydrochloride may experience nausea, vomiting, stomach upset, abdominal cramping and diarrhea, or constipation. If you are allergic to this drug, you may show typical reactions associated with drug allergies including sore throat, fever, difficulty in breathing, and various effects on the blood system. Propranolol Hydrochloride may induce bronchospasms (spasms of muscles in the bronchi), which will make any existing asthmatic condition or any severe upper respiratory disease worse.

Possible Adverse Drug Effects

Occasionally, patients taking Propranolol Hydrochloride may experience emotional instability, or a somewhat detached or unusual personality appearance, or they may show unusual effects on the blood system.

Drug Interactions

This drug will interact with any psychotropic drug, including the MAO inhibitors, which stimulates one of the adrenergic segments of the nervous system. Since this information is not generally available, you should discuss the potential problem of using Propranolol Hydrochloride with your doctor if you are taking any psychotropic or psychiatric drug.

Propranolol Hydrochloride may cause increased effectiveness of Insulin or oral antidiabetic drugs. If you are diabetic, discuss the situation with your doctor; a reduction in dose of antidiabetic medication will probably be made.

Propranolol Hydrochloride may reduce the effectiveness of Digitalis on your heart. Any dose of Digitalis medication will have to be altered. If you are taking Digitalis for a purpose other than congestive heart failure, the effectiveness of the Digitalis may be increased by Propranolol Hydrochloride, and the dose of Digitalis may have to be reduced.

Propranolol Hydrochloride may interact with certain other drugs to produce lowering of blood pressure. This interaction has positive results in the treatment of patients with high blood pressure.

Do not self-medicate with over-the-counter cold, cough, or allergy remedies which may contain stimulant drugs that will aggravate certain types of heart disease and high blood pressure, or other ingredients that may antagonize the effects of Propranolol Hydrochloride. Double-check with your doctor or pharmacist before taking any over-the-counter medication.

Usual Dose

From 30 to 700 milligrams per day depending on disease treated and patient's response. The drug is given in the smallest effective dose; that is, the smallest dose which will produce the desired therapeutic effect.

Overdosage

Symptoms are slowed heart rate, heart failure, lowered blood pressure, and spasms of the bronchial muscles which make it difficult to breathe. The patient should be taken to a hospital emergency room where proper therapy can be given. ALWAYS bring the medicine bottle with you.

Special Information

Take Propranolol Hydrochloride before meals for maximum effectiveness.

There have been reports of serious effects on the heart when this drug is stopped abruptly. Rather, the dose should be lowered gradually from what you are taking to nothing over a period of 2 weeks.

Generic Name

Pseudoephedrine

Brand Names

D-Feda	Sudadrine Syrup
Neofed	Sudafed
Novafed	Sudecon
Pseudo-Bid	

Type of Drug

Bronchodilator-decongestant.

Prescribed for

Symptomatic relief of stuffy nose, upper respiratory congestion, or bronchospasm associated with asthma, asthmatic bronchitis, or a similar disorder.

General Information

This drug will produce central nervous system stimulation, and it should not be taken by people with heart disease or high blood pressure. Elderly people are more likely to experience adverse effects from this and other stimulant drugs; overdosage of stimulants in this age group may cause hallucinations, convulsions, depression, and even death.

Pseudoephedrine should be used with caution if you are pregnant or nursing a newborn child. It is possible to transfer a small amount of this drug to the unborn child through the placenta, or to the newborn child through the mother's breast milk.

Cautions and Warnings

Do not take Pseudoephedrine if you are allergic or sensitive to this or similar drugs or if you have severe high blood pressure, coronary artery disease (angina pectoris), or abnormal heart rhythms.

Possible Side Effects

Excessive tiredness or drowsiness, restlessness, nervousness with an inability to sleep. Less frequent: tremor, headache, palpitations, elevation of blood pressure, sweating, sleeplessness, loss of appetite, nausea, vomiting, dizziness, constipation.

Drug Interactions

Interaction with alcoholic beverages may produce excessive drowsiness and/or sleepiness, and/or inability to concentrate.

Do not self-medicate with additional over-the-counter drugs for the relief of cold symptoms: taking Pseudoephedrine with such drugs may result in aggravation of high blood pressure, heart disease, diabetes, or thyroid disease.

Do not take Pseudoephedrine if you are taking or suspect you may be taking a monoamine oxidose (MAO) inhibitor: severe elevation in blood pressure may result.

Usual Dose

Adult: 60 milligrams every 4 hours.
Child (ages 6 to 12): 30 milligrams every 4 hours.
Child (ages 2 to 6): 15 milligrams every 4 hours.
Liquid form contains 30 milligrams per teaspoon; tablets contain 30 or 60 milligrams depending upon strength prescribed; time-release dosage contains 60 to 120 milligrams (taken twice per day).

Brand Name

Quibron

Ingredients

Guiafenesin
Theophylline

Type of Drug

Antiasthmatic combination product.

Prescribed for

Relief of asthma symptoms or other upper respiratory disorders.

General Information

Quibron is one of several antiasthmatic combination products prescribed for the relief of asthmatic symptoms and other breathing problems. These products contain drugs which help relax the bronchial muscles, drugs which increase the diameter of the breathing passages, and a mild tranquilizer to help relax the patient. Other products in this class may contain similar ingredients with additional medicine to help eliminate mucus from the breathing passages.

Possible Side Effects

Large doses of Quibron can produce excitation, shakiness, sleeplessness, nervousness, chest pains, rapid or irregular heartbeat. Occasionally, patients have been known to develop hesitation or difficulty in urination.

Cautions and Warnings

Do not use this drug if you are allergic or sensitive to it or to any related drug, such as Aminophylline. If you have a stomach ulcer or heart disease, you should use this drug with caution. If you are pregnant or think that you may be pregnant you should carefully discuss the use of this drug with your doctor, since Quibron may induce an adverse effect in the unborn child.

Possible Adverse Drug Effects

Excessive urination, heart stimulation, drowsiness, muscle weakness, muscle twitching, unsteady walk. These effects are usually controlled by having your doctor adjust the dose.

Usual Dose

Capsules, 1 to 2 every 6 to 8 hours. Elixir, 1 to 2 tablespoons every 6 to 8 hours.

Special Information

Take this drug with food to avoid upset stomach.

Brand Name

Quibron Plus

Ingredients

Butabarbital
Ephedrine
Guiafenesin
Theophylline

Type of Drug

Antiasthmatic combination product.

Prescribed for

Relief of asthma symptoms or other upper respiratory disorders.

General Information

Quibron Plus is one of several antiasthmatic combination products prescribed for the relief of asthmatic symptoms and other breathing problems. These products contain drugs which help relax the bronchial muscles, drugs which increase the diameter of the breathing passages, and a mild tranquilizer to help relax the patient. Other products in this class may contain similar ingredients with additional medicine to help eliminate mucus from the breathing passages.

Possible Side Effects

Large doses of Quibron Plus can produce excitation, shakiness, sleeplessness, nervousness, chest pains, rapid or irregular heartbeat, dizziness, dryness of the nose and throat, headache, and sweating. Occasionally, patients have been known to develop hesitation or difficulty in urination.

Cautions and Warnings

Do not use this drug if you are allergic or sensitive to it or to any related drug, such as Aminophylline. If you have a stomach ulcer or heart disease, you should use this drug with caution. If you are pregnant or think that you may be pregnant you should carefully discuss the use of this drug with your doctor, since Quibron Plus may induce an adverse effect in the unborn child.

Possible Adverse Drug Effects

Excessive urination, heart stimulation, drowsiness, muscle weakness, muscle twitching, unsteady walk. These effects are usually controlled by having your doctor adjust the dose.

Drug Interactions

Quibron Plus may cause sleeplessness and/or drowsiness. Do not take this drug with alcoholic beverages.

Taking Quibron Plus or similar medicines with MAO

inhibitors can produce severe interaction. Consult your physician first.

Usual Dose

Capsules, 1 to 2 every 6 to 8 hours. Elixir, 1 to 2 table-spoons every 6 to 8 hours.

Special Information

Take this drug with food to avoid upset stomach.

Generic Name

Quinidine Sulfate

Brand Names

Cin-Quin	Quinora
Quinidex Extentabs	SK-Quinidine Sulfate

Type of Drug

Antiarrhythmic.

Prescribed for

Abnormal heart rhythms.

General Information

Derived from the bark of the cinchona tree (which gives us Quinine), the drug works by affecting the flow of potassium into and out of cells of the heart muscle (myocardium). Its basic action is slowing down of the pulse. Its action allows normal control mechanisms in the heart to take over and keep the heart beating at a normal rate and rhythm.

Cautions and Warnings

Do not take Quinidine Sulfate if you are allergic to it or a related drug. If you are pregnant use this drug only after a careful review of your state of health with your doctor.

Possible Side Effects

High doses of Quinidine Sulfate can give you rash, changes in hearing, dizziness, ringing in the ears, headache, nausea, or disturbed vision: this group of symptoms, called cinchonism, is due to ingestion of large amounts of Quinidine Sulfate and is not necessarily a toxic reaction. However, report signs of cinchonism to your doctor immediately.

Possible Adverse Drug Effects

Quinidine Sulfate may cause unusual heart rhythms, but such effects are generally found by your doctor during routine examination or electrocardiogram. It can cause nausea, vomiting, stomach pain, and diarrhea. It may affect components of the blood system and can cause headache, fever, dizziness, feeling of apprehension or excitement, confusion, delirium, disturbed hearing, blurred vision, changes in color perception, sensitivity to bright lights, double vision, difficulty seeing at night, flushing of the skin, itching, nausea, vomiting, cramps, unusual urge to defecate or urinate, and cold sweat.

Drug Interactions

If you are taking an oral anticoagulant (blood-thinning medicine) and have been given a new prescription for Quinidine Sulfate, be sure your doctor knows about the blood-thinning medication because Quinidine Sulfate may affect the ability of the anticoagulant to do its job. The anticoagulant dose may have to be adjusted for the effect of Quinidine Sulfate.

If you are taking Phenobarbital or Phenytoin, it may reduce the time that Quinidine Sulfate is effective in your body, and may increase your need for Quinidine Sulfate.

Avoid over-the-counter cough, cold, allergy, or diet preparations. These medications may contain drugs which will stimulate your heart and can be dangerous while you are taking Quinidine Sulfate. Ask your pharmacist if you have any questions about the contents of a particular cough, cold, or allergy remedy.

Usual Dose

Extremely variable, depending on disease and patient's response. Most doses are between 800 to 1200 milligrams per day.

Overdosage

Produces abnormal effects on the heart and symptoms of cinchonism. Patient should be taken to a hospital emergency room where proper therapy can be given. ALWAYS bring the medicine bottle.

Special Information

If Quinidine Sulfate gives you stomach upset, take it with food. If this does not solve the problem, contact your doctor.

Brand Name

Regroton

Ingredients

Chlorthalidone
Reserpine

Type of Drug

Antihypertensive.

Prescribed for

High blood presure.

General Information

Regroton is a good example of a drug taking advantage of a drug interaction. Each of the drug ingredients works by different mechanisms to lower your blood pressure. The Chlorthalidone relaxes the muscles in your veins and arteries and also helps reduce the volume of blood flowing through those blood vessels. Reserpine works on the nervous system to decrease the quality of nerve transmissions which are contributing to the increased pressure. These drugs complement each other so that their combined effect is better than the effect of the two individually.

It is essential that you take your medicine exactly as prescribed, for maximum benefit.

An ingredient in this drug may cause excessive loss

of potassium, which may lead to a condition called hypokalemia. Warning signs are dryness of mouth, excessive thirst, weakness, drowsiness, restlessness, muscle pains or cramps, muscle fatigue, lack of urination, abnormal heart rhythm, and upset stomach. If this happens, call your doctor. You may need potassium from some outside source which may be done by taking a potassium supplement or by eating foods such as bananas, citrus fruits, melons, and tomatoes which have high concentrations of potassium.

This drug should be stopped at the first sign of despondency, early morning insomnia, loss of appetite, or sexual impotence. Drug-induced depression may persist for several months after the drug has been discontinued; it has been known to be severe enough to result in suicide attempts. This drug should be used with care by women of childbearing age.

Cautions and Warnings

Do not take this drug if you are sensitive or allergic to either of its ingredients or if you have a history of mental depression, active peptic ulcer, or ulcerative colitis.

Possible Side Effects

People taking Regroton may experience the following: loss of appetite, stomach irritation, nausea, vomiting, cramps, diarrhea, constipation, dizziness, headache, tingling in the arms and legs, restlessness, chest pains, abnormal heart rhythms, drowsiness, depression, nervousness, anxiety, nightmares, glaucoma, blood disorders, rash, itching, fever, difficulty in breathing, muscle spasms, weakness, high blood sugar, sugar in the urine, blurred vision, stuffed nose, dryness of the mouth, or rash. Occasionally, impotence or decreased sex drive occurs.

Drug Interactions

Interaction with Digitalis or Quinidine may cause abnormal heart rhythms.

Interaction with drugs containing lithium may lead to toxic effects of lithium.

Avoid over-the-counter cough, cold, or allergy remedies containing stimulant drugs which may raise your blood pressure.

Usual Dose

Must be individualized to patient's response.

Salutensin

Ingredients

Hydroflumethiazide
Reserpine

Type of Drug

Antihypertensive.

Prescribed for

High blood pressure.

General Information

Salutensin is a good example of a drug taking advantage of a drug interaction. Each of the drug ingredients works by different mechanisms to lower your blood pressure. The Hydroflumethiazide relaxes the muscles in your veins and arteries and also helps reduce the volume of blood flowing through those blood vessels. Reserpine works on the nervous system to decrease the quality of nerve transmissions which are contributing to the increased pressure. These drugs complement each other so that their combined effect is better than the effect of the two individually.

It is essential that you take your medicine exactly as prescribed, for maximum benefit.

An ingredient in this drug may cause excessive loss of potassium, which may lead to a condition called hypokalemia. Warning signs are dryness of mouth, excessive thirst, weakness, drowsiness, restlessness, muscle pains or cramps, muscular fatigue, lack of urination, abnormal heart rhythms, and upset stomach. If this happens, call your doctor. You may need potassium from some outside source which may be done by taking a potassium supplement or by eating foods such as bananas, citrus fruits, melons, and tomatoes which have high concentrations of potassium.

This drug should be stopped at the first sign of despondency, early morning insomnia, loss of appetite, or sexual impotence. Drug-induced depression may persist for several months after the drug has been discontinued; it has been known to be severe enough to result in suicide attempts. This drug should be used with care by women of childbearing age.

Cautions and Warnings

Do not take this drug if you are sensitive or allergic to either of its ingredients or if you have a history of mental depression, active peptic ulcer, or ulcerative colitis.

Possible Side Effects

People taking Salutensin may experience the following: loss of appetite, stomach irritation, nausea, vomiting, cramps, diarrhea, constipation, dizziness, headache, tingling in the arms and legs, restlessness, chest pains, abnormal heart rhythms, drowsiness, depression, nervousness, anxiety, nightmares, glaucoma, blood disorders, rash, itching, fever, difficulty in breathing, muscle spasms, weakness, high blood sugar, sugar in the urine, blurred vision, stuffed nose, dryness of the mouth, or rash. Occasionally, impotence or decreased sex drive occurs.

Drug Interactions

Interaction with Digitalis or Quinidine may cause abnormal heart rhythms.

Interaction with drugs containing lithium may lead to toxic effects of lithium.

Avoid over-the-counter cough, cold, or allergy remedies containing stimulant drugs which may raise your blood pressure.

Usual Dose

Must be individualized to patient's response.

Brand Name

Septra

Ingredients

Sulfamethoxazole
Trimethoprim

Other Brand Name

Bactrim

Type of Drug

Urinary anti-infective.

Prescribed for

Urinary tract infections. Septra can also be used to treat infection caused by *Pneumocystis carinii*.

General Information

Septra is one of many combination products used to treat urinary tract infections. This is a unique combination because it attacks the infecting organism in two separate ways and is effective in many situations where other drugs are not.

Cautions and Warnings

Do not take this medication if you are allergic or sensitive to either ingredient or to any sulfa drug or if you are pregnant. Infants under age 2 months should not be given this combination product. Symptoms such as unusual bleeding or bruising, extreme tiredness, rash, sore throat, fever, pallor, or yellowing of the skin or whites of the eyes may be early indications of serious blood disorders. If any of these effects occur, contact your doctor immediately and stop taking the drug.

Possible Side Effects

Effects on components of the blood system, allergic reactions including itching, rash, drug fever, swelling around the eyes, arthritislike pains. Septra can also cause nausea, stomach upset, vomiting, abdominal pain, diarrhea, coating on the tongue, headache, tingling in

the arms and/or legs, depression, convulsions, hallucinations, ringing in the ears, dizziness, difficulty sleeping, feeling of apathy, tiredness, weakness, and nervousness. Septra may affect your kidneys and cause you to
produce less urine.

Usual Dose

1 to 2 tablets every 12 hours for 10 to 14 days. Oral
suspension, 2 to 4 teaspoons every 12 hours for 10 to 14
days.

Special Information

Take Septra in the exact dosage and for the exact period
of time prescribed. Do not stop taking it just because
you are beginning to feel better.

You may develop unusual sensitivity to sun or bright
light. If you have a history of light sensitivity or if you
have sensitive skin, avoid prolonged exposure to sunlight while using Septra.

Drink lots of fluid to help decrease the chances of
crystals forming in your kidneys. Take each dose with
a full glass of water.

Brand Name

Ser-Ap-Es Tablets

Ingredients

Hydralazine
Hydrochlorothiazide
Reserpine

Other Brand Name

Unipres Tablets

Type of Drug

Antihypertensive combination.

Prescribed for

High blood pressure.

General Information

Be sure to take this medicine exactly as prescribed: if you don't, the medicine will not be able to work best for you.

An ingredient in this drug may cause you to lose an excessive amount of potassium, and this may lead to a condition known as hypokalemia. Warning signs of hypokalemia are dryness of the mouth, excessive thirst, weakness, drowsiness, restlessness, muscle pain or cramps, muscular fatigue, lack of urination, abnormal heart rhythms, and upset stomach. If you notice these warning signs, call your doctor. You may need to take extra potassium to replace the loss caused by the drug. You may do this either by taking a potassium supplement (liquid, powder, or tablet), or by increasing the amounts of foods in your diet which are unusually high in potassium. Some of these foods are bananas, citrus fruits, melons, and tomatoes.

One of the ingredients in Ser-Ap-Es Tablets may cause mental depression. If you have a history of depressive problems, make sure your doctor knows, so that the appropriate changes can be made. Stop taking this drug at the first sign of despondency, early morning insomnia, loss of appetite, or sexual impotence. Drug-induced depression may persist for several months after the drug has been stopped; it has been known to be severe enough to result in suicide attempts. This drug should be used with care by women of childbearing age.

Cautions and Warnings

Do not take Ser-Ap-Es Tablets if you are sensitive or allergic to any of its ingredients or if you have a history of mental depression, active peptic ulcer, or ulcerative colitis. Long-term administration in large doses may produce symptoms similar to arthritis in a few patients. This usually resolves itself when you stop taking the drug. The recurrence of fever, chest pains, not feeling well, or other unexplained problems should be investigated further by your doctor.

Possible Side Effects

Common: headache, loss of appetite, vomiting, nausea, diarrhea, abnormal heart rate, chest pains, stomach upset, cramps, tingling in the arms and legs, restlessness, drowsiness, depression, nervousness, anxiety, nightmares, glaucoma, blood disorders, rash, itching, fever, difficulty in breathing, muscle spasms, weakness, high blood sugar, sugar in the urine, blurred vision, stuffed nose, dry mouth, rash. Impotence and decreased sex drive have also been reported.

Possible Adverse Drug Effects

Flushing of the skin, tearing of the eyes, conjunctivitis, disorientation, and anxiety are infrequent. Rarely, long-term users have developed symptoms of hepatitis.

Drug Interactions

Ser-Ap-Es Tablets may interact with MAO inhibitor drugs, Digitalis, or Quinidine.

Ser-Ap-Es Tablets will interact with drugs containing lithium, producing a higher incidence of adverse effects from the lithium products.

Avoid over-the-counter cough, cold, or allergy remedies which contain stimulant drugs, as these can counteract the effect of your antihypertensive medication.

Usual Dose

Must be individualized to patient response.

Overdosage

Symptoms are extreme lowering of blood pressure, rapid heartbeat, headache, generalized skin flushing, chest pains, and poor heart rhythms. The patient should be treated in a hospital where proper facilities and procedures are available. ALWAYS bring the medicine bottle to the emergency room.

Special Information

It is important to eat a well-balanced diet or follow the special diet given to you by your doctor. You must take your medicine exactly as prescribed.

Slight stomach upset from Ser-Ap-Es Tablets can be overcome by taking each dose with some food. If stomach pain continues or becomes severe, call your doctor.

313

Brand Name

Singlet Tablets

Ingredients

Acetaminophen
Chlorpheniramine Maleate
Phenylephrine Hydrochloride

Type of Drug

Decongestant-antihistamine.

Prescribed for

Relief of runny nose, congestion, headache, pain, and other general symptoms associated with the common cold, influenza, or other upper respiratory diseases.

General Information

Singlet Tablets is one of many products marketed to relieve the symptoms of the common cold. Most of these products contain ingredients to relieve nasal congestion or to dry up runny noses or relieve a scratchy throat. Some may contain ingredients to suppress cough, or to help eliminate unwanted mucus. All these products are good only for the relief of symptoms and do not treat the underlying problem such as the cold virus or other infections.

Cautions and Warnings

Avoid taking Singlet Tablets if you are pregnant.

Possible Side Effects

Excessive tiredness or drowsiness, restlessness, nervousness with an inability to sleep. Less frequent: tremor, headache, palpitations, elevation of blood pressure, sweating, sleeplessness, loss of appetite, nausea, vomiting, dizziness, constipation.

Drug Interactions

Interaction with alcoholic beverages may produce excessive drowsiness and/or sleepiness, or inability to concentrate.

Do not self-medicate with additional over-the-counter drugs for the relief of cold symptoms: taking Singlet Tablets with such drugs may result in aggravation of high blood pressure, heart disease, diabetes, or thyroid disease.

Do not take Singlet Tablets if you are taking or suspect you may be taking an MAO inhibitor: severe elevation in blood pressure may result.

Usual Dose

1 tablet 3 times per day.

Generic Name

Spironolactone

Brand Name

Aldactone

Type of Drug

Diuretic.

Prescribed for

High blood pressure; fluid in the body due to other diseases.

General Information

Spironolactone is a specific physiologic antagonist of aldosterone. Therefore, it provides an extremely useful approach to the treatment of excess fluid in the body related to the presence of high levels of aldosterone (hyperaldosteronism) when used alone or in combination with other diuretics.

Cautions and Warnings

Should not be used if you know you have kidney failure or high blood levels of potassium. Patients taking Spironolactone should not take potassium or foods rich in potassium.

Possible Side Effects

Drowsiness, lethargy, headache, gastrointestinal upset, cramping and diarrhea, rash, mental confusion, fever, feeling of ill health, enlargement of the breasts, inability to achieve or maintain erection in males, irregular menstrual cycles or deepening of the voice in females. These side effects are generally reversible.

Drug Interactions

Spironolactone will potentiate (increase the action of) other antihypertensive drugs; frequently it is used for this effect. The dosage of other antihypertensive drugs may be reduced as much as 50 percent when Spironolactone is added to the regimen.

Patients taking Spironolactone for the treatment of high blood pressure should not self-medicate with over-the-counter cough, cold, or allergy remedies containing stimulant drugs which may counteract its effectiveness and have an adverse effect on their hearts.

Usual Dose

Adult: High blood pressure, initial dose 2 to 4 tablets per day in divided doses; excess fluids related to other diseases, 4 tablets per day in divided doses.

Child: 1 to 1.5 milligrams per pound of body weight, if deemed necessary.

Special Information

Take the drug exactly as it has been prescribed, for maximum therapeutic effect. High blood levels of potassium associated with use of Spironolactone may cause weakness, lethargy, drowsiness, muscle pains or cramps, and muscular fatigue.

Generic Name

Sulfamethoxazole

Brand Name

Gantanol

Type of Drug

Urinary anti-infective.

Prescribed for

Urinary tract infections.

General Information

Sulfamethoxazole is a member of the group of drugs called sulfa drugs. Some sulfa drugs are used for the treatment of urinary tract infections. Others may be used for high blood pressure, diabetes mellitus, or as diuretic (water-losing) drugs. When taking Sulfamethoxazole for urinary tract infections it is essential that you take your medicine for the full course prescribed by your doctor. If you don't, your infection will not be cured and may actually become more difficult to treat. Sulfa drugs may be used to treat infections other than in the urinary tract, but they are usually the best choice for urinary infections.

Cautions and Warnings

Do not take Sulfamethoxazole if you know you are allergic to sulfa drugs, salicylates, or similar agents. Do not take this drug if you are pregnant or nursing a young child since the drug can pass from the mother into the child. Sulfamethoxazole should not be considered if you have advanced kidney disease.

Possible Side Effects

Headache, itching, skin rash, sensitivity to strong sunlight, nausea, vomiting, abdominal pains, feeling of tiredness or lassitude, hallucinations, dizziness, ringing in the ears, chills, feeling of ill health.

Possible Adverse Drug Effects

Blood diseases or alterations of normal blood components, itching of the eyes, arthritis-type pain, diarrhea, loss of appetite, stomach cramps or pains, hearing loss, drowsiness, fever, chills, loss of hair, yellowing of the skin and/or eyes, reduction in sperm count.

Drug Interactions

When Sulfamethoxazole is taken with an anticoagulent (blood-thinning) drug, any drug used to treat diabetes,

317

or Methotrexate, it will cause unusually large amounts of these drugs to be released into the bloodstream, producing symptoms of overdosage. If you are going to take Sulfamethoxazole for an extended period, your physician should reduce the dosage of these interactive drugs. Also avoid large doses of Vitamin C.

Usual Dose

Adult: First dose, 4 tablets; then 2 tablets 2 to 3 times per day.

Child (suspension): First dose, 25 to 30 milligrams per pound of body weight; then 12.5 to 15 milligrams per pound morning and evening. No more than 34 milligrams per pound per day.

Take each dose with a full glass of water.

Therapy should continue 1 to 2 days after symptoms have subsided. Take the medicine for the time prescribed by your doctor: do not stop just because you have begun to feel better.

Overdosage

Induce vomiting and give a rectal enema; then take the patient to a hospital emergency room. ALWAYS bring the medicine bottle.

Special Information

Sulfamethoxazole can cause photosensitivity—a severe reaction to strong sunlight. Avoid prolonged exposure to strong sunlight while you are taking it.

Sore throat, fever, unusual bleeding or bruising, rash, and feeling tired are early signs of serious blood disorders and should be reported to your doctor immediately.

Generic Name

Sulfasalazine

Brand Names

Azulfidine	S.A.S.-500
Azulfidine En-Tabs	Sulcolon

Type of Drug

Sulfonamide.

Prescribed for

Treatment of ulcerative colitis.

General Information

Sulfasalazine is a member of the group of drugs called sulfa drugs. Some sulfa drugs are used for their effects as anti-infectives, others are diuretics or can be used to treat diabetes mellitus. This particular drug has a unique effect in that it reduces the intestinal inflammation of ulcerative colitis.

Cautions and Warnings

Do not take Sulfasalazine if you know you are allergic to sulfa drugs, salicylates, or similar agents. Do not take this drug if you are pregnant or nursing a young child, since the drug can pass from the mother into the child. Sulfasalazine should not be considered if you have advanced kidney disease.

Possible Side Effects

Headache, itching, skin rash, sensitivity to strong sunlight, nausea, vomiting, abdominal pains, feeling of tiredness or lassitude, hallucination, dizziness, ringing in the ears, chills, feeling of ill health.

Possible Adverse Drug Effects

Blood diseases or changes in normal blood components, itching of the eyes, arthritis-type pain, diarrhea, loss of appetite, stomach cramps or pains, hearing loss, drowsiness, fever, chills, loss of hair, yellowing of the skin and/or eyes, reduction in sperm count.

Drug Interactions

When Sulfasalazine is taken with an anticoagulant (blood-thinning) drug, any drug used to treat diabetes, or Methotrexate, it will cause unusually large amounts of these drugs to be released into the bloodstream, producing symptoms of overdosage. If you are going to take Sulfasalazine for an extended period, your physician should reduce the dosage of these interactive drugs. Avoid large doses of Vitamin C.

Usual Dose

Adult: 6 to 8 tablets per day to start. Adjust dose as needed. Usual maintenance dose is 4 tablets per day.

Child: 20 to 40 milligrams per pound of body weight per day to start. Adjust dose as needed. Usual maintenance dose is 15 milligrams per pound per day.

Overdosage

Induce vomiting and give a rectal enema; then take the patient to a hospital emergency room. ALWAYS bring the medicine bottle.

Special Information

Sulfasalazine can cause photosensitivity—a severe reaction to strong sunlight. Avoid prolonged exposure to strong sunlight while you are taking it.

Sore throat, fever, unusual bleeding or bruising, rash, and feeling tired are early signs of serious blood disorders and should be reported to your doctor immediately.

Generic Name

Sulfisoxazole

Brand Names

Gantrisin	Rosoxol
J-Sul	SK-Soxazole
Lipo Gantrisin	Sulfalar

Type of Drug

Urinary anti-infective.

Prescribed for

Urinary tract infections.

General Information

Sulfisoxazole is a member of the group of drugs called sulfa drugs. Some sulfa drugs are used for the treatment of urinary tract infections. Others may be used for high blood pressure, diabetes mellitus, or as diuretic (water-losing) drugs. When taking Sulfisoxazole for urinary tract infections it is essential that you take your medicine for the full course prescribed by your doctor. If you don't, your infection will not be cured and may actually become more difficult to treat. Sulfa drugs may be used to treat infections other than in the urinary tract, but they are usually the best choice for urinary infections.

Cautions and Warnings

Do not take Sulfisoxazole if you know you are allergic to sulfa drugs, salicylates, or similar agents. Do not take this drug if you are pregnant or nursing a young child, since the drug can pass from the mother into the child. Sulfisoxazole should not be considered if you have advanced kidney disease.

Possible Side Effects

Headache, itching, skin rash, sensitivity to strong sunlight, nausea, vomiting, abdominal pains, feeling of tiredness or lassitude, hallucinations, dizziness, ringing in the ears, chills, feeling of ill health.

Possible Adverse Drug Effects

Blood diseases or changes in normal blood components, itching of the eyes, arthritis-type pain, diarrhea, loss of appetite, stomach cramps or pains, hearing loss, drowsiness, fever, chills, loss of hair, yellowing of the skin and/or eyes, reduction in sperm count.

Drug Interactions

When Sulfisoxazole is taken with an anticoagulant (blood-thinning) drug, any drug used to treat diabetes, or Methotrexate, it will cause unusually large amounts of these drugs to be released into the bloodstream, producing symptoms of overdosage. If you are going to take Sulfisoxazole for an extended period, your physician should reduce the dosage of these interactive drugs. Avoid large doses of Vitamin C.

Usual Dose

Adult: First dose, 4 to 8 tablets; then 2 to 3 tablets 4 times per day (not to exceed 12 tablets daily).

Child (over 50 pounds): Liquid suspension (Lipogantrisin), 1 teaspoon 4 times per day; liquid syrup (Gantrisin Syrup), 2 teaspoons 4 times per day.

Overdosage

Induce vomiting and give a rectal enema; then take the patient to a hospital emergency room. ALWAYS bring the medicine bottle.

Special Information

Sulfisoxazole can cause photosensitivity—a severe reaction to strong sunlight. Avoid prolonged exposure.

Sore throat, fever, unusual bleeding or bruising, rash, and feeling tired are early signs of serious blood disorders and should be reported to your doctor immediately.

Brand Name

Synalgos-DC

Ingredients

Aspirin
Caffeine
Dihydrocodeine Bitartrate
Phenacetin
Promethazine Hydrochloride

Type of Drug

Narcotic analgesic combination.

Prescribed for

Relief of mild to moderate pain.

General Information

Synalgos-DC is one of many combination products containing narcotics and analgesics. These products often also contain barbiturates or tranquilizers, and Acetaminophen may be substituted for Aspirin, or Phenacetin and/or Caffeine may be omitted. All these products are used for the relief of mild to moderate pain.

Cautions and Warnings

Do not take Synalgos-DC if you know you are allergic or sensitive to it. Long-term use of Synalgos-DC may cause drug dependence or addiction. Synalgos-DC is a respiratory depressant. Use this drug with extreme caution if you suffer from asthma or other breathing problems. Synalgos-DC affects the central nervous system, producing sleepiness, tiredness, and/or inability to concentrate. If you are pregnant or suspect that you are pregnant do not take this drug.

Possible Side Effects

Most frequent: light-headedness, dizziness, sleepiness, nausea, vomiting, loss of appetite, sweating. If these effects occur, consider calling your doctor and asking him about lowering the dose you are taking. Usually the side effects disappear if you simply lie down.

More serious side effects of Synalgos-DC are shallow breathing or difficulty in breathing.

Possible Adverse Drug Effects

Euphoria (feeling high), weakness, sleepiness, headache, agitation, uncoordinated muscle movement, minor hallucinations, disorientation and visual disturbances, dry mouth, loss of appetite, constipation, flushing of the face, rapid heartbeat, palpitations, faintness, urinary difficulties or hesitancy, reduced sex drive and/or potency, itching, skin rashes, anemia, lowered blood sugar, and a yellowing of the skin and/or whites of the eyes. Narcotic analgesics may aggravate convulsions in those who have had convulsions in the past.

Drug Interactions

Interaction with alcohol, tranquilizers, barbiturates, or sleeping pills produces tiredness, sleepiness, or inability to concentrate, and seriously increases the depressive effect of Synalgos-DC.

The Aspirin component of Synalgos-DC can affect

anticoagulant (blood-thinning) therapy. Be sure to discuss this with your doctor so that the proper dosage adjustment can be made.

Interaction with adrenal cortical steroids, Phenylbutazone, or alcohol can cause severe stomach irritation with possible bleeding.

Usual Dose

2 capsules every 4 hours.

Overdosage

Symptoms are depression of respiration (breathing), extreme tiredness progressing to stupor and then coma, pinpointed pupils of the eyes, no response to stimulation such as a pin stick, cold and clammy skin, slowing down of heartbeat, lowering of blood pressure, convulsions, and cardiac arrest. The patient should be taken to a hospital emergency room immediately. ALWAYS bring the medicine bottle.

Special Information

Drowsiness may occur: be careful when driving or operating hazardous machinery.

Take with food or ½ glass of water to prevent stomach upset.

The Phenacetin ingredient of Synalgos-DC may be toxic to your kidneys: do not take this medication for longer than 10 days unless directed by your doctor.

Brand Name

Tedral

Ingredients

Ephedrine
Phenobarbital
Theophylline

Type of Drug

Antiasthmatic combination product.

Prescribed for

Relief of asthma symptoms or other upper respiratory disorders.

General Information

Tedral is one of several antiasthmatic combination products prescribed for the relief of asthmatic symptoms and other breathing problems. These products contain drugs which help relax the bronchial muscles, other drugs which increase the diameter of the breathing passages, and a mild tranquilizer to help relax the patient. Other products in this class may contain similar ingredients plus other medicine to help eliminate mucus from the breathing passages.

Cautions and Warnings

It is recommended that you take this drug with food to help prevent stomach upset.

Possible Side Effects

Large doses of Tedral can produce excitation, shakiness, sleeplessness, nervousness, chest pains, rapid or irregular heartbeat, dizziness, dryness of the nose and throat, headache, and sweating. Occasionally, patients have been known to develop hesitation or difficulty in urination.

Possible Adverse Drug Effects

Excessive urination, heart stimulation, drowsiness, muscle weakness, muscle twitching, unsteady walk. These effects are usually controlled by having your doctor adjust the dose.

Drug Interactions

Tedral may cause sleeplessness and/or drowsiness. Do not take this drug with alcoholic beverages.

Taking Tedral or similar medicines with MAO inhibitors can produce severe interaction. Consult your doctor first.

Usual Dose

From 1 to 2 tablets every 4 hours. Sustained action

tablet, 1 tablet every 12 hours. Expectorant or suspension, 1 teaspoon per 60 pounds of body weight every 4 hours.

Terpin Hydrate with Codeine

Brand Names

Cotussis Cough Syrup
Prunicodeine Liquid

Type of Drug

Cough suppressant.

Prescribed for

Relief of coughs due to colds or other respiratory infections.

General Information

Terpin Hydrate with Codeine may make you tired or drowsy. Avoid other drugs which may have the same effect, since they will add to the drowsiness.

Cautions and Warnings

Terpin Hydrate is supposed to decrease the production of mucus and other bronchial secretions which can cause cough, but the usual dose of Terpin Hydrate with Codeine does not contain enough Terpin Hydrate to achieve this effect in most patients. The cough suppressant effect of Terpin Hydrate with Codeine is primarily due to the Codeine.

Do not take Codeine if you know you are allergic or sensitive to this drug. Long-term use of Codeine may cause drug dependence or addiction. Codeine is a respiratory depressant. Use this drug with extreme caution if you suffer from asthma or other breathing problems. Codeine affects the central nervous system, producing sleepiness, tiredness, and/or inability to concentrate. Be careful if you are driving, operating machinery, or performing other functions requiring concentration. If you are pregnant or suspect that you are pregnant do not take this drug.

Possible Side Effects

Most frequent: light-headedness, dizziness, sedation or sleepiness, nausea, vomiting, sweating. Because Terpin Hydrate with Codeine liquid contains 42 percent alcohol (84 proof), it is an easily abused drug product.

Possible Adverse Drug Effects

Euphoria (feeling high), weakness, sleepiness, headache, agitation, uncoordinated muscle movement, minor hallucinations, disorientation and visual disturbances, dry mouth, loss of appetite, constipation, flushing of the face, rapid heartbeat, palpitations, faintness, urinary difficulties or hesitancy, reduced sex drive and/or potency, itching, skin rashes, anemia, lowered blood sugar, and a yellowing of the skin and/or whites of the eyes. Narcotic analgesics may aggravate convulsions in those who have had convulsions in the past.

Drug Interactions

Because of its depressant effect and potential effect on breathing, Codeine should be taken with extreme care in combination with alcohol, sedatives, tranquilizers, antihistamines, or other depressant drugs.

Usual Dose

One to 2 teaspoons 3 or 4 times a day as needed for relief of cough.

Special Information

Try to cough up as much mucus as possible while taking this medication. This will help reduce the cough and help you get better more quickly.

Generic Name

Tetracycline

Brand Names

Achromycin	Retet
Achromycin V	Robitet
Bristacycline	Ro-Cycline
Centet	Sarocycline
Cyclopar	SK-Tetracycline
Fed-Mycin	Sumycin
G-Mycin	Tetrachel
Maytrex	Tetracyn
Paltet	Tetrex
Panmycin	T-250

Type of Drug

Broad-spectrum antibiotic effective against gram-positive and gram-negative organisms.

Prescribed for

Bacterial infections such as gonorrhea, infections of the mouth, gums, and teeth, Rocky Mountain spotted fever and other fevers caused by ticks and lice from a variety of carriers, urinary tract infections, and respiratory system infections such as pneumonia and bronchitis.

These diseases are produced by gram-positive and gram-negative organisms such as diplococci, staphylococci, streptococci, gonococci, *E. coli,* and *Shigella.*

Tetracycline has also been successfully used to treat some skin infections, but it is not considered the first-choice antibiotic for the treatment of general skin infections or wounds.

General Information

Tetracycline works by interfering with the normal growth cycle of the invading bacteria, preventing them from reproducing and thus allowing the body's normal defenses to fight off the infection. This process is referred to as bacteriostatic action. Tetracycline has also been used along with other medicines to treat amoebic infections of the intestinal tract, known as amoebic dysentery. It is also prescribed for diseases caused by ticks, fleas, and lice.

Tetracycline has been successfully used in the treatment of adolescent acne, using small doses over a long period of time. Adverse effects or toxicity in this type of therapy are almost unheard of.

Since the action of this antibiotic depends on its concentration within the invading bacteria, it is imperative that you, the patient, completely follow the doctor's directions.

Cautions and Warnings

You should not use Tetracycline if you are pregnant. Tetracycline when used in children has been shown to interfere with the development of the long bones and may retard growth.

Exceptions would be when Tetracycline is the only effective antibiotic available and all risk factors have been made known to the patient.

Tetracycline should not be given to people with known liver disease or kidney or urine excretion problems. You should avoid taking high doses of Tetracycline or undergoing extended Tetracycline therapy if you will be exposed to sunlight for a long period because this antibiotic can interfere with your body's normal sun-screening mechanism, possibly causing a severe sunburn. If you have a known history of allergy to Tetracycline you should avoid taking this drug or other drugs within this category such as Aureomycin, Terramycin, Rondomycin, Vibramycin, Declomycin, and Minocin.

Possible Side Effects

As with other antibiotics, the common side effects of Tetracycline are stomach upset, nausea, vomiting, diarrhea, and skin rash. Less common side effects include hairy tongue, itching and irritation of the anal and/or vaginal region. If these symptoms appear, consult your physician immediately. Periodic physical examinations and laboratory tests should be given to patients who are on long-term Tetracycline.

Possible Adverse Drug Effects

Tetracycline may produce loss of appetite, peeling of the skin, sensitivity to the sun, fever, chills, anemia, possible brown spotting of the skin, decrease in kidney function, and damage to the liver.

Drug Interactions

Tetracycline (a bacteriostatic drug) may interfere with the action of bactericidal agents such as Penicillin. It is not advisable to take both during the same course of therapy.

The antibacterial effect of Tetracycline is neutralized when taken with food, some dairy products (such as milk and cheese), and antacids.

Don't take multivitamin products containing minerals at the same time as Tetracycline, or you may reduce the antibiotic's effectiveness. You may take these two medicines at least 2 hours apart.

People receiving anticoagulation therapy (blood-thinning agents) should consult their doctor, since Tetracycline will interfere with this form of therapy. An adjustment in the anticoagulation dosage may be required.

Usual Dose

Adult: 250 to 500 milligrams 4 times per day.

Child (age 9 and over): 50 to 100 milligrams 4 times a day.

Take on an empty stomach 1 hour before or 2 hours after meals.

Child (up to age 8): Should avoid Tetracycline as it has been shown to produce serious discoloration of the permanent teeth.

Storage

Tetracycline can be stored at room temperature.

Special Information

Do *not* take after the expiration date on the label. The decomposition of Tetracycline produces a highly toxic substance which can cause serious kidney damage.

Theophylline

Brand Names

Accurbron	Somophyllin
Adophyllin	Synophylate-L.A. Cenules
Aerolate	Theobid
Aqualin Supprettes	Theo-dur
(suppositories)	Theolair
Bronkodyl	Theo-Lix
Elixicon	Theolixer
Elixophyllin	Theon
Lanophyllin	Theophyl
Liquophylline	Theophyl-225
Norophylline	Theospan
Slo-Phyllin	Theotal

Type of Drug

Xanthine bronchodilator.

Prescribed for

Relief of bronchial asthma and spasms of bronchial muscles associated with emphysema, bronchitis, and other diseases.

General Information

Theophylline is one of several drugs known as xanthine derivatives which are the mainstay of therapy for bronchial asthma and similar diseases. Other members of this group are Aminophylline, Dyphylline, and Oxtriphylline. Although the dosage for each of these drugs is different, they all work by relaxing bronchial muscles and helping reverse spasms in these muscles.

Cautions and Warnings

Do not use this drug if you are allergic or sensitive to it or to any related drug, such as Aminophylline. If you have a stomach ulcer or heart disease, you should use this drug with caution. If you are pregnant or think that you may be pregnant you should carefully discuss the use of this drug with your doctor, since Theophylline may induce an adverse effect in the unborn child.

Possible Side Effects

Possible side effects from Theophylline or other xan-thine derivatives are nausea, vomiting, stomach pain, diarrhea, irritability, restlessness, difficulty sleeping, excitability, muscle twitching or spasms, heart palpita-tions, other unusual heart rates, low blood pressure, rapid breathing, and local irritation (particularly if a suppository is used).

Possible Adverse Drug Effects

Infrequent: vomiting blood, fever, headache, dehydra-tion.

Drug Interactions

Taking Theophylline at the same time as another xan-thine derivative may increase side effects. Don't use together except under the direct care of a doctor.

Theophylline is often given in combination with a stimulant drug such as Ephedrine. Such combinations can cause excessive stimulation and should be used only as specifically directed by your doctor.

Some reports have indicated that combining Eryth-romycin and Theophylline will give you higher blood levels of Theophylline. Remember that higher blood levels mean the possibility of more side effects.

Usual Dose

Adult: 100 to 200 milligrams every 6 hours.

Child: 50 to 100 milligrams every 6 hours. On the basis of body weight, 1 to 2½ milligrams per pound every 6 hours.

The best dose of Theophylline for you is tailored to your needs and severity of your disease: the lowest dose that will produce maximum control of your symp-toms.

Overdosage

The first symptoms are loss of appetite, nausea, vomit-ing, difficulty sleeping, and restlessness, followed by unusual behavior patterns, frequent vomiting, and ex-treme thirst, with delirium, convulsions, very high tem-perature, and collapse. These serious toxic symptoms are rarely experienced after overdose by mouth, which produces loss of appetite, nausea, vomiting, and stimulation. The overdosed patient should be taken to a hospital emergency room where proper treatment can be given.

Special Information

Take on an empty stomach, at least 1 hour before or 2 hours after meals; but occasional mild stomach upset can be minimized by taking the dose with some food (note if you do this a reduced amount of drug will be absorbed into your bloodstream).

Generic Name

Thioguanine

Brand Name

Thioguanine

Type of Drug

Antimetabolite, antineoplastic.

Prescribed for

Treatment of leukemia.

General Information

Thioguanine is a member of the antimetabolite group of drugs used to treat neoplastic diseases. These drugs work by interfering with the metabolism of the cancerous cells. In doing so, they disrupt the cell division cycle of the disease and slow its progress.

Cautions and Warnings

Blood counts should be taken once a week while on Thioguanine to avoid excessive lowering of white-cell counts. It should be used with extreme care by pregnant women (and then only after the first 3 months of pregnancy), and by patients with kidney or liver disease.

Possible Side Effects

Nausea, vomiting, loss of appetite, stomach irritation or pains.

Usual Dose

1 to 1½ milligrams per pound of body weight per day, given in a single dose, adjusted to patient response.

Overdosage

Overdosage with Thioguanine leads to an excessive drop in white blood cell counts. In case of overdosage, bring the patient to a hospital emergency room immediately. ALWAYS bring the medicine bottle.

Special Information

Because of the nature of the disease treated with this drug, it is absolutely essential that you remain in close contact with the doctor providing your treatment, to obtain maximum benefit with minimum side effect.

Generic Name

Thioridazine Hydrochloride

Brand Name

Mellaril

Type of Drug

Phenothiazine antipsychotic.

Prescribed for

Psychotic disorders, moderate to severe depression with anxiety, control of agitation or aggressiveness of disturbed children, alcohol withdrawal symptoms, intractable pain, and senility.

General Information

Thioridazine Hydrochloride and other members of the phenothiazine group act on a portion of the brain called the hypothalamus. They affect parts of the hypothalamus that control metabolism, body temperature, alertness, muscle tone, hormone balance, and vomiting, and may be used to treat problems related to any of these functions.

Cautions and Warnings

Thioridazine Hydrochloride should not be taken if you are allergic to one of the phenothiazine drugs. Do not take Thioridazine Hydrochloride if you have any blood, liver, kidney, or heart disease, very low blood pressure, or Parkinson's disease. This medication is a tranquilizer and can have a depressive effect, especially during the first few days of therapy. Care should be taken when performing activities requiring a high degree of concentration, such as driving. If you are taking this medication and become pregnant contact your doctor immediately.

Possible Side Effects

Most common: drowsiness, especially during the first or second week of therapy. If drowsiness becomes troublesome, contact your doctor.

Possible Adverse Drug Effects

Thioridazine Hydrochloride can cause jaundice (yellowing of the whites of the eyes or skin), usually in 2 to 4 weeks. The jaundice usually goes away when the drug is discontinued, but there have been cases when it did not. If you notice this effect or if you develop symptoms such as fever and generally not feeling well, contact your doctor immediately. Less frequent: changes in components of the blood including anemias, raised or lowered blood pressure, abnormal heart rates, heart attack, feeling faint or dizzy.

Phenothiazines can produce "extrapyramidal effects," such as spasm of the neck muscles, severe stiffness of the back muscles, rolling back of the eyes, convulsions, difficulty in swallowing, and symptoms associated with Parkinson's disease. These effects look very serious but go away after the drug has been withdrawn; however, symptoms of the face, tongue, and jaw may persist for as long as several years, especially in the elderly with a history of brain damage. If you experience extrapyramidal effects, contact your doctor immediately.

Thioridazine Hydrochloride may cause an unusual increase in psychotic symptoms or may cause paranoid reactions, tiredness, lethargy, restlessness, hyperactivity, confusion at night, bizarre dreams, inability to sleep, depression, and euphoria. Other reactions are itching, swelling, unusual sensitivity to bright lights, red skin, and rash. There have been cases of breast enlargement, false positive pregnancy tests, changes in menstrual flow in females, and impotence and changes in sex drive in males. Thioridazine Hydrochloride may also cause dry mouth, stuffy nose, headache, nausea, vomiting, loss of appetite, change in body temperature, loss of facial color, salivation, perspiration, constipation, diarrhea, changes in urine and stool habits, worsening of glaucoma, blurred vision, weakening of eyelid muscles, and spasms in bronchial and other muscles, as well as increased appetite, fatigue, excessive thirst, and changes in the coloration of skin, particularly in exposed areas.

Drug Interactions

Thioridazine Hydrochloride should be taken with caution in combination with barbiturates, sleeping pills, narcotics, or any other medication which may produce a depressive effect. Avoid alcohol.

Usual Dose

Adult: For the treatment of psychosis, 50 to 100 milligrams 3 times per day at first; then 50 to 800 milligrams per day as required to control symptoms effectively without overly sedating the patient.
Child (ages 2 to 12): 0.5 to 1.5 milligrams per pound of body weight per day.

Overdosage

Symptoms are depression, extreme weakness, tiredness, desire to go to sleep, coma, lowered blood pressure, uncontrolled muscle spasms, agitation, restlessness, convulsions, fever, dry mouth, and abnormal heart rhythms. The patient should be taken to a hospital emergency room immediately. ALWAYS bring the medicine bottle.

Generic Name
Thiothixene

Brand Name
Navane

Type of Drug
Thioxanthene antipsychotic.

Prescribed for
Psychotic disorders.

General Information
Thiothixene is one of many nonphenothiazine agents used in the treatment of psychosis. The drugs in this group are usually about equally effective when given in therapeutically equivalent doses. The major differences are in type and severity of side effects. Some patients may respond well to one and not at all to another: this variability is not easily explained and is thought to relate to inborn biochemical differences.

Cautions and Warnings
Thiothixene should not be used by patients who are allergic to it. Patients with blood, liver, kidney or heart disease, very low blood pressure, or Parkinson's disease should avoid this drug.

Possible Side Effects
Most common: drowsiness, especially during the first or second week of therapy. If the drowsiness becomes troublesome, contact your doctor.

Possible Adverse Drug Effects
Thiothixene can cause jaundice (yellowing of the whites of the eyes or skin), usually in 2 to 4 weeks. The jaundice usually goes away when the drug is discontinued, but there have been cases when it did not. If you notice this effect or if you develop symptoms such as fever and generally do not feel well, contact your doctor immediately. Less frequent: changes in components

337

of the blood including anemias, raised or lowered blood pressure, abnormal heartbeat, heart attack, feeling faint or dizzy.

Thioxanthene drugs can produce extrapyramidal effects such as spasms of the neck muscles, severe stiffness of the back muscles, rolling back of the eyes, convulsions, difficulty in swallowing, and symptoms associated with Parkinson's disease. These effects look very serious but go away after the drug has been withdrawn; however, symptoms of the face, tongue, and jaw may persist for several years, especially in the elderly with a long history of brain damage. If you experience extrapyramidal effects contact your doctor immediately.

Thiothixene may cause an unusual increase in psychotic symptoms or may cause paranoid reactions, tiredness, lethargy, restlessness, hyperactivity, confusion at night, bizarre dreams, inability to sleep, depression, or euphoria. Other reactions are itching, swelling, unusual sensitivity to bright lights, red skin, and rash. There have been cases of breast enlargement, false positive pregnancy tests, changes in menstrual flow in females, and impotence and changes in sex drive in males.

Thiothixene may also cause dry mouth, stuffy nose, headache, nausea, vomiting, loss of appetite, change in body temperature, loss of facial color, salivation, perspiration, constipation, diarrhea, changes in urine and stool habits, worsening of glaucoma, blurred vision, weakening of eyelid muscles, and spasms in bronchial and other muscles, as well as increased appetite, fatigue, excessive thirst, and changes in the coloration of skin, particularly in exposed areas.

Drug Interactions

Thiothixene should be taken with caution in combination with barbiturates, sleeping pills, narcotics, or any other medication which produces a depressive effect. Avoid alcohol.

Usual Dose

Adult (and child age 12 and over): 2 milligrams 3

times per day to start. Dose is increased according to patient need and may go to 60 milligrams per day.

Child (under age 12): Not recommended.

Overdosage

Symptoms are depression, extreme weakness, tiredness, desire to go to sleep, coma, lowered blood pressure, uncontrolled muscle spasms, agitation, restlessness, convulsions, fever, dry mouth, and abnormal heart rhythms. The patient should be taken to a hospital emergency room immediately. ALWAYS bring the medicine bottle.

Generic Name

Thyroglobulin

Brand Name

Proloid

Type of Drug

Thyroid replacement.

Prescribed for

Replacement of thyroid hormone or low output of hormone from the thyroid gland.

General Information

Thyroglobulin is used to replace the normal output of the thyroid gland when it is unusually low. The drug is obtained from purified extract of frozen hog thyroid and is chemically standardized according to its iodine content. Thyroglobulin, or other forms of thyroid therapy, may be used for short periods in some people or for long periods in others. Some people take a thyroid replacement drug for their entire lives. It is important for your doctor to check periodically that you are receiving the correct dose. Occasionally a person's need for thyroid changes. As this need changes, the dose should also be changed: your doctor can only do this by checking certain blood tests.

Thyroglobulin is one of several thyroid replacement products available. The major difference between these products is in effectiveness in treating certain phases of thyroid disease.

Cautions and Warnings

If you have hyperthyroid disease or high output of thyroid hormone you should not use Thyroglobulin. Symptoms of hyperthyroid disease include headache, nervousness, sweating, rapid heartbeat, chest pains, and other signs of central nervous system stimulation. If you have heart disease or high blood pressure, thyroid replacement therapy should not be used unless it is clearly indicated and supervised by your doctor. If you develop chest pains or other signs of heart disease while you are taking thyroid medication, contact your doctor immediately.

Possible Side Effects

Most common: palpitations of the heart, rapid heartbeat, abnormal heart rhythms, weight loss, chest pains, shaking of the hands, headache, diarrhea, nervousness, inability to sleep, heat discomfort, and sweating. These symptoms may be controlled by adjusting the dose of the medication. If you are suffering from one or more side effects, you must contact your physician immediately so that the proper dose adjustment can be made.

Drug Interactions

Interaction of Thyroglobulin with Cholestyramine (Questran) can be avoided by spacing the two doses at least 4 hours apart.

Avoid over-the-counter products containing stimulant drugs, such as many drugs used to treat coughs, colds, or allergies, which will affect your heart and may cause symptoms of overdosage.

Thyroid replacement therapy may increase the effect of anticoagulant (blood-thinning) drugs such as Warfarin or Bishydroxycoumarin. Be sure you report this to your physician as it will be necessary to reduce the dose of your anticoagulant drug by approximately one-third at the beginning of thyroid therapy (to avoid hemorrhage). Further adjustments may be made later after your doctor reviews your blood tests.

Diabetics may have to increase their dose of Insulin or oral antidiabetic drugs. Changes in dose must be made by a physician.

Usual Dose

Initial dose, 16 milligrams (¼ grain) per day, then increase at intervals of 1 to 2 weeks until response is satisfactory. Maintenance dose, 32 to 190 milligrams per day or even higher.

Overdosage

Symptoms are headache, irritability, nervousness, sweating, rapid heartbeat with unusual stomach rumbling and with or without cramps, chest pains, heart failure, and shock. The patient should be taken to a hospital emergency room immediately. ALWAYS bring the medicine bottle.

Generic Name

Thyroid Hormone

Brand Names

Delcoid	Thyrocrine
S-P-T	Thyroglandular
Thyrar	Thyro-Teric

Type of Drug

Thyroid replacement.

Prescribed for

Replacement of thyroid hormone or low output of hormone from the thyroid gland.

General Information

Thyroid Hormone is one of several thyroid replacement products available. The major difference between these products is in effectiveness in treating certain phases of thyroid disease.

Cautions and Warnings

If you have hyperthyroid disease or high output of thyroid hormone you should not use Thyroid Hormone. Symptoms of hyperthyroid disease include headache, nervousness, sweating, rapid heartbeat, chest pains, and other signs of central nervous system stimulation. If you have heart disease or high blood pressure, thyroid replacement therapy should not be used unless it is clearly indicated and is supervised by your doctor. If you develop chest pains or other signs of heart disease while you are taking thyroid medication, contact your doctor immediately.

Possible Side Effects

Most common: palpitations of the heart, rapid heartbeat, abnormal heart rhythms, weight loss, chest pains, shaking of the hands, headache, diarrhea, nervousness, inability to sleep, heat discomfort and sweating. These symptoms may be controlled by adjusting the dose of the medication. If you are suffering from one or more side effects, contact your doctor immediately so that the proper dose adjustment can be made.

Drug Interactions

Interaction of Thyroid Hormone with Questran can be avoided by spacing the two doses at least 4 hours apart.

Avoid over-the-counter products containing stimulant drugs used to treat coughs, colds, or allergies, which will affect your heart and may cause symptoms of overdosage.

Thyroid replacement therapy may increase the effect of anticoagulant (blood-thinning) drugs such as Warfarin or Bishydroxycoumarin. Be sure you report this to your physician as it will be necessary to reduce the dose of your anticoagulant drug by approximately one-third at the beginning of thyroid therapy (to avoid hemorrhage). Further adjustments may be made later after your doctor reviews your blood tests.

Diabetics may have to increase their dose of Insulin or oral antidiabetic drugs. Changes in dose must be made by a doctor.

Usual Dose

The dose is tailored to the individual.

Adult: Initial dose, 15 to 30 milligrams per day depending on severity of disease; then increase gradually to 180 milligrams per day.

Child: Initial dose, same as adult; but children may require greater maintenance doses because they are growing.

Take in 1 dose before breakfast.

Overdosage

Symptoms are headache, irritability, nervousness, sweating, rapid heartbeat with unusual stomach rumbling and with or without cramps, chest pains, heart failure, and shock. The patient should be taken to a hospital emergency room immediately. ALWAYS bring the medicine bottle.

Generic Name

Tolazamide

Brand Name

Tolinase

Type of Drug

Oral antidiabetic.

Prescribed for

Diabetes mellitus (sugar in the urine).

General Information

Tolazamide is one of several oral antidiabetic drugs that work by stimulating the production and release of insulin from the pancreas. The primary difference between these drugs lies in their duration of action. Because these drugs do not lower blood sugar directly, they require some function of pancreas cells.

Cautions and Warnings

Mild stress such as infection, minor surgery, or emotional upset reduces the effectiveness of Tolazamide. Remember that while you are taking this drug you should be under your doctor's continuous care.

Tolazamide is used as an aid to, not a substitute for, a diet. Diet remains of primary importance in the treatment of your diabetes. Follow the diet plan your doctor has prescribed for you.

Tolazamide and similar drugs are not oral Insulin, nor are they a substitute for Insulin. They do not lower blood sugar by themselves.

The treatment of diabetes is your responsibility. You should follow all instructions about diet, body weight, exercise, personal hygiene, and all measures to avoid infection. If you are not feeling well, or if you have symptoms such as itching, rash, yellowing of the skin or eyes, abnormally light-colored stools, low-grade fever, sore throat, or diarrhea—contact your doctor immediately.

Possible Side Effects

Common: loss of appetite, nausea, vomiting, stomach upset. At times you may experience weakness or tingling in the hands and feet. These effects can be eliminated by reducing the daily dose or, if necessary, by switching to a different oral antidiabetic drug. This decision must be made by your doctor.

Possible Adverse Drug Effects

Tolazamide may produce abnormally low levels of blood sugar when too much is taken for your immediate requirements. (Other medical factors which may cause lowering of blood sugar are liver or kidney disease, malnutrition, age, drinking alcohol, and diseases of the glands.)

Tolazamide may cause a yellowing of the whites of the eyes or skin, itching, rash, or changes in laboratory tests made by your doctor. Usually these reactions will disappear in time. If they persist you should contact your doctor.

Drug Interactions

Thiazide diuretics may call for a higher dose of Tolazamide, while Insulin, sulfa drugs, Oxyphenbutazone, Phenylbutazone, Aspirin and other salicylates, Probenecid, Dicoumarol, Bishydroxycoumarin, Warfarin, Phenyramidol, and MAO inhibitor drugs prolong and enhance the action of Tolazamide, possibly requiring dose reduction.

Interaction with alcoholic beverages will cause flushing of the face and body, throbbing pain in the head and neck, difficult breathing, nausea, vomiting, sweating, thirst, chest pains, palpitations, lowered blood pressure, weakness, dizziness, blurred vision, and confusion. If you experience these reactions contact your doctor immediately.

Because of the stimulant ingredients in many over-the-counter drug products for the relief of coughs, colds, and allergies, avoid them unless your doctor advises otherwise.

Usual Dose

Moderate diabetes, 100 to 250 milligrams daily. Severe diabetes, 500 to 1000 milligrams daily.

Overdosage

A mild overdose of Tolazamide lowers the blood sugar, which can be treated by eating sugar in such forms as candy and orange juice. A patient with a more serious overdose should be taken to a hospital emergency room immediately. ALWAYS bring the medicine bottle.

Generic Name

Tolbutamide

Brand Name
Orinase

Type of Drug
Oral antidiabetic.

Prescribed for
Diabetes mellitus (sugar in the urine).

General Information

Tolbutamide is one of several oral antidiabetic drugs that work by stimulating the production and release of insulin from the pancreas. The primary difference between these drugs lies in their duration of action. Because they do not lower blood sugar directly, they require some function of pancreas cells.

Cautions and Warnings

Mild stress such as infection, minor surgery, or emotional upset reduces the effectiveness of Tolbutamide. Remember that while taking this drug you should be under your doctor's continuous care.

Tolbutamide is an aid to, not a substitute for, a diet. Diet remains of primary importance in the treatment of your diabetes. Follow the diet plan your doctor has prescribed for you.

Tolbutamide and similar drugs are not oral Insulin, nor are they a substitute for Insulin. They do not lower blood sugar by themselves.

The treatment of diabetes is your responsibility. You should follow all instructions about diet, body weight, exercise, personal hygiene, and all measures to avoid infection. If you are not feeling well, or if you have symptoms such as itching, rash, yellowing of the skin or eyes, abnormally light-colored stools, a low-grade fever, sore throat, or diarrhea—contact your doctor immediately.

Possible Side Effects

Common: loss of appetite, nausea, vomiting, stomach upset. At times you may experience weakness or tingling in the hands and feet. These effects can be eliminated by reducing the daily dose of Tolbutamide or, if necessary, switching to a different oral antidiabetic drug. This decision must be made by your doctor.

Possible Adverse Drug Effects

Tolbutamide may produce abnormally low levels of blood sugar when too much is taken for your immediate requirements. (Other factors which may cause lower-

346

ing of blood sugar are liver or kidney disease, malnutrition, age, drinking alcohol, and diseases of the glands.)

Tolbutamide may cause a yellowing of the whites of the eyes or skin, itching, rash, or changes in the results of laboratory tests made by your doctor. Usually these reactions will disappear in time. If they persist you should contact your doctor.

Drug Interactions

Thiazide diuretics may call for a higher dose of Tolbutamide, while Insulin, sulfa drugs, Oxyphenbutazone, Phenylbutazone, Aspirin and other salicylates, Probenecid, Dicoumarol, Bishydroxycoumarin, Warfarin, Phenyramidol, and MAO inhibitor drugs prolong and enhance the action of Tolbutamide, possibly requiring dose reduction.

Interaction with alcoholic beverages will cause flushing of the face and body, throbbing pain in the head and neck, difficult breathing, nausea, vomiting, sweating, thirst, chest pains, palpitations, lowered blood pressure, weakness, dizziness, blurred vision, and confusion. If you experience these reactions contact your doctor immediately.

Because of the stimulant ingredients in many over-the-counter drug products for the relief of coughs, colds, and allergies, avoid them unless your doctor advises otherwise.

Usual Dose

Begin with 1 to 2 grams per day; then increase or decrease according to patient's response. Maintenance dose, 250 milligrams to 2 (or, rarely, 3) grams per day.

Overdosage

A mild overdose of Tolbutamide lowers the blood sugar, which can be treated by eating sugar in such forms as candy and orange juice. A patient with a more serious overdose should be taken to a hospital emergency room immediately. ALWAYS bring the medicine bottle.

Tolmetin Sodium

Brand Name

Tolectin

Type of Drug

Nonsteroid anti-inflammatory.

Prescribed for

Relief of pain and inflammation of joints and muscles; arthritis.

General Information

Tolmetin Sodium is one of several new drugs used to treat various types of arthritis. These drugs reduce inflammation and share side effects, the most common of which is possible formation of ulcers and upset stomach. The drugs are roughly comparable to Aspirin in controlling the symptoms of arthritis, and are used by some people who cannot tolerate Aspirin.

Cautions and Warnings

Do not take Tolmetin Sodium if you are allergic or sensitive to this drug, Aspirin, or other nonsteroid anti-inflammatory drugs. Tolmetin Sodium may cause stomach ulcers.

Possible Side Effects

Stomach upset, blurred vision, darkening of stool, changes in color vision, skin rash, weight gain, retention of fluids.

Possible Adverse Drug Effects

Most frequent: stomach upset, dizziness, headache, drowsiness, ringing in the ears. Other: heartburn, nausea, vomiting, bloating, gas in the stomach, stomach pain, diarrhea, constipation, dark stool, nervousness, insomnia, depression, confusion, tremor, lack of appetite, fatigue, itching, rash, double vision, abnormal heart rhythm, anemia or other changes in the composition of the blood, changes in liver function, loss of hair, tingling in the hands and feet, fever, breast enlargement, lowered blood sugar, occasional effects on the kidneys. If symptoms appear, stop taking the medicine and see your doctor immediately.

Drug Interactions

Tolmetin Sodium increases the action of Phenytoin, sulfa drugs, drugs used to control diabetes, and drugs used to thin the blood. If you are taking any of these medicines, be sure you discuss it with your doctor, who will probably change the dose of the other drug.

Usual Dose

Adult: 400 milligrams 3 times per day, to start. Dosage must then be adjusted to individual need. Do not take more than 2000 milligrams per day. If upset stomach occurs, take each dose with food, milk, or antacid.

Child (age 2 and over): 9 milligrams per pound of body weight given in divided doses 3 to 4 times per day, to start. Adjust dose to individual need. Do not give more than 13.5 milligrams per pound of body weight to a child.

Child (under age 2): Not recommended.

Generic Name

Triamcinolone Acetonide Ointment/Cream/Gel

Brand Names

Aristocort	Kenalog
Aristoderm	Tramacin
Aristogel	

Type of Drug

Corticosteroid.

Prescribed for

Relief of inflammation in a local area, itching, or some other dermatological (skin) problem.

General Information

Triamcinolone Acetonide is used to relieve the symptom of any itching, rash, or inflammation of the skin. It does not treat the underlying cause of the skin problem, only the symptom. It exerts this effect by interfering with natural body mechanisms that produced the rash, itching, etc., in the first place. If you use this drug without finding the cause of the problem, the problem may return after you stop using the drug. Triamcinolone Acetonide should not be used without your doctor's consent because it could cover an important reaction, one that may be valuable to him in treating you.

Cautions and Warnings

Triamcinolone Acetonide should not be used if you have viral diseases of the skin (herpes), fungal infections of the skin (athlete's foot), or tuberculosis of the skin, nor should it be used in the ear if the eardrum has been perforated. People with a history of allergies to any of the components of the ointment, cream, or gel should not use this drug.

Possible Side Effects

After topically applying this drug, some people may experience burning sensations, itching, irritation, dryness, and secondary infection.

Special Information

Clean the skin before applying Triamcinolone Acetonide to prevent secondary infection. Apply in a very thin film (effectiveness is based on contact area and not on the thickness of the layer applied).

Brand Name

Triavil

Ingredients

Amitriptyline Hydrochloride
Perphenazine

Other Brand Name

Etrafon

Type of Drug

Antidepressant-tranquilizer combination.

Prescribed for

Relief of symptoms of anxiety and/or depression associated with chronic physical or psychiatric disease.

General Information

Triavil and other psychotherapeutic agents are effective in treating various symptoms of psychological or psychiatric disorders. These disorders may come from organic disease or may be signs of psychiatric illness. Triavil must be used only under the supervision of a doctor. Triavil usually takes several weeks to work, so don't expect instant results. It will take a minimum of 2 weeks to 1 month for this medication to show beneficial effect. If you feel there has been no change in symptoms after 6 to 8 weeks, contact your doctor and discuss it with him. He may tell you to continue taking the medicine and give it more time, or he may give you another drug which he feels will be more effective.

Cautions and Warnings

Do not take Triavil if you are allergic to it or to any related compound. For more information on drugs related to the ingredients found in Triavil, consult the entries for Amitriptyline and Chlorpromazine. Do not take Triavil if you have glaucoma or difficulty passing urine, unless specifically directed by your physician. Triavil may make you sleepy or tired and it may also cause difficulty in concentration. Be extremely careful when driving a car or operating machinery while taking this drug, especially during the first couple of weeks of therapy. If you are pregnant and are taking this medication, consider asking your doctor to change drug therapy, since the ingredients found in Triavil will pass into the unborn child.

Possible Side Effects

Most frequent: dry mouth, difficulty in urination, constipation, blurred vision, rapid heartbeat, numbness and tingling sensation in the arms and legs, yellowing of the skin and/or whites of the eyes, unusually low blood pressure, drowsiness, sleepiness.

Possible Adverse Drug Effects

Infrequent: dizziness, nausea, excitement, fainting, slight twitching of the muscles, jittery feeling, weakness, headache, heartburn, loss of appetite, increased perspiration, loss of coordination, skin rash with unusual sensitivity to bright lights, itching, redness, peeling away of large sections of skin. You may experience an allergic reaction: difficulty in breathing, retention of fluids in arms and legs, drug fever, swelling of the face and tongue.

Also infrequent: effects on the hormone and blood system, convulsions, development of unusual skin colorations and spots, effect on sex drive and sexual performance.

Drug Interactions

Avoid depressive drugs such as other tranquilizers, sleeping pills, antihistamines, barbiturates, or alcohol. Interaction will cause excessive drowsiness, inability to concentrate, and/or sleepiness.

One of the ingredients in Triavil may increase your response to common stimulant drugs found in over-the-counter cough and cold preparations, causing stimulation, nervousness, and difficulty in sleeping.

Avoid large amounts of Vitamin C, which may cause you to release larger than normal amounts of Triavil from your body.

Both of the ingredients in Triavil may neutralize drugs used to treat high blood pressure. If you have high blood pressure and are taking Triavil, discuss this potential difficulty with your doctor or pharmacist to be sure that you are taking adequate doses of blood pressure medicine.

If you are taking a drug which is an MAO inhibitor, discuss this matter with your doctor, because there have been severe interactions.

Usual Dose

1 to 2 tablets 3 to 4 times per day. Milligrams in dose to be specified by physician.

Overdosage

Symptoms are central nervous system depression to the point of possible coma, low blood pressure, agitation, restlessness, convulsions, fever, dry mouth, abnormal heart rhythms, confusion, hallucinations, drowsiness, unusually low body temperature, dilated eye pupils, and abnormally rigid muscles. The patient should be taken to a hospital emergency room immediately. ALWAYS bring the medicine bottle.

Generic Name

Trifluoperazine

Brand Name

Stelazine

Type of Drug

Phenothiazine antipsychotic.

Prescribed for

Psychotic disorders, moderate to severe depression with anxiety, control of agitation or aggressiveness of disturbed children, alcohol withdrawal symptoms, intractable pain, and senility.

General Information

Trifluoperazine and other members of the phenothiazine group act on a portion of the brain called the hypothalamus. They affect parts of the hypothalamus that control metabolism, body temperature, alertness, muscle tone, hormone balance, and vomiting, and may be used to treat problems related to any of these functions.

Cautions and Warnings

Trifluoperazine should not be taken if you are allergic to one of the drugs in the broad classification of phenothiazine drugs. Do not take Trifluoperazine if you have any blood, liver, kidney, or heart disease, very low blood pressure, or Parkinson's disease. This medication is a tranquilizer and can have a depressive effect, especially during the first few days of therapy. Care should be taken when performing activities requiring a high degree of concentration, such as driving. If you are taking this medication and become pregnant contact your doctor immediately.

Possible Side Effects

Most common: drowsiness, especially during the first or second week of therapy. If the drowsiness becomes troublesome, contact your doctor.

Possible Adverse Drug Effects

Trifluoperazine can cause jaundice (yellowing of the whites of the eyes or skin), usually in 2 to 4 weeks. The jaundice usually goes away when the drug is discontinued, but there have been cases when it did not. If you notice this effect or if you develop symptoms such as fever and generally not feeling well, contact your doctor immediately. Less frequent: changes in components of the blood including anemias, raised or lowered blood pressure, abnormal heart rate, heart attack, feeling faint or dizzy.

Phenothiazines can produce "extrapyramidal effects," such as spasms of the neck muscles, severe stiffness of the back muscles, rolling back of the eyes, convulsions, difficulty in swallowing, and symptoms associated with Parkinson's disease. These effects look very serious, but go away after the drug has been withdrawn; however, symptoms of the face, tongue, and jaw may persist for as long as several years, especially in the elderly with a history of brain damage. If you experience extrapyramidal effects contact your doctor immediately.

Trifluoperazine may cause an unusual increase in psychotic symptoms or may cause paranoid reactions, tiredness, lethargy, restlessness, hyperactivity, confusion at night, bizarre dreams, inability to sleep, depression, and euphoria. Other reactions are itching, swelling, unusual sensitivity to bright lights, red skin, and rash. There have been cases of breast enlargement, false positive pregnancy tests, and changes in menstrual flow in females, and impotence and changes in sex drive in males. Trifluoperazine may also cause dry mouth, stuffy nose, headache, nausea, vomiting, loss of appetite, change in body temperature, loss of facial color, salivation, perspiration, constipation, diarrhea, changes in urine and stool habits, worsening of glaucoma, blurred vision, weakening of eyelid muscles, and spasms in bronchial and other muscles, as well as increased appetite, fatigue, excessive thirst, and changes in the coloration of skin, particularly in exposed areas.

Drug Interactions

Trifluoperazine should be taken with caution in combination with barbiturates, sleeping pills, narcotics, or any other medication which may produce a depressive effect. Avoid alcohol.

Usual Dose

Adult: 2 to 40 milligrams per day (the lowest effective dose should be used). This long-acting drug will then be taken once or twice per day.

Elderly: Lower dose, because of greater sensitivity to phenothiazines.

Child (ages 6 to 12): 1 to 2 milligrams per day, slowly increased (to as much as 15 milligrams per day) until satisfactory control is achieved.

Overdosage

Symptoms are depression, extreme weakness, tiredness, desire to go to sleep, coma, lowered blood pressure, uncontrolled muscle spasms, agitation, restlessness, convulsions, fever, dry mouth, and abnormal heart rhythms. The patient should be taken to a hospital emergency room immediately. ALWAYS bring the medicine bottle.

Generic Name

Trihexyphenidyl

Brand Names

Artane
Hexyphen
Tremin

Type of Drug

Anticholinergic.

Prescribed for

Treatment of Parkinson's disease or prevention or control of muscle spasms caused by other drugs, particularly the phenothiazine drugs.

General Information

The drug has an action on the body similar to that of Atropine Sulfate. As an anticholinergic it has the ability to reduce muscle spasm: this makes the drug useful in treating Parkinson's disease and other diseases associated with spasm of skeletal muscles.

Cautions and Warnings

Trihexyphenidyl should be used with caution if you have narrow angle glaucoma, stomach ulcers, obstructions in the gastrointestinal tract, prostatitis, or myasthenia gravis.

Possible Side Effects

The same as with any other anticholinergic drug: dry mouth, difficulty in urination, constipation, blurred vision, and increased sensitivity to strong light. The effects may increase if Trihexyphenidyl is taken with antihistamines, phenothiazines, antidepressants, or other anticholinergic drugs.

Side effects are less frequent and severe than those seen with Atropine Sulfate, to which this drug is therapeutically similar.

Drug Interactions

Interaction with other anticholinergic drugs, including tricyclic antidepressants, may cause severe stomach upset or unusual abdominal pain. If this happens, contact your doctor.

Avoid over-the-counter remedies which contain Atropine or similar drugs. Your pharmacist can tell you the ingredients of over-the-counter drugs.

Usual Dose

From 1 to 15 milligrams per day, depending on disease and patient's response.

Special Information

Side effects of dry mouth, constipation, and increased sensitivity to strong light may be relieved by, respectively, chewing gum or sucking on hard candy, taking a stool softener, and wearing sunglasses. Such side effects are easily tolerated in the absence of undesirable drug interaction.

Generic Name

Trimethobenzamide Hydrochloride

Brand Name

Tigan

Type of Drug

Antiemetic.

Prescribed for

Control of nausea and vomiting.

General Information

Trimethobenzamide Hydrochloride works on the "chemoreceptor trigger zone" of the brain through which impulses are carried to the vomiting center. It can help control nausea and vomiting.

Cautions and Warnings

Do not use this drug if you are allergic or sensitive to it. Trimethobenzamide Hydrochloride rectal suppositories contain a local anesthetic and should not be used for newborn infants or patients who are allergic to local anesthetics. Some drugs, when taken by children with a viral illness that causes vomiting, may contribute to the development of Reye's syndrome, a potentially fatal, acute childhood disease. Although this relationship has not been confirmed, caution must be exercised. Reye's syndrome is characterized by the rapid onset of persistent severe vomiting, tiredness, and irrational behavior. It can progress to coma, convulsions, and death—usually following a nonspecific illness associated with a high fever. It has been suspected that Trimethobenzamide Hydrochloride and other drugs which can be toxic to the liver may unfavorably alter the course of Reye's syndrome; such drugs should be avoided in children exhibiting signs and symptoms associated with Reye's syndrome.

Trimethobenzamide Hydrochloride can obscure the signs of overdosage by other drugs or signs of disease because of its effect of controlling nausea and vomiting.

Possible Side Effects

Muscle cramps and tremors, low blood pressure (especially after an injection of this medication), effects on components of the blood, blurred vision, drowsiness, headache, jaundice (yellowing of skin or whites of the eyes). If you experience one of these side effects report it to your doctor. If you develop a skin rash or other allergic effects from Trimethobenzamide Hydrochloride, stop taking the drug and tell your doctor. Usually these symptoms will disappear by themselves, but additional treatment may be necessary.

Drug Interactions

Trimethobenzamide Hydrochloride may make you sleepy or cause you to lose concentration. Avoid alcoholic beverages, antihistamines, sleeping pills, tranquilizers, and other depressant drugs which may aggravate these effects.

Usual Dose

Adult: A 250-milligram capsule 3 to 4 times per day. Rectal suppository form, 200 milligrams 3 to 4 times per day.

Child (30 to 90 pounds): 100 to 200 milligrams 3 to 4 times per day. Rectal suppository form, 100 to 200 milligrams 3 to 4 times per day.

Child (under 30 pounds): Rectal suppository form, 100 milligrams 3 to 4 times per day.

Dose must be adjusted according to disease severity and patient's response.

Special Information

Severe vomiting should not be treated with an antiemetic drug alone: the cause of the vomiting should be established and treated. Overuse of antiemetic drugs may delay diagnosis of the underlying condition or problem and obscure the signs of toxic effects from other drugs. Primary emphasis in the treatment of vomiting is on reestablishment of body fluid and electrolyte balance, relief of fever, and treatment of the causative disease process.

Generic Name

Tripelennamine

Brand Names

PBZ-SR
Pyribenzamine
Ro-Hist

Type of Drug

Antihistamine.

Prescribed for

Seasonal allergy, stuffed and runny nose, itching of the eyes, scratching of the throat caused by allergy, and other allergic symptoms such as itching, rash, or hives.

General Information

Antihistamines generally, and Tripelennamine specifically, act by blocking the release of the chemical substance histamine from the cell. Antihistamines work by drying up the secretions of the nose, throat, and eyes.

Cautions and Warnings

Tripelennamine should not be used if you are allergic to this drug. It should be avoided or used with extreme care if you have narrow angle glaucoma (pressure in the eye), stomach ulcer or other stomach problems, enlarged prostate, or problems passing urine. It should not be used by people who have deep-breathing problems such as asthma.

Tripelennamine can cause dizziness, drowsiness, and lowering of blood pressure, particularly in the elderly patient. Young children can show signs of nervousness, increased tension, and anxiety.

Possible Side Effects

Occasional: itching, rash, sensitivity to light, perspiration, chills, dryness of the mouth, nose, and throat, lowering of blood pressure, headache, rapid heartbeat, sleeplessness, dizziness, disturbed coordination, confusion, restlessness, nervousness, irritability, euphoria (feeling high), tingling of the hands and feet, blurred vision, double vision, ringing in the ears, stomach upset, loss of appetite, nausea, vomiting, constipation, diarrhea, difficulty in urination, tightness of the chest, wheezing, nasal stuffiness.

Possible Adverse Drug Effects

Use with care if you have a history of asthma, glaucoma, thyroid disease, heart disease, high blood pressure, or diabetes.

Drug Interactions

Tripelennamine should not be taken with MAO inhibitors. Interaction with tranquilizers, sedatives, and sleeping medication will increase the effects of these drugs; it is extremely important that you discuss this with your doctor so that doses of these drugs can be properly adjusted.

Be extremely cautious when drinking while taking Tripelennamine, which will enhance the intoxicating effect of alcohol. Alcohol also has a sedative effect.

Usual Dose

Adult: 25 to 50 milligrams every 4 to 6 hours. Up to 600 milligrams per day may be used. Adult patients may take up to 3 of the 100-milligram long-acting (PBZ-SR) tablets per day, although this much is not usually needed.

Infant and child: 2 milligrams per pound of body weight per day in divided doses. No more than 300 milligrams should be given per day. Older children may take up to 3 of the extended release (long-acting) tablets per day, if needed.

Overdosage

Symptoms are depression or stimulation (especially in children), fixed or dilated pupils, flushing of the skin, and stomach upset. Take the patient to a hospital emergency room immediately, if you cannot make him vomit. ALWAYS bring the medicine bottle.

Special Information

Antihistamines produce a depressing effect: be extremely cautious when driving or operating heavy equipment.

The safety of Tripelennamine in pregnancy has not been established. A breast-feeding mother should avoid taking this medication, since it is known to pass from the mother to the baby through the milk.

Brand Name

Tri-Vi-Flor Drops

Ingredients

Sodium Fluoride
Vitamin A
Vitamin C
Vitamin D

Type of Drug

Multivitamin supplement with a fluoride.

Prescribed for

Vitamin deficiencies and prevention of dental cavities in infants and children.

General Information

Tri-Vi-Flor Drops is a vitamin supplement containing a fluoride. Fluorides taken in small daily doses have been effective in preventing cavities in children by strengthening their teeth and making them resistant to cavity formation. Too much of a fluoride can cause damage to the teeth. Because of this, vitamins with a fluoride should only be used in areas where the water supply is not fluoridated.

Cautions and Warnings

Tri-Vi-Flor Drops should not be used in areas where the fluoride content exceeds 0.7 ppm (part per million). Your pediatrician or local water company can tell you the fluoride content of the water you drink.

Possible Side Effects

Occasional skin rash, itching, stomach upset, headache, weakness.

Usual Dose

One milliliter per day.

Brand Name

Tuss-Ornade Spansules/Liquid

Ingredients

Caramiphen Edisylate
Chlorpheniramine Maleate
Isopropamide Iodide
Phenylpropanolamine Hydrochloride

Type of Drug

Decongestant; expectorant.

Prescribed for

Relief of cough, nasal congestion, runny nose, and other symptoms associated with the common cold, viruses, or other upper respiratory diseases. It may also be used to treat allergies, asthma, ear infections, or sinus infections.

General Information

Tuss-Ornade is one of almost 100 products marketed to relieve the symptoms of the common cold and other respiratory infections. These products contain medicine to relieve congestion, act as an antihistamine, relieve or suppress cough, and help cough up mucus. They may contain medicine for each purpose, or may contain a combination of medicines. Some combinations leave out the antihistamine, the decongestant, or the expectorant. You must realize while taking Tuss-Ornade or similar products that these drugs are good only for the relief of symptoms and will not treat the underlying problem, such as a cold virus or other infections.

Cautions and Warnings

Can cause excessive tiredness or drowsiness.

Possible Side Effects

Dry mouth, blurred vision, difficulty passing urine, (possibly) constipation, nervousness, restlessness, or even inability to sleep.

Drug Interactions

Taking Tuss-Ornade with an MAO inhibitor can produce severe interaction, so consult your doctor before combining them.

Since Tuss-Ornade contains ingredients which may cause sleepiness or difficulty in concentration, do not drink alcoholic beverages while taking this drug. The combination can cause excessive drowsiness or sleepiness, and result in inability to concentrate and carry out activities requiring extra concentration and co-ordination.

Usual Dose

Spansules, 1 every 12 hours. Liquid, 1 to 2 teaspoons 3 to 4 times per day as needed for relief of cough, nasal congestion, runny nose, or other symptoms associated with the common cold or other upper respiratory diseases.

Special Information

Take with a full glass of water to remove excessive mucus from the throat and reduce stomach upset.

Brand Name

Tylenol with Codeine

Ingredients

Acetaminophen
Codeine Phosphate

Other Brand Names

Aceta with Codeine
Acetaminophen with
   Codeine
Capital with Codeine
Coastaldyne Tablets
Codap Tablets

Empracet with Codeine
Hasacode Tablets
Liquix-C Capsules
Phenaphen with Codeine
Proval Capsules
SK-APAP with Codeine

Type of Drug

Narcotic analgesic combination.

Prescribed for

Relief of mild to moderate pain.

General Information

Tylenol with Codeine and equivalent brand names are generally prescribed for the patient who is in pain but is allergic to Aspirin. Tylenol with Codeine is probably not effective for arthritis or other pain caused by inflammation because the ingredient Acetaminophen does not have the ability to reduce inflammation. Aspirin with Codeine will produce an anti-inflammatory effect, and this is the major difference between these two products.

Cautions and Warnings

Do not take Codeine if you know you are allergic or sensitive to it. Long-term use of Codeine may cause drug dependence or addiction. Codeine is a respiratory depressant. Use this drug with extreme caution if you suffer from asthma or other breathing problems. Codeine affects the central nervous system, producing sleepiness, tiredness, and/or inability to concentrate. Be careful if you are driving, operating machinery, or performing other functions requiring concentration. If you are pregnant or suspect that you are pregnant do not take this drug.

Possible Side Effects

Most frequent: light-headedness, dizziness, sleepiness, nausea, vomiting, loss of appetite, sweating. If these effects occur, consider calling your doctor and asking him about lowering the dose of Codeine you are taking. Usually the side effects disappear if you simply lie down.

More serious side effects of Codeine are shallow breathing or difficulty in breathing.

Possible Adverse Drug Effects

Adverse effects of Codeine include euphoria (feeling high), weakness, sleepiness, headache, agitation, uncoordinated muscle movement, minor hallucinations, disorientation and visual disturbances, dry mouth, loss of appetite, constipation, flushing of the face, rapid heartbeat, palpitations, faintness, urinary difficulties or hesitancy, reduced sex drive and/or potency, itching, skin rashes, anemia, lowered blood sugar, and a yellowing of the skin and/or whites of the eyes. Narcotic analgesics may aggravate convulsions in those who have had convulsions in the past.

Drug Interactions

Because of its depressant effect and potential effect on breathing, Codeine should be taken with extreme care in combination with alcohol, sleeping medicine, tranquilizers, or other depressant drugs.

Usual Dose

Adult: 1 to 2 tablets every 4 hours.
Child: Not recommended for children.

Overdosage

Symptoms are depression of respiration (breathing), extreme tiredness progressing to stupor and then coma, pinpointed pupils of the eyes, no response to stimulation such as a pin stick, cold and clammy skin, slowing down of the heart rate, lowering of blood pressure, yellowing of the skin and/or whites of the eyes, bluish color in skin of hands and feet, fever, excitement, delirium, convulsions, cardiac arrest, and liver toxicity (shown by nausea, vomiting, pain in the abdomen, and diarrhea). The patient should be taken to a hospital emergency room immediately. ALWAYS bring the medicine bottle.

Special Information

Tylenol with Codeine is best taken with food or at least ½ glass of water to prevent stomach upset.

Brand Name

Vioform-Hydrocortisone Cream/Lotion/Ointment

Ingredients

Hydrocortisone
Iodochlorhydroxyquin

Other Brand Names

Caquin

Cortin

Cort-Quin

Domeform-HC

Formtone-HC

Hexaderm-I.Q.

Hydrocortisone with
   Iodochlorhydroxyquin

Hydroquin

Hysone

Iodocort

Mity-Quin

Oxyquin

Racet

Vio-Hydrocort

Vioquin-HC

Viotag

Vytone

Type of Drug

Topical corticosteroid combination.

Prescribed for

Inflamed conditions of the skin such as eczema, athlete's foot, and other fungal infections.

General Information

Hydrocortisone is used to relieve the symptom of any itching, rash, or inflammation of the skin. It does not treat the underlying cause of the skin problem, only the symptom. It exerts this effect by interfering with natural body mechanisms that produced the rash, itching, etc, in the first place. If you use this drug without finding the cause of the problem, the problem may return after you stop using the drug. Hydrocortisone should not be used without your doctor's consent because it could cover an important reaction, one that may be valuable to him in treating you. Iodochlorhydroxyquin is used because of its antifungal, antibacterial, and antieczema effects.

Cautions and Warnings

Keep this medication away from the eyes. Because there is some question about the safety of topical Hydrocortisone in pregnant females, these products should not be used extensively or in large amounts for a long time if you are pregnant. If local irritation worsens, or develops where there was none, stop using the drug and contact your physician immediately.

Possible Side Effects

Burning sensation, itching, irritation, dryness, secondary infection, pimples similar to acne.

Usual Dose

Apply to affected area only, 2 to 3 times per day.

Generic Name

Warfarin

Brand Names

Athrombin-K
Coumadin Sodium
Panwarfin

Type of Drug

Oral anticoagulant.

Prescribed for

Anticoagulation (thinning of the blood). This is generally a secondary form of treatment for other diseases —such as pulmonary embolism, heart attack, or abnormal heart rhythms—in which the formation of blood clots may cause serious problems.

General Information

Anticoagulants act by depressing the body's normal production of various factors which are known to take part in the coagulation mechanism. If you are taking Warfarin it is absolutely essential that you take the exact dose in the exact way prescribed by your doctor. Notify your doctor at the earliest sign of unusual bleeding or bruising (that is, the formation of black-and-blue marks), if you pass blood in your urine or stool, and/or if you pass a black tarry stool. The interactions of this class of drugs are extremely important and are discussed in detail below.

Warfarin can be extremely dangerous if not used properly. Periodic blood tests of the time it takes your blood or various factors in your blood to begin to coagulate are required for proper control of oral anti-coagulant therapy.

If you are pregnant or think that you may be pregnant, you must discuss this with your doctor immediately: Warfarin can cause problems with the mother and will also pass into the fetus. It can cause and has caused bleeding and death of the fetus. A nursing mother should be careful, since the Warfarin will appear in the mother's milk. There are situations where the potential benefits to be gained from the use of Warfarin or one of the other oral anticoagulants may outweigh possible negative effects of these drugs in the pregnant patient: the decision to use one of these drugs is an important one which should be made cooperatively by you and your doctor.

Cautions and Warnings

Warfarin must be taken with care if you have a pre-existing blood disease associated with coagulation or lack of coagulation. Other conditions in which the use of Warfarin should be discussed with your doctor are threatened abortion, Vitamin C deficiency, stomach ulcers or bleeding from the genital or urinary areas, severe high blood pressure, diseases of the large bowel such as diverticulitis or ulcerative colitis, and subacute bacterial endocarditis.

Possible Side Effects

The principal side effect experienced by patients taking Warfarin or other oral anticoagulant drugs is bleeding, which may occur within therapeutic dosage ranges and even when blood tests normally used to monitor anti-coagulant therapy are within normal limits. If you bleed abnormally while you are taking anticoagulants and have eliminated the possibility of drug interactions, you should discuss this matter immediately with your doctor: it may indicate the presence of an underlying problem.

Possible Adverse Drug Effects

People taking oral anticoagulant drugs have reported bleeding from peptic ulcers, nausea, vomiting, diarrhea, blood in the urine, anemia, adverse effects on components of the blood, hepatitis, jaundice or yellowing of the skin and whites of the eyes, itching, rash, loss of hair, sore throat and mouth, and fever.

Drug Interactions

Warfarin and other oral anticoagulant (blood-thinning) drugs are probably involved in more drug interactions than any other drug. Contact your pharmacist or doctor to discuss any other medications which you may be taking in order to avoid serious adverse interactions, which may increase the effectiveness of Warfarin to the point of causing severe bleeding or hemorrhage, or decrease its effectiveness to the point of causing formation of blood clots. Your doctor and your pharmacist should have records of all medications which you are taking.

Drugs that may *increase* the effect of Warfarin include broad-spectrum antibiotics such as Neomycin, mineral oil, Chlorestyramine, Phenylbutazone, Oxyphenbutazone, Clofibrate, Indomethacin, sulfa drugs, Chloral Hydrate, Ethacrynic Acid, Mefenamic Acid, Nalidixic Acid, Aspirin, oral antidiabetic drugs (Tolbutamide, Chlorpropamide, Tolazamide), and Phenytoin (see p. 276 for interaction resulting in Phenytoin toxicity). Chloramphenicol, Allopurinol, Nortriptyline, Methylphenidate, Disulfiram, Chlortetracycline, Quinidine, Haloperidol, Ascorbic Acid in large quantities, MAO inhibitors, Meperidine, and Thyroid Hormone and antithyroid drugs such as Propylthiouracil and Methylthiouracil will also increase the effects of oral anticoagulants.

There are fewer drugs that will *decrease* the effect of Warfarin, but the potential interaction can be just as dangerous with barbiturates, Glutethimide, Ethchlorvynol, Meprobamate, Griseofulvin, estrogens, oral contraceptive drugs, Chlorthalidone, corticosteroids, and Rifampin.

No matter what the interaction, it is essential that you discuss all medications you are taking with your doctor or pharmacist, including not only prescription drugs but over-the-counter drugs containing Aspirin or other ingredients which may interact with Warfarin. Consult your physician or pharmacist before buying any over-the-counter drug.

Usual Dose

2 to 10 or more milligrams daily, but dose is extremely variable and must be individualized for maximum effect.

Overdosage

The primary symptom is bleeding. A laboratory test will show longer blood-clotting time, and bleeding can make itself known by appearance of blood in the urine or stool, an unusual number of black-and-blue marks, oozing of blood from small cuts made while shaving or from other trivial nicks or cuts, or bleeding from the gums after brushing the teeth. If bleeding does not stop within 10 to 15 minutes, your doctor should be called. He may tell you to skip a dose of anticoagulant and continue normal activities, or to go to a local hospital or doctor's office where blood evaluations can be made; or he may give you a prescription for Vitamin K, which antagonizes the effect of Warfarin. The latter has dangers because it can complicate subsequent anticoagulant therapy, but this is a decision that your doctor must make.

The Top 200
Prescription Drugs

The following is a list of the top 200 prescription drugs in the United States in 1977.*

Rank	Name of Product	Rank	Name of Product
1	Valium	20	Darvon Compound-65
2	Ampicillin	21	Indocin
3	Lasix Oral	22	Donnatal
4	Inderal	23	Keflex
5	Tetracycline systemic	24	Ovral
6	Dyazide	25	Erythromycin systemic
7	Tylenol with Codeine	26	Penicillin VK
8	Aldomet	27	Elavil
9	Dimetapp	28	Benadryl Cap/Tab.
10	Lanoxin	29	Lomotil
11	HydroDIURIL	30	Aldoril
12	Actifed	31	Fiorinal
13	Dalmane	32	Phenobarbital
14	Empirin Compound with Codeine	33	Hygroton
		34	Dilantin Sodium
15	Premarin Oral	35	Prednisone oral
16	V-Cillin K	36	Ilosone
17	Librium	37	Librax
18	Darvocet-N 100	38	Ortho-Novum 1/50-21
19	Motrin		

---

* Reprinted by permission of Pharmacy Times, based on the annual National Prescription Audit (NPA) which is conducted by IMS America, Ltd., Ambler Pa.

Rank	Name of Product	Rank	Name of Product
39	Mellaril	77	Parafon Forte
40	Antivert	78	Hydropres
41	Butazolidin Alka	79	Macrodantin
42	Isordil	80	Sinequan
43	Thyroid	81	Esidrix
44	Diabinese	82	Coumadin Oral
45	Diuril	83	Gantrisin Systemic
46	Ser-Ap-Es	84	Talwin Tabs.
47	Aldactazide	85	E-Mycin
48	Mycolog	86	Naldecon
49	Percodan	87	Atarax
50	Triavil	88	Equagesic
51	Ornade	89	Tuss-Ornade
52	Tranxene	90	Phergan VC Expectorant with Codeine
53	Drixoral		
54	Achromycin-V		
55	E.E.S.	91	Bendectin
56	Synthroid	92	Combid
57	Pavabid	93	Darvon
58	Digoxin	94	Demulen-21
59	Ovulen-21	95	Serax
60	Erythrocin	96	Apresoline
61	Phenaphen with Codeine	97	Butisol Sodium
		98	Kenalog Derm.
62	Valisone	99	Quinidine Sulfate
63	Zyloprim	100	Compazine
64	Pen-Vee-K	101	Larotid
65	Sumycin	102	Nitroglycerin
66	Orinase	103	Actifed-C Expectorant
67	Thorazine		
68	Ortho-Novum 1/80-21	104	Stelazine
		105	Cortisporin Otic
69	Atromid-S	106	Benadryl Elixir
70	Vibramycin	107	Tofranil
71	Slow-K	108	Ionamin
72	Meprobamate	109	Vasodilan
73	Phenergan Expectorant with Codeine	110	Monistat
		111	Hydrochlorothiazide
74	Chlor-Trimeton Tabs.	112	Omnipen
		113	Penicillin G systemic
75	Tenuate		
76	Lo/Ovral	114	Equanil

Rank	Name of Product	Rank	Name of Product
115	Naprosyn	150	Phenergan VC
116	Marax		Expectorant
117	Periactin	151	Vistaril
118	Amoxil	152	Cordran
119	Neosporin Ophth.	153	Cyclospasmol
120	Poly-Vi-Flor	154	Pronestyl
	Chewable	155	Sorbitrate
121	Phenergan	156	Mycostatin Vaginal
	Expectorant	157	Provera
122	Lidex	158	Catapres
123	Amoxicillin	159	Tigan
124	Salutensin	160	Pro-Banthine
125	Kwell	161	Pyridium
126	Flagyl Oral	162	Norinyl-1/50-21
127	Isopto-Carpine	163	Bactrim DS
128	Pentids	164	Gantanol
129	Bentyl	165	Quibron
130	Fiorinal with	166	Potassium Chloride
	Codeine	167	Doriden
131	Teldrin	168	Norgesic
132	Norlestrin-21	169	Darvocet-N 50
133	Synalgos-DC	170	Tolectin
134	Amcill	171	DBI-TD
135	Synalar	172	Dimetane Expecto-
136	Nitrobid		rant-DC
137	Enduron	173	Hydergine
138	Persantine	174	Benylin Cough
139	Azo Gantrisin		Syrup
140	Tolinase	175	Medrol Oral
141	Dimetane	176	Fastin
	Expectorant	177	Aristocort Derm.
142	Ambenyl	178	Polaramine Tabs.
	Expectorant	179	Ritalin
143	Regroton	180	Elixophyllin
144	Nalfon	181	Aminophyllin
145	Diupres	182	Lotrimin
146	Aldactone	183	Placidyl
147	Proloid	184	Norgesic Forte
148	Tandearil	185	Dimetane Tabs.
149	Vioform-	186	K-Lyte
	Hydrocortisone	187	Tri-Vi-Flor Drops

Rank	Name of Product	Rank	Name of Product
188	Diamox Oral	195	AVC Cream
189	Feosol	196	Haldol
190	Ovral-28	197	Anusol-HC
191	Polycillin	198	Insulin NPH
192	Robaxin-750	199	Principen
193	Minocin	200	Pediamycin
194	Paregoric		

How Drug Types Work

ANTIBIOTICS

Antibiotics are used to treat infections which may be caused by any of hundreds of microorganisms. You must take an antibiotic specific for the organism causing your problem; otherwise, your infection cannot be cured.

How do we identify the trouble-making organism? By running specific tests called "cultures." Your doctor, a nurse, or a specifically trained technician takes a small sample from the infected area and puts it in a medium where it can multiply and grow, for example, agar, from which it can draw appropriate nutrients. The culture is placed in an environment which promotes growth. Within 2 days the organisms multiply to form a colony; samples of the colony can be examined under a microscope and identified.

The organisms may be tested against various antibiotics to see which is the best choice for treatment. This is called testing for sensitivity.

Your doctor often has a good idea of what the infecting organisms are as soon as he evaluates the location and appearance of the infection and correlates this information with your symptoms. However, he must confirm his hypothesis by taking a culture.

If you are already taking an antibiotic there is a difficulty in taking a culture: the culture may give a false negative by not growing even if you have an infection. Even small amounts of antibiotic in your body can grossly interfere with this test.

Many infections, including the common cold, the flu, and some other upper respiratory (lung) infections, are caused by viruses. Viruses are not fully living organisms like bacteria; for the most part, they are not affected by antibiotics, so taking an antibiotic will have no effect on your disease. You must depend upon your doctor to distinguish between bacterial and virus infections, which often present the same general symptoms. Often the only way to tell them apart is through a culture.

Can taking an antibiotic when you don't need one hurt you? Yes. Taking any drug unnecessarily exposes you to potential side effects and adverse reactions. Also, unwarranted use of an antibiotic can sensitize you to it, so that the next time you use it, perhaps in a situation where you badly need it, you may develop an allergic reaction. Self-medication with antibiotics is unwise for other reasons: you may take too much or too little, or you may have an infection caused by an organism not affected by the antibiotic. Do not take any antibiotic unless specifically directed to do so by your doctor.

In general, antibiotics are considered either bactericidal or bacteriostatic. Bactericidal antibiotics kill the microorganisms they affect, by interfering with natural processes such as development of cell wall or normal chemical reactions. Bactericidal antibiotics include Penicillin, Ampicillin, Amoxicillin, Cephalexin, Polymyxin, Bacitracin, Amphotericin, and Nystatin.

Bacteriostatic antibiotics interfere with microorganisms by disturbing chemical processes (usually, stages of protein production) necessary to their reproduction. Bacteriostatic antibiotics include Tetracycline, Doxycycline, Minocycline, Erythromycin, Griseofulvin, and Chloramphenicol. (Chloramphenicol may be bactericidal in some situations.)

ANTIHYPERTENSIVE DRUGS

High blood pressure is a major problem in the United States, since many people have it and there are problems associated with treating it. Twelve percent of Americans have high blood pressure but don't know it. Of those who know they have high blood pressure, only half have achieved constant pressure readings in the acceptable range.

High blood pressure can cause heart attack, heart failure, stroke, aneurysm (ballooning out of a major blood vessel—death can result if the blood vessel wall bursts like a balloon), and kidney failure.

How do you know if you have high blood pressure?

For diagnosis a series of blood pressure readings, on at least three visits, are taken to be sure that the high pressure is persistent. The way your high blood pressure is treated depends upon how high the pressure is and also on an evaluation of how much damage has already been done.

Drugs usually play a major role in the treatment of high blood pressure. Three types of drugs are used to help reduce muscle tension in veins and arteries: diuretics, vasodilators, and drugs that interfere with nervous system activity.

Diuretics help lower blood pressure by lowering the amount of water in the body. They decrease the amount of fluid that must be handled by the circulatory system and lower the blood pressure by reducing fluid volume inside blood vessels. Diuretics alone can often control mild or moderate hypertension. Some diuretics used to treat hypertension are Hydrochlorothiazide, Chlorothiazide, Chlorthalidone, and Furosemide.

Vasodilators work directly on the muscles in the walls of arteries to relax them, reducing blood pressure, so they are called direct-acting vasodilators. An example is Hydralazine, an ingredient in the drug SerApEs and available by itself in tablet form; it is always used in combination with another antihypertensive drug.

The third group of drugs act on the nervous system to help control muscle tone in blood vessels. Some of these drugs work in the brain or spinal cord (central nervous system); some at intermediate centers for nervous system control called autonomic ganglia; some at nerve endings where control of muscle tone actually takes place; and some at points in muscle tissue (receptor sites) where chemical messages from the nervous system are received. Some of the more important drugs in this group are Reserpine, Methyldopa, Clonidine, Guanethidine, and Propranolol (also used for heart disease).

More than one drug is usually prescribed in the treatment of hypertension. By mixing medications from the three major groups we can get drugs that complement one another, resulting in more efficient lowering of blood pressure.

One of the problems in the treatment of high blood

pressure is that people often don't do what is best for them. They don't take their medicines as directed, they don't follow special diets given to them, and they don't follow other instructions relating to exercise and weight control. In high blood pressure, as in many other diseases, effective treatment can only be accomplished by you. The medication prescribed for your hypertension can help only if taken exactly as directed.

HEART DRUGS

This section is about drugs that have a direct effect on the heart rather than drugs that have only a secondary effect, for example, by reducing high blood pressure. We will discuss digitalis drugs, drugs used to correct abnormal heart rhythm, and drugs used to treat angina pectoris.

Digitalis Group

The members of the digitalis group are chemically similar. Originally derived from the garden plant *Digitalis purpurea* (foxglove), they are chemically synthesized today. Most commonly used are Digoxin and Digitoxin. Digitalis drugs may differ in how long it takes the drug to start working, how long the drug effect lasts, how the drug is eliminated from the body, and how well the drug is tolerated by patients.

What are the effects of Digitalis on your heart? First, it makes your heart beat more forcefully, which helps people with congestive heart failure by helping the heart to work more efficiently and increase the amount of blood pumped with each contraction, or beat. The heart is essentially a pump; the more efficiently it works, the better off we are.

Second, Digitalis slows the rate at which the heart beats. This is also important in helping the heart to be more efficient. When a person gets heart failure, the heart muscle contracts with less force and pumps less blood with each beat. The normal response of the heart is to try to work faster and keep a sufficient supply of blood flowing. But a faster heartbeat creates another problem: like any pump, the heart can only work when there is sufficient fluid (blood) inside the pump chamber. When the heart beats too rapidly, the pump chambers of the heart (ventricles) do not fill enough between beats, reducing the potential output of the heart.

Correcting Abnormal Heart Rhythms

When abnormalities in the conduction of nervous impulses through the heart muscle are present, they cause the heart to beat in uneven cycles or in an uncoordinated manner. Arrhythmias (abnormal heart rhythms) have many causes, including:

- Imbalances in body levels of potassium or sodium.
- Thyroid or other disease.
- Adverse drug effects.
- Cardiac disease directly affecting nerve pathways in the heart.

Arrhythmias, which come in many sizes, shapes, and styles, are classified according to heart area affected, cause (if one can be found), and severity. Classification aids in drug selection. Commonly used drugs include Phenytoin, Procainamide, Propranolol, and Quinidine. They slow down the rate of nerve impulse conduction and nerve response in the heart, which decreases the rate of contraction of various parts of the heart.

When drugs do not satisfactorily control abnormal heart rhythms an electrical device called a pacemaker may be inserted. The pacemaker controls heart rate by sending out an electrical impulse of its own that overrides or counterbalances abnormal impulses being transmitted within the heart. It may be implanted permanently if use for some time does not convert the heart to a normal rhythm of its own.

Treatment of Angina

Angina pectoris is characterized by a squeezing, choking, or heavy pain or discomfort in the chest. These symptoms can also be found in or can extend to the arm, shoulder, back, neck, or lower jaw. Angina usually sets in or gets worse while or immediately after the patient has undergone physically strenuous activity. It is thought to be caused by a decrease in oxygen supply to the heart. Oxygen deficit develops when blood flow to the heart is partly blocked by blood vessels with deposits of cholesterol or other materials in them. Development of this kind of blockage is called atherosclerosis and the disease (such as angina) resulting from it is called atherosclerotic heart disease. Oxygen deficit can also occur if the blood vessels develop a spasm and choke off blood supply.

Drugs used to treat angina help dilate (open) the blood vessels serving the heart. Nitroglycerin, the main example of the nitrate group, is taken in tablets under the tongue and can provide almost immediate relief from angina as the tablets are absorbed directly into the bloodstream and help relax the muscles in the walls of blood vessels serving the heart. Other drugs of this group, such as Isosorbide Dinitrate (Isordil Sorbitrate), Erythrityl Tetranitrate (Cardilate), and Pentaerythrityl Tetranitrate (Peritrate, Duotrate) have different durations of activity. A long-acting drug may not give as prompt relief, but it is hoped that by keeping the blood vessels dilated, the frequency of angina attacks will be reduced. An attack that occurs while a person is taking a long-acting drug can be treated by the faster-acting Nitroglycerin.

Propranolol (Inderal) does not affect blood vessels by dilating them. It slows the activity of the heart so that the heart requires less oxygen to work; this decreases the likelihood of an angina attack. Most effective when used with one of the drugs discussed above, it can only prevent an angina attack; it cannot be used to treat an acute angina attack.

ANTICOAGULANTS

Anticoagulants are popularly known as blood-thinning drugs: by preventing blood from clotting, they keep it "thinner." They have been in use for some 400 years and are prescribed to anyone who has a disease that increases the chance of forming a blood clot or who has had some damage from a blood clot in the brain (stroke), heart, lung, or other critical area. Those who have had a myocardial infarction (heart attack) may be given an anticoagulant to keep heart damage from causing the formation of a blood clot.

The clotting process is a complex set of chemical reactions; anything that upsets one or more of these reactions will prevent clot formation.

If you are taking an anticoagulant, its effectiveness

should be carefully monitored by blood tests, which can easily and conveniently be performed in your doctor's office and are used to help decide if you need more or less medication. Anticoagulants should not be used if you have a history of severe bleeding episodes, have an active bleeding ulcer, have had a recent stroke with continued bleeding in the head, or are pregnant (especially if your doctor feels you may spontaneously lose your baby).

Most people taking anticoagulant drugs have no major problems so long as they take care of themselves, follow instructions, and avoid unnecessary medications, including over-the-counter drugs containing Aspirin. (Guidance on specific over-the-counter drugs can be obtained from your doctor or pharmacist.) Aspirin and other over-the-counter drugs can interact with oral anticoagulants to increase the action of the anticoagulant, causing bleeding, most commonly at first from the nose or gums. If you are taking an anticoagulant and begin to ooze blood from the nose or gums, contact your doctor *immediately*.

Or the action of the anticoagulant may be decreased, which increases the risk of a blood clot—exactly what you were trying to prevent in the first place. This interaction is more insidious because the first sign you see may be the formation of a clot. The best policy is to avoid drugs which can interfere with anticoagulant activity, including barbiturates, Glutethimide, oral contraceptive drugs, and Phenytoin.

Interactions with anticoagulant drugs can be compensated for by adjusting the dosage of anticoagulant. For example, if you must take Phenytoin on a long-term basis, the doctor can give you more anticoagulant drug than he otherwise would.

DRUGS FOR THE COMMON COLD

Have you ever felt unwell and had a runny or stuffed nose, postnasal drip, muscle aches, cough, headache, or fever? If so, you probably have been told, "It's just a cold." The common cold is a catchall name given to a set of symptoms that can be caused by over 150 different viruses. Although we know what causes a cold we cannot prevent or cure it: we can only let it run its

382

course and take medicine to make us more comfortable and help relieve the symptoms. Antibiotic drugs are not effective against cold viruses. How, then, can you make yourself more comfortable during a cold? You can take nasal decongestants, antihistamines, cough suppressants, expectorants, analgesics (pain relievers), or antipyretics (fever reducers). Usually, if you get a prescription for a cold remedy it will contain drugs in two or three of these categories. Let us consider each type of drug and how it helps relieve our suffering.

Nasal Decongestants

When your nose is stuffed or runny, tissue in the lining of the nose and blood vessels are dilated and produce more secretions (mucus) than normal. There has to be someplace for the extra material to go, so it either goes out the front way (runny nose) or the back way (postnasal drip). Dilated tissues give one the feeling of nasal congestion or stuffiness. Decongestant drugs are stimulants which, when they reach the congested area, act on the swollen vessels and tissues to cause them to return to normal size by vasoconstriction. By allowing nasal passages to clear, this can improve sinus drainage and help relieve sinus headache.

Decongestants can be applied topically as nose drops or sprays, or can be swallowed in tablet or liquid form. People often use the drugs in both forms—the tablet or liquid to produce a deeper, longer-lasting constriction, and the spray to produce almost immediate response by constriction of surface vessels and tissues. In tablet or liquid form, decongestants are frequently combined with antihistamines.

People with high blood pressure, diabetes, heart disease, or thyroid disease should avoid decongestants because they could worsen their disease. People taking antidepressant drugs or MAO inhibitors should not take decongestants because of possible drug interaction.

Antihistamines

Antihistamines block the effects of histamine, a naturally occurring chemical in the body which is released into the bloodstream as part of its response to outside challenge. This response is sometimes called the allergic response and when we experience it we say we have an allergy, whether the challenge is from an insect bite, pollen or other allergenic (allergy-provoking) substance, or a virus, as in the common cold. Antihistamines can only block histamine after it is in the bloodstream; they cannot prevent histamine from being released.

People's response to antihistamine drugs is variable. As there are four major chemical types of antihistamines, there is great variability in human response to these drugs.

Cough Suppressants

Coughing can be good for you! It is a natural reflex designed to protect you by helping to clear the respiratory tract of any unwanted material, be it foreign matter or unusually heavy natural secretions. When you take a cough medicine it suppresses this natural reflex. It cannot and does not do anything about the reason for your cough.

Cough medicine is helpful when it allows you to get a restful night's sleep when you might otherwise have been kept up by a cough. Also, reducing the amount of coughing can be good because frequent, deep coughing tends to cause irritation of the respiratory tract. Cough suppressants act either on the cough control center (there actually is such a place!) in the part of the brain called the medulla, or on the source of irritation in your throat causing the cough center to be activated. Most commercial cough suppressants (both prescription and over-the-counter) tend to combine a centrally acting drug (such as Codeine or Dextromethorphan) with an ingredient that will help reduce local irritation (such as glycerin, honey, or some other soothing syrupy medicine). Expectorants such as Terpin Hydrate, Guiafenesin, and Potassium Iodide are often used in cough formulas on the theory that by making mucus secretions in the throat thinner and perhaps easier to bring up, they will help reduce cough.

Expectorants

Expectorants stimulate the production of mucus and other respiratory secretions, helping loosen thick, tenacious secretions by diluting them with more secretory material. Once diluted, they can be removed by natural action. They work well in respiratory diseases that cause very thick secretions. Their effectiveness with coughs due to colds, however, is questionable because thickness of secretions is not a major problem. When purchasing a cough medicine, especially one sold over the counter, be sure that if there is an expectorant in it, there is also a cough suppressant. If you are not sure, consult your pharmacist.

Analgesics and Antipyretics

The two antipyretic analgesics (reducing fever, reducing pain) commonly used in cold medicines are Aspirin and Acetaminophen (Tylenol, Datril, etc.). Aspirin also reduces inflammation. Aspirin or Acetaminophen should only be used if you have fever, pain, or inflammation (Aspirin only, not Acetaminophen). Taking these drugs unnecessarily may expose you to drug-induced side effects without gaining any counterbalancing benefit. If your doctor has given you a prescription drug to relieve pain, fever, or inflammation, don't take the medicine again unless you consult him first.

PSYCHOTROPIC DRUGS

Psychotropic drugs are used to alleviate symptoms in psychiatric disorders. They are extremely useful in today's stressful society and often enable people to function normally on a day-to-day basis.

Psychotropic drugs affect brain chemicals or chemical systems called neurotransmitters, which mediate such basic functions as sleep, wakefulness, and memory, by increasing or blocking their effects. There are three major classes of psychotropic drugs: antianxiety drugs, antipsychotic drugs, and antidepressants.

Antianxiety Drugs

These are the minor tranquilizers such as Diazepam (Valium), Chlordiazepoxide (Librium), Oxazepam (Serax), and related benzodiazepines, and Meprobamate, which are used to treat anxiety neurosis. People with an anxiety neurosis experience waves of anxiety characterized by apprehension, tension, sudden fatigue, and a panic reaction; these feelings may be accompanied by sweating, rapid heartbeat (palpitation), weakness, dizziness, and irritability, which are defenses set up by the brain to avoid the actual source of the anxiety. Antianxiety drugs generally direct their activity at brain centers involved with emotion.

Antipsychotic Drugs

The antipsychotic (neuroleptic) drugs alter the activity of dopamine, norepinephrine, and serotonin in the brain, with a profound effect on psychotic disorder, whether paranoid or schizophrenic. People with psychotic disorders show severe personality disintegration and distortion of the world around them, have difficulty separating reality from fantasy, and often suffer from hallucinations and delusions.

The three major groups of antipsychotic drugs are the phenothiazines, such as Chlorpromazine (Thorazine), Trifluoperazine (Stelazine), and Thioridazine (Mellaril); the butyrophenones, such as Haloperidol (Haldol); and the thioxanthenes, such as Thiothixene (Navane). All of them tend to exhibit more side effects than antianxiety drugs and are reserved for the more severe situations.

Antidepressants

Depressed people tend to be self-critical, self-deprecating, brooding; they have a feeling of extreme helplessness. Loss of self-esteem, withdrawal from personal relationships, and inhibition of normal aggressive activity may result. Those suffering from depression also frequently suffer from anxiety. Here the depression is thought to be a defense against the underlying anxiety and is accompanied by physical complaints of headache, tiredness, loss of appetite, and constipation.

The two classes of antidepressant drugs are the tricyclic antidepressants, such as Amitriptyline (Elavil and Endep) and Imipramine (Tofranil), and the MAO inhibitors, such as Isocarboxazid (Marplan), Tranylcypromine Sulfate (Parnate), and Phenelzine Sulfate (Nardil). Both classes are effective in relieving depressive symptoms, but they do not cure depression; they only help the patient to deal more effectively with his problems.

MAO INHIBITORS

MAO inhibitor drugs block a naturally occurring enzyme system called monoamine oxidase, where the name MAO comes from. One of its important functions is to break down other naturally occurring chemicals called amines. Amines are responsible for much of the stimulating effects of the central nervous system. By giving an MAO inhibitor we *increase* the amount of amines available. Too much MAO inhibitor can produce excess amine effects such as overstimulation, very high blood pressure, agitation, changes in heart rate and rhythm, muscle spasms and tremors, and sleeplessness; but taken under the supervision of a physician, MAO inhibitors can be valuable, relatively safe therapeutic agents.

We saw above that some MAO inhibitor drugs are used to treat severe depression. Others are used to treat high blood pressure (Pargyline [Eutonyl]), Hodgkin's disease (Procarbazine [Matulane]), and infections (Furazolidone [Furoxone]); here the beneficial effects may not be related directly to MAO inhibition, but many of the adverse effects and all the drug interactions are so related.

When an MAO inhibitor is given along with a drug which is broken down, at least in part, by the MAO enzyme system, the result is *higher concentration* of the second drug. For example, when antidepressant drugs are given with an MAO inhibitor, unusually high antidepressant levels can cause fever and convulsions. Similarly, when a diabetic patient is given an MAO inhibitor drug, his blood sugar will be lowered, if he is taking either an oral antidiabetic drug or Insulin.

MAO inhibitors have also been implicated in serious interactions with certain foods—those containing large amounts of naturally occurring amines (tyramine or dopa). The MAO inhibitor makes you lose the ability to rapidly destroy these chemicals, with possible results of headache, rapid rise in blood pressure, hemorrhaging due to bursting of small blood vessels, and general stimulation. Several deaths have been caused by this interaction!

Some foods to be avoided if you are taking an MAO inhibitor are broad beans, Chianti wine, chicken or beef liver, pickled herring, and cheddar cheese, as well as Camembert, Stilton, Brie, Emmentaler, and Gruyère cheese. Avoid large amounts of chocolate, sour cream, canned figs, raisins, soy sauce, pineapple, and bananas.

CORTICOSTEROIDS

Corticosteroid drugs are chemically related to hydrocortisone, corticosterone, aldosterone, and deoxycorticosterone (naturally produced hormones that are essential to normal body functions). The first two hormones control the storage of carbohydrates (sugars) in the body, affect the breakdown of body proteins, and reduce inflammation. The last two primarily control the regulation of sodium and potassium in the body, although they possess some activity similar to that of hydrocortisone and corticosterone.

Some of the corticosteroid drugs most commonly used in patient treatment are related to the hormones hydrocortisone and corticosterone: Betamethasone, Cortisone, Dexamethasone, Fluprednisolone, Hydrocortisone, Meprednisone, Methylprednisolone, Paramethasone, Prednisolone, Prednisone, and Triamcinolone.

Others are related to the hormone deoxycorticosterone: Deoxycorticosterone and Fludrocortisone.

Corticosteroids are used to treat a wide variety of conditions. They can be used to replace naturally produced hormones in patients who cannot make enough of their own. They can also be used to treat diseases in which it is desirable to administer a potent anti-inflammatory drug. Some of the host of diseases in which corticosteroids are used for this effect are those which affect collagen (connective) tissue such as lupus erythematosus and pemphigus vulgaris; allergic disorders including asthma, hay fever, and allergic rhinitis (nasal inflammation due to allergy); and reactions to drugs, serum, and blood transfusions. Skin rashes of various types, causes, and severities are also treated with corticosteroids. The drugs can be especially helpful in treating itchy, inflamed rashes and in psoriasis, neurodermatitis, and similar conditions. Corticosteroids are also given to treat inflammation of areas of the body including tendons, muscles, eye, brain, and liver. They are of great value in shock and are often used as part of the treatment of certain cancers.

Because of the wide variety of diseases for which corticosteroids are used, your doctor must individualize treatment for you, depending upon the drug being used and the disease being treated.

Corticosteroids can have many serious side effects. The possibility of experiencing side effects increases with the amount of drug being taken and the length of time it is taken. Some of the possible side effects of corticosteroids are irritation of the stomach (possibly leading to peptic ulcer), loss of body potassium, infection (due to temporary disabling of body defense mechanisms), behavioral and personality changes, loss of calcium from bone leading to subsequent bone weakness and possible ease of fracture in elderly patients, increased pressure inside the eye, excessive breakdown of body proteins, change in the quality and appearance of skin to which corticosteroids are topically applied, muscle weakness, aggravation of diabetes, and unusual or excessive retention of water in the body, leading to fluid accumulation under the skin.

Corticosteroids are remarkable drugs which can be lifesaving. They should only be used under the direct supervision of your doctor because of the many serious side effects which can develop. The carefully supervised use of corticosteroids is quite safe, in most cases. If you must take one of these drugs, be sure to follow your doctor's directions explicitly: only then will you get the maximum benefit.

ANALGESICS

Analgesics are drugs used to relieve pain. They act on centers in the nervous system to affect your response to painful stimuli. They don't take the pain away, they simply reduce the response produced by the pain.

Analgesics are classified by the severity of pain they relieve. Those that relieve severe pain are called strong analgesics; those that relieve mild to moderate pain are called mild analgesics.

Strong analgesics have the additional quality of altering the psychological response to pain and alleviating the anxiety and apprehension which often accompanies the painful situation. Some drugs considered to be strong analgesics are narcotics, such as Morphine, Meperidine (Demerol), Opium, Oxymorphone (Numorphan), Oxycodone (found in Percodan), Pentazocine (Talwin), and Methotrimeprazine (Levoprome). They all exert basically the same effect on the central nervous system. Their usefulness is related to the length of their effective pain relief, how fast they start working, and the type and degree of side effects and adverse reactions. The differences among them are not that great and selection of one is usually related to the doctor's training and experience. Patients may express a strong feeling for one of these drugs according to past experience.

Strong analgesics should not be used for mild to moderate pain because of their relative potency and the definite potential for addiction after prolonged use. Other side effects associated with these drugs are difficulty in breathing, nausea, vomiting, constipation, lowered blood pressure, slowed heart rate, and drug reaction or allergy.

Mild analgesics are divided into two categories: those which are chemical derivatives of one of the strong analgesics such as Codeine Sulfate, Propoxyphene (Darvon, Dolene, SK-65), Ethoheptazine (Zactane), and those considered to also be antipyretic (fever-reducing) such as Aspirin, Sodium Salicylate, Salicylamide, Acetaminophen, Phenacetin, Dipyrone, and Mefenamic Acid (Ponstel).

Of the mild analgesics which are derivatives of one of the strong analgesics, Codeine Sulfate is the most effective, although it can become addicting after long periods. It is generally considered more effective than Aspirin and is therefore held in reserve by most doctors for patients who either cannot be effectively treated by the milder drugs or who cannot take them for some reason.

The analgesic-antipyretic drugs are among the most widely used in the world, primarily because most members of this group are available without a prescription. They are used to treat any mild or moderate pain of headache or muscle ache, or from arthritis (inflammation of bone joints), sprains, strains, and so on. They may also be prescribed as part of the treatment of pain due to surgical procedures, cancer, and periodic cramps, and for the reduction of fever. The two drugs most used are Aspirin and Acetaminophen.

Aspirin, which was first synthesized from salicin, a substance found in willow bark, has strong analgesic, antipyretic, and anti-inflammatory properties. It not only works on the central nervous system but has a well-documented effect directly on the source of pain, usually as a result of its anti-inflammatory activity. Care must be taken when Aspirin is kept around the house, since it is the most common cause of drug poisoning in young children. Furthermore, Aspirin and the other salicylates have important side effects, including irritation of the gastrointestinal system (possibly leading to or aggravating preexisting ulcers), stimulation, dizziness, ringing in the ears, inability to hear high tones, delirium, stupor and coma in very high doses, and prolongation of the time it takes for blood to clot. (One dose of 650 milligrams—2 tablets—approximately doubles clotting time in normal persons for 4 to 7 days.) Aspirin should not be taken for long periods in high doses unless you are under your doctor's care. Animal studies have indicated that large doses of Aspirin over long periods can cause adverse effects on the fetus; however, this effect has never been reported in a human. Pregnant women who take Aspirin (or other salicylates) for long periods in high doses do have increased length of gestation and prolonged spontaneous labor.

See page 3 for information on Acetaminophen.

Drugs and Foods

Recently, much attention has been paid to the effect of diet on drug therapy and the effect of drugs on diet and nutrition.

How Does Diet Affect Drug Therapy?

Food can interfere with the ability of drugs to be absorbed into the blood through the gastrointestinal system. For this reason, most medications are best taken at least 1 hour before or 2 hours after meals, unless directed otherwise by your doctor.

Among drugs which are best taken with meals because the food reduces the amount of stomach irritation caused by the drug are Indomethacin, Phenylbutazone, and Oxyphenbutazone. Other drugs, for example Amoxicillin, may not be affected at all by food. Consult the monographs for specific information about the best time to take medicines.

Some food effects interfere with a drug by reducing the amount of medication available to be absorbed. Juice or milk taken to help you swallow drugs can interfere with them. Many fruit juices, because of their acid content, break down Penicillin-G, Erythromycin, and other antibiotics. Milk or milk products (such as ice cream) can interfere with the absorption of Tetracycline antibiotics through the gastrointestinal tract.

Investigators have questioned the seriousness of such effects; it is generally difficult to prove that people don't get well as fast as a result of them. Probably there is some effect, but its extent is not known.

Some medications react with specific diets. People taking anticoagulant (blood-thinning) drugs should avoid foods rich in fats because they may cause a reduction in anticoagulant effectiveness. People taking Levo-Dopa

(L-dopa) should avoid high-protein diets rich in Vitamin B$_6$ (Pyridoxine), which can reduce the effectiveness of Levo-Dopa.

Raw vegetables (cabbage, okra, and some others) contain Vitamin K, which specifically interferes with oral anticoagulant drugs. This interaction can contribute to the development of potentially fatal blood clots.

An ingredient in licorice can cause you to retain sodium and lose potassium. This can be dangerous if you have high blood pressure (increased sodium = increased water = higher blood pressure) or if you are taking a Digitalis drug for your heart (less potassium = more Digitalis side effects).

Many foods interact with MAO inhibitors (see p. 387). Foods containing potassium can be useful to people taking diuretics who need to add potassium to their diet:

Apricots (dried)	Prune juice
Dates	Orange juice
Raisins	Watermelon
Peaches (dried)	Turkey
Cantaloupe	Steak
Figs (dried)	Milk
Bananas	

How Do Drugs Affect Diet and Nutrition?

Drugs can affect your appetite. Drugs that can stimulate your appetite include tricyclic antidepressants and phenothiazine tranquilizers.

Drugs that can cause you to lose your appetite include antibiotics (especially Penicillin) and any medication with a possible side effect of nausea and vomiting.

Many drugs can interfere with the normal absorption of one or more body nutrients:

Antacids	Isoniazid
Cathartics (laxatives)	Clofibrate
Colchicine	Glutethimide
Barbiturates	Methotrexate
Anticonvulsants	Neomycin Sulfate
Chloramphenicol	Oral contraceptives
Anticholinergics (Atropine, etc.)	Sulfa drugs

Twenty Questions to Ask About Medicine

1. What is the name of this medicine?
2. What results can be expected from taking it?
3. How long should I wait before reporting if this medicine does not help me?
4. How does the medicine work?
5. What is the exact dose of the medicine?
6. What time of day should I take it?
7. Can I drink alcoholic beverages while taking this medicine?
8. Do I have to take special precautions with this medicine in combination with other prescription drugs I am taking?
9. Do I have to take special precautions with this medicine in combination with nonprescription (over-the-counter) drugs?
10. Can I take this medicine without regard to whether it's mealtime?
11. Are there any special instructions I should have about how to use this medicine?
12. How long should I continue to take this medicine?
13. Is my prescription renewable?
14. For how long a period can my prescription be renewed?
15. Which side effects should I report and which can I disregard?
16. Can I save any unused portion of this medicine for future use?
17. How should I store this medicine?
18. How long can I keep this medicine without its losing strength?

19. What should I do if I forget to take a dose of this medicine?

20. Is this medicine available in a less expensive, generic form? If so, is the less expensive form of equal quality?

Other Points to Remember for Safe Drug Use

- Make sure you tell the doctor everything that is wrong with you. The more information he has, the more effectively he can treat you.
- Make sure each doctor you see knows all the medicines you use regularly, including prescription and nonprescription drugs.
- Keep a record of any bad reaction you have had to a medicine.
- Fill each prescription you are given. If you don't fill a prescription, make sure the doctor knows it.
- Don't take extra medicine without consulting your doctor or pharmacist.
- Follow the label instructions EXACTLY. If you have any questions, call your doctor or pharmacist.
- Report any unusual symptoms that develop after taking medicine.
- Don't save unused medicine for future use unless you have consulted your doctor. Dispose of unused medicine by flushing it down the toilet.
- Never have medicine where children can see or reach it.
- Always read the label before taking your medicine. Don't trust your memory.
- Consult your pharmacist for guidance on the use of over-the-counter (nonprescription) drugs.
- Don't share your medicine with anyone. Your prescription was written for you and only you.
- Be sure the label stays on the container until the medicine is used or destroyed.

- Keep the label facing up when pouring liquid medicine from the bottle, so that the label remains clean.
- Don't use a prescription medicine unless it has been specifically prescribed for you.
- When you travel, take your prescription with you in its original container.
- If you move to another city, ask your pharmacist to forward your prescription records to your new pharmacy.
- Carry important medical facts about you in your wallet. Such things as drug allergies, chronic diseases (diabetes, etc.), or special requirements can be very useful.
- Don't hesitate to discuss the cost of your medical care with your doctor or pharmacist.
- Exercise your right to make decisions about buying medicines:

1. If you suffer from a chronic condition, you can probably save by buying in larger quantities.

2. Choose your pharmacist as carefully as you choose your doctor.

3. Remember, the cost of your prescription includes the professional services offered by your pharmacy. If you want more service you will have to pay more for it.

Glossary

Addiction—Habituation to the use of a drug or other substance. Withdrawal of the addicting agent gives rise to physical symptoms and an overwhelming desire for the agent.

Adrenal corticosteroid—Drug related to hydrocortisone, corticosterone, or deoxycorticosterone used primarily for its ability to reduce inflammation. Also used to replace natural corticosteroids in deficient patients.

Allergy—Unusual response produced in some people when exposed to a drug, food, or other substance. The response can vary widely from a simple rash to life-threatening symptoms.

Amoebicide—Drug used to treat infections caused by amoebas, tiny microorganisms commonly found in nature.

Analgesic—Pain-relieving.

Androgen—Drug or hormone that stimulates activity in male sex organs or prevents changes in male sex characteristics already present.

Anemia—Condition in which the number or size of red blood cells or the amount of oxygen-carrying hemoglobin contained in red blood cells is deficient. Anemia is usually further defined according to the causative agent or disease.

Anesthetic—Drug that produces loss of sensation or of response to stimulation.

Angina pectoris—Severe chest pain, often extending down the left shoulder and arm, relieved by Nitroglycerin.

Antacid—Drug used to neutralize excess acid in the stomach.

Antianxiety drug—Drug used to treat symptoms of anxiety (feeling of apprehension or danger accompanied by restlessness).

Antiarrhythmic drug—Drug used to help regulate unusual or abnormal heart rhythms.

Antiasthmatic drug—Drug used to treat symptoms of asthma, including difficulty in breathing, with wheezing.

Antibacterial drug—Drug that is destructive to or prevents the growth of bacteria.

398

Antibiotic—Substance derived from a mold or bacteria which slows or stops the growth of other bacteria.

Anticholinergic drug—Drug that antagonizes or counteracts the effects of acetylcholine, a natural hormone responsible for certain nervous system activities.

Anticoagulant drug—Drug used to extend the time it normally takes for blood to clot.

Anticonvulsant drug—Drug used to prevent or treat any disease associated with violent involuntary muscle contractions.

Antidepressant—Drug used to treat the symptoms of depression (dejection, sinking of one's spirits).

Antidiabetic drug—Drug used to treat diabetes mellitus.

Antidiarrheal drug—Drug used to treat diarrhea.

Antidote—Drug used to counteract the adverse effects of a drug or chemical.

Antiemetic drug—Drug to control vomiting.

Antiflatulent drug—Drug used to relieve discomfort due to excessive gas in the stomach or intestines.

Antihelminthic drug—Drug used to treat infections caused by helminths (worms).

Antihistamine—Drug used for its ability to neutralize or antagonize the effects of histamine, a naturally occurring substance; used to relieve the symptoms of allergy.

Antihyperlipidemic drug—Drug used to help control high levels of fats (cholesterol; triglycerides) in the blood.

Anti-infective—Relating to any agent used to treat an infection.

Antineoplastic drug—Drug used to treat neoplasms (unusual growths of tissue). Cancers are neoplastic diseases. Benign (noncancerous) growths are also neoplastic.

Antipruritic drug—Drug used to relieve itching.

Antipyretic drug—Drug used to reduce fever.

Antirheumatic drug—Drug used to treat or prevent rheumatism.

Antitoxin—Drug that neutralizes the effects of toxins (poisons, usually produced by bacteria invading the body).

Antitussive drug—Drug used to relieve cough.

Arrhythmia—Unusual or irregular heartbeat.

Ataxia—Loss of ability to coordinate muscular movements.

Bacteria—Living organisms, visible only under a microscope, which may infect humans and cause disease. Bacteria are classified according to shape, chemical reactivity, and nutrients they require.

Bactericidal drug—Drug that kills bacteria.

Bacteriostatic drug—Drug that inhibits the reproduction of bacteria.

Blood count—Number of red and white blood cells found in a standard sample of blood.

Blood dyscrasia—General term for any blood disease.

Blood sugar—Sugar normally found in the blood and burned for energy. Normal level of blood sugar is approximately 100 mg %.

Bradycardia—Slowing of the heartbeat, usually to less than 60 beats per minute.

Bronchodilator—Drug used to help relax the bronchial muscles and to widen the bronchial passages.

Calorie—Unit of measure used to determine the energy (heat) value of foods to the body.

Cancer—General term used to describe malignant neoplasms which tend to spread rapidly and will result in illness and death if left untreated.

Capillary—Microscopic blood vessel connecting veins with arteries.

Carcinoma—Cancer.

Cardiac—Having to do with the heart.

Cardiac arrest—Stoppage of heart activity.

Cardiac glycoside—Type of drug that has the ability to increase the strength of and help regulate the rate of the heartbeat.

Cataract—Condition in which the lens of the eye loses its transparency, so that light cannot pass through it normally.

Cerebrum—Portion of the brain that is the seat of conscious mental processes.

Cerumen—Earwax.

Chilblain—Frostbite.

Climacteric—Menopause.

Coagulant drug—Drug which causes clotting of the blood.

Coma—State of unconsciousness from which one cannot be awakened. Causes include diabetes, liver disease, and thyroid disease.

Conception—Act of becoming pregnant.

Congestion—Presence of abnormal amounts of fluids due to increased flow into the area or decreased drainage.

Corticosteroid—See **Adrenal corticosteroid.**

Decongestant—Drug that reduces congestion.

Decubitus—Bedsore.

Delirium—Condition of extreme mental excitement marked by a stream of confused, unconnected ideas.

Dementia—General mental deterioration.

Demulcent—Agent applied to the skin or mucous membranes to relieve an irritation.

Dermatologic drug—Agent applied directly to the skin.

Dextrose—See **Glucose.**

Diabetes—Disease of body metabolism in which there is an insufficient supply of natural insulin. This reduces the body's ability to store or burn glucose.

Diagnostic drug—Agent used by a physician to assist in the diagnosis of a disease.

Dilate—To enlarge a cavity, canal, blood vessel, or opening.

Disinfectant—Agent that inhibits or destroys bacteria which cause disease.

Diuretic—Drug that stimulates the production and passing of urine.

Dose—Quantity of a drug or medicine to be taken or applied all at once or over a designated period.

Drug dependence—Term used to describe drug habituation or addiction.

Drug interaction—Situation where one drug affects (increases or decreases) the ability of a second drug to exert a therapeutic effect.

Drug sensitivity—Reaction or allergy to a drug.

Edema—Accumulation of clear watery fluid.

EEG—Electroencephalogram.

EKG—Electrocardiogram.

Electrolytes—Chemicals such as sodium, potassium, calcium, and bicarbonate found in body tissues and fluids.

Embolism—Obstruction of a blood vessel, caused by a blood clot or a large mass of bacterial or foreign material.

Emollient—Agent that softens or smooths irritated skin or mucous membranes.

Endocarditis—Inflammation of the membrane lining the heart.

Endocrine glands—Glands that produce hormones and release them directly into the bloodstream.

Enzyme—Protein, produced by body cells, which stimulates a chemical reaction in the body and remains unchanged during the reaction.

Epilepsy—Chronic disease characterized by periods of unconsciousness, convulsions, or both.

Eruption—Redness, spotting, or breaking out in a rash on the skin.

Estrogen—Drug or hormone that stimulates activity in female sex organs or prevents changes in female sex characteristics already present.

Euphoria—Feeling of exaggerated well-being.

Exfoliation—Profuse scaling of large areas of skin.

Expectorant—Drug that stimulates the production of secretions from mucous membranes.

Fever—Body temperature above 98.6°F (37°C).

Ganglia—Aggregations or groups of nerve cells.

Gastritis—Inflammation of the stomach.

Generic name—Standard name accepted for a drug. Manufacturers often use their own trade name that correspond to the generic name.

Glucose—Principal sugar used by the body for energy; also called dextrose.

Gonad—Sexual gland.

Hallucination—Perception of something which does not exist.

Hemorrhoids—Piles.

Hepatitis—Inflammation of the liver.

Histamine—Substance produced by the body as part of an allergic reaction; it causes dilation of blood vessels, lowered blood pressure, and stimulation of secretions from the stomach and other organs.

Hyperacidity—Abnormally large amounts of acid in the stomach.

Hyperglycemia—Presence of high level of sugar (glucose) in the blood.

Hyperkalemia—Presence of high potassium level in the blood.

Hyperlipidemia—High blood level of cholesterol and/or triglycerides.

Hypertension—High blood pressure.

Hypoacidity—Unusually low level of stomach acid.

Hypoglycemia—Low blood sugar (glucose) level.

Hypokalemia—Low blood potassium level.

Hypotension—Low blood pressure.

Immunity—Resistance to the effects of a specified disease or of some other abnormal condition.

Ketonuria—The passage of ketone bodies (acetone) in the urine. This condition may be present in diabetes or as a result of an unbalanced high-protein diet.

Laudanum—Tincture of opium.

Laxative—Drug that can loosen the bowels (act as a cathartic). Types of laxatives are bulk, saline, and stimulant.

Lesion—Wound or injury.

Lethargy—Drowsiness.

Malaise—Feeling of general discomfort or of being out of sorts.

Metastasis—Shifting of a disease, or its local effect, from one part of the body to another.

Migraine headache—Pain on one side of the head; complex of effects consisting of head pain, dizziness, nausea and vomiting, and extreme sensitivity to bright light.

Myopia—Nearsightedness.

Nebulizer—Atomizer or vaporizer.

Neoplasm—New or abnormal growth of tissue usually associated with a tumor.

Normotension—Blood pressure in the normal range.

Nystagmus—Rapid uncontrolled eye movement.

Obesity—Body weight at least 10 to 20 percent greater than the expected value.

Over-the-counter drug—Medication sold without a prescription. May be purchased in pharmacies and other outlets.

Palpitation—Rapid heart beat in which the patient feels throbbing in his chest.

Paralysis—Loss of power in one or more muscles because of injury or disease.

Pill—Small mass of material containing a medication and taken by swallowing.

Plasma—Fluid portion of circulating blood.

Platelet—Component of the blood whose primary role is in the clotting mechanism.

Pneumonia—Inflammation of the lungs, from any cause.

Polydipsia—Excessive thirst.

Polyuria—Excessive urination.

Prescription—Written formula for the preparation and administration of any remedy or medicine, by a qualified, licensed medical practitioner.

Progestins—Female hormones that cause changes in the uterus to prepare it for the fertilized egg. Progestins may also affect other female sex characteristics.

Pruritis—Itching.

Psychotherapeutic drug—Drug used as treatment or part of the treatment of emotional disorders.

Rash—Local or generalized eruption.

Respiration—Breathing.

Rhinorrhea—Running nose.

Somnifacient drug—Drug that produces sleep.

Sulfa drug—Drug belonging to the chemical group of sulfonamides. Members of this group can have anti-infective, diuretic, and antidiabetic properties.

Sulfonamide—See **Sulfa drug**.

Sympathomimetic drug—Drug with stimulating action, also causing relief of congestion, increase in blood pressure, and other effects.

Symptom—Any change in function, appearance, or sensation related to a disease.

Syndrome—Group of symptoms which, when taken together, indicate the presence of a specific disease.

Tablet—Solid dosage form containing medicine. Tablets from different manufacturers may vary in size, color, shape, and content.

Testosterone—Male sex hormone.

Tinnitus—Ringing or noise in the ears, often as a drug side effect.

Toxic—Poisonous or harmful.

Toxin—Substance produced by a cell or group of cells, or by bacteria during their growth, that produces a poisonous effect.

Toxoid—Toxin that has been treated with chemicals to destroy its harmful properties. After this treatment it can be injected into the human body and will provide immunity to the original toxin.

Tremor—Involuntary trembling or quivering.

Tumor—Swelling or neoplasm that grows at an unusual rate.

Ulcer—Lesion on the surface of the skin or mucous membrane.

Urticaria—Hives or itching rash.

Vaccine—Solution of modified virus or bacteria that, when injected, provides immunity to the original virus or bacteria.

Vasodilator—Drug that causes opening or widening of the blood vessels.

Vitamin—Chemical present in foods that is essential to normal body functions and to normal chemical reactions in the body.

Sources Used in Compiling the Information in This Book

Abramowicz, Mark, ed., *The Medical Letter on Drugs and Therapeutics,* Medical Letter, New Rochelle, N.Y., 1974, 1975, 1976, 1977, 1978.

American Medical Association, Department of Drugs, *AMA Drug Evaluations,* 3d ed., Publishing Sciences Group, Acton, Mass., 1977.

American Pharmaceutical Association, *Evaluations of Drug Interactions,* 2d ed., American Pharmaceutical Association, Washington, D.C., 1976.

American Pharmaceutical Association, *Handbook of Nonprescription Drugs,* 5th ed., American Pharmaceutical Association, Washington, D.C., 1977.

American Society of Hospital Pharmacists, *American Hospital Formulary Service,* American Society of Hospital Pharmacists, Washington, D.C., 1978.

Conn, H. F., ed., *Current Therapy 1977,* W. B. Saunders, Philadelphia, 1977.

Deichman, W. B., and Gerarde, H. W., *Toxicology of Drugs and Chemicals,* Academic Press, New York, 1969.

Dorlands Illustrated Medical Dictionary, 24th ed., W. B. Saunders Co., Philadelphia, 1965.

Gleason, M. N., Gosselin, R. E., Hodge, H. C., and Smith, R. P., *Clinical Toxicology of Commercial Products,* 3d ed., Williams & Wilkins, Baltimore, 1969.

Goldstein, A., Aronow, L., and Kalman, S., *Principles of Drug Action: The Basis of Pharmacology,* 2d ed., John Wiley & Sons, New York, 1974.

Goodman, L. S., and Gilman, A., *The Pharmacological Basis of Therapeutics,* 5th ed., Macmillan, New York, 1975.

Greenblatt, D. J., and Shader, R. I., *Benzodiazepines in Clinical Practice,* Raven Press, New York, 1974.

Hansten, P. D., *Drug Interactions,* 3d ed., Lea & Febiger, Philadelphia, 1975.

Kastrup, E. K., and Schwach, G., eds., *Facts and Comparisons,* Facts and Comparisons, St. Louis, 1978.

Langley, L., Cheraskin, F., and Sleeper, R., *Dynamic Anatomy and Physiology,* 2d ed., McGraw-Hill, New York, 1963.

Long, J. S., *The Essential Guide to Prescription Drugs,* Harper & Row, New York, 1977.

Medical Economics, *Physicians' Desk Reference,* 32d ed., Medical Economics, Oradell, N.J., 1978.

Parish, P., *The Doctors and Patients Handbook of Medicines and Drugs,* Alfred A. Knopf, New York, 1977.

Silverman, H. M., "Anticoagulant Therapy," *New Environment of Pharmacy* 3:5 (Nov./Dec.) 1976.

Silverman, H. M., "Antineoplastic Therapy," *Physician Assistant* 1:23 (May/June) 1976.

Silverman, H. M., "Classification of Antibiotics," *Hospital Formulary Management* 7:26 (Feb.) 1972.

Silverman, H. M., "Fetal and Newborn Adverse Drug Reactions," *Drug Intelligence and Clinical Pharmacy* 8:690 (Dec.) 1974.

Silverman, H. M., "MAO Inhibitors," *Hospital Formulary Management* 8:14 (March) 1973.

Silverman, H. M., "The Proper Time for Taking Drugs," *Hospital Formulary Management* 9:18 (Feb.) 1974.

Strauss, S., *Your Prescription and You,* 3d ed., Medical Business Services, Ambler, Pa., 1978.

Thomas, C. L., ed., *Tabers Cyclopedic Medical Dictionary,* 12th ed., F. A. Davis, Philadelphia, 1973.

Index of Generic and Brand Name Drugs

414

Index of Drug Types

ABOUT THE AUTHORS

Harold M. Silverman, Pharm.D., currently serves as associate director of the department of pharmacy at Lenox Hill Hospital, New York City. Dr. Silverman has been associated with the hospital since 1967 and has been responsible for the development of many of that hospital's advanced pharmacy practice programs, including clinical pharmacy, drug information and the computerization of pharmacy services. He has contributed extensively to the professional pharmacy literature, including published articles and papers, textbook chapters and is the author of the *Med-File* Drug Interaction System. He has served as consultant to the State of New York and City of New York, as well as to several corporations in the areas of pharmacy and pharmacology. He has served as contributing editor to several professional publications. Dr. Silverman holds two degrees from Columbia University, where he was elected to the Rho Chi Pharmaceutical Honor Society. He has served on the faculties of Columbia University and Long Island University, where he now holds the rank of assistant professor. He is listed in *Outstanding Young Men of America* for 1976, 1977 and 1979. Dr. Silverman resides with his wife and two daughters in Rye, N.Y.

Gilbert I. Simon, Sc.D., is director of the department of pharmacy, Lenox Hill Hospital, New York City. He has held this position since 1960. Dr. Simon received his B.S. from Fordham University, his M.S. from Long Island University, and his doctorate, Honoris Causa, from the College of Pharmacy Sciences, City of New York (Columbia University). He was an assistant professor of pharmaceutical sciences at Columbia University from 1964 to 1976. An active member in the American Society of Hospital Pharmacists, the New York State Council of Hospital Pharmacists, and the New York City Society of Hospital Pharmacists, Dr. Simon has served as president to both the New York State and the New York City societies. In 1973 he was honored with the Award of Merit from the New York City Society of Hospital Pharmacists for his contribution to the practice of institutional pharmacy. He has been a member of the Pharmacy Advisory Committee of the Greater New York Hospital Association and served on committees of the Hospital Association of the State of New York. Dr. Simon is currently a member of the New York State Medical Advisory Committee, Department of Social Services, and has served as a consultant to the pharmacy industry. He has been a principal speaker on contemporary hospital pharmacy practice throughout the United States and in Europe. In 1975, Drs. Simon and Silverman co-authored *Med-File*, a book on common nonprescription drugs and their interactions. Dr. Simon and his wife, Mimi, live in Bronxville, New York.

How's Your Health?

Bantam publishes a line of informative books, written by top experts to help you toward a healthier and happier life.

MS READ-a-thon— a simple way to start youngsters reading.

Boys and girls between 6 and 14 can join the MS READ-a-thon and help find a cure for Multiple Sclerosis by reading books. And they get two rewards—the enjoyment of reading, and the great feeling that comes from helping others.

Parents and educators: For complete information call your local MS chapter, or call toll-free (800) 243-6000. Or mail the coupon below.

Kids can help, too!